Tennis, Apartheid and Social Justice

Tennis, Apartheid and Social Justice
The First Non-Racial International Tennis Tour, 1971

Saleem Badat

UNIVERSITY OF KwaZulu-Natal Press

Published in 2023 by University of KwaZulu-Natal Press
Private Bag X01
Scottsville, 3201
Pietermaritzburg
South Africa
Email: books@ukzn.ac.za
Website: www.uknpress.co.za

© 2023 Saleem Badat

All rights reserved. No part of this publication may be reproduced or transmitted in any form or by electrical or mechanical means, including information storage and retrieval systems, without prior permission in writing from the publishers.

ISBN: 978 1 86914 514 9
e-ISBN: 978 1 86914 515 6

Project manager: Sally Hines
Editor: Christopher Merrett
Layout: Susan Elliott
Proofreader: Catherine Munro
Indexer: Judith Shier
Cover design: Marise Bauer, M Design
Cover image: The Dhiraj Squad and their tour bus in the Netherlands, 1971

Printed and bound by CPI Group (UK) Ltd, Croydon, CR0 4YY

Here comes the story of the '71 non-racial overseas tennis tour
The one about which the apartheid authorities were rather dour
A tour that the non-racial tennis union and black players had never undertaken
Playing opponents without reference to colour was verboten
Just as were dreams of being champions of the world
      — Inspired by Bob Dylan's 'Hurricane' about the wrongful imprisonment of black boxer Rubin (Hurricane) Carter

Contents

Foreword *by Professor Paulus Zulu*	ix
Preface	xi
Acknowledgements	xiii
Abbreviations	xvi
1971 Tennis Tour Timeline	xviii
Introduction	1

PART ONE

1 Fifty-Two Years Ago	9
2 Sport and Social Justice	13
3 Reclaiming the Narrative on Tennis History	23
4 From Colonialism to Apartheid in Sport	37
5 Tennis under Apartheid	50
6 International Collusion with Apartheid Sport	56
7 The Historic 1971 Tour	71
8 UK Tournaments: April to June 1971	89
9 The Rest of the Tour	102
10 Lighter Moments and Tour Lessons	108
11 Conclusion	114

PART TWO

12 The Dhiraj Squad	133
13 Jasmat (Dhiraj) Soma	136
14 Hiralal (Dhiraj) Soma	154

15	Alwyn Solomon	166
16	Oscar Woodman	179
17	Hoosen Bobat	187
18	Cavan Bergman	209

Notes 230
Bibliography 260
Index 269

Foreword

The sport of tennis, like all areas of life in colonial and apartheid South Africa, was by law and social convention segregated along lines of race. Facilities, opportunities, sponsorship and participation in international tournaments were the preserve largely of the small white minority. Only whites were permitted to represent South Africa in international competition between countries.

Despite brutal repression, black South Africans courageously resisted racism and other oppressive practices on and off the tennis court and sports field in myriad ways.

Black people played tennis and established sports clubs from at least the late 1800s. In time, they forged regional and national associations to administer, co-ordinate and promote competitive tennis, instituted coaching and convened tournaments.

In 1962, the Southern Africa Lawn Tennis Union (SnALTU) was formed with a deep commitment to non-racialism. It subsequently affiliated to the South African Council on Sport (SACOS), which was the sport wing of the anti-apartheid liberation movement. SACOS was a powerful advocate of non-racial sport and popularised the slogan 'no normal sport in an abnormal society'. This year it celebrates the 50th anniversary of its founding.

I had the honour to serve the noble cause of non-racial tennis as an executive member of the Southern Natal Tennis Union in the late 1970s, at a time when non-racial tennis was growing and was a vibrant feature of black communities, and when there was burgeoning resistance to apartheid oppression and inequities.

Focusing on the first SnALTU-sponsored international tour in 1971 by talented young black tennis players, *Tennis, Apartheid and Social Justice* documents vividly how, in the face of apartheid repression, players and administrators upheld equality and human dignity as opposed to racism in sport, often at great personal cost to themselves. The book also describes the political, social and sporting conditions locally and internationally, under which the tour took place.

As Saleem Badat argues, under a democratic government, there has been neither recognition nor reparations for outstanding apartheid-era black tennis players. Nor has there been substantive transformation in social relations or opportunities for black people, either on the tennis courts, on the sports fields or in the wider society.

Adding salt to the wound is observing a post-1994 minister of sport call for racial quotas in sport when most black schools have no sporting facilities besides a primordial soccer ground, should the natural terrain permit one.

This book is a powerful and timely reminder that in tennis the struggle for equity and social justice continues. We owe a great debt to the author for highlighting conditions in South African tennis, past and present.

Professor Paulus Zulu

Preface

At a birthday celebration in 2019 at Richmond in the pleasant KwaZulu-Natal Midlands, my good friend Hoosen Bobat regaled us with the story of 'three wise men' (the alternative version) who were born on the same date. As narrated, the angel deposited Hoosen in Mansfield Road, in the Botanic Gardens suburb of Durban, and Yusuf (Chewie) Khan in High Street, Richmond; both on 12 November 1952. Then, the angel lost her way; alas, there was no GPS and Google Maps in those days. So only one year later was Moosa Cassimjee safely deposited in Wasbank, either wiser or less wise for his 'delayed deposit', depending on your point of view of course!

An entertaining raconteur, Bobat's reminiscences about his participation, at the age of 18, in the first non-racial tennis tour of Europe in 1971 inspired this book. Six young black players undertook the historic tour under the auspices of the avowedly non-racial Southern Africa Lawn Tennis Union (SnALTU). The book is not only about Bobat's tennis achievements. Instead, it is a critical account of the 1971 international tour against the destructive backdrop of apartheid-era sports conditions and the talented, pioneering young black tennis players who embarked on that tour. It draws on media reports of the time, published literature, a journal kept by Bobat's father and interviews with the players who participated in the tour. Dubbed the Dhiraj Squad, after Jasmat Dhiraj the indisputable non-racial tennis champion of that time, the other players were Hiralal Dhiraj, Alwyn Solomon, Oscar Woodman, Hoosen Bobat and Cavan Bergman, who was still a secondary school student then and the youngest member of the squad.

Stimulating the publication is the Constitution's call to 'recognise the injustices of the past' and to 'honour those who suffered for justice and freedom in our land'. *Tennis, Apartheid and Social Justice* illuminates the circumstances in which the 1971 tour occurred, the outstanding and talented young tennis players who undertook the tour, and the dynamics associated with it. In doing so, the publication honours those who stood firm on the principle and practice of non-racial sport despite the impediments and hardships experienced by them.

Colonialism and apartheid perpetrated great injustices against black sportspersons and denied them the facilities, opportunities and human dignity to realise their talents. To achieve social justice in sport and other domains in South Africa requires determined cultivation of prophetic memory. This entails remembrance of our brutal and traumatic past and the sacrifices that were made to achieve democracy. It necessitates critique of the dulling amnesia that effectively obscures or diminishes the injustices of the past and threatens to undermine the achievement of our constitutional ideals. It requires sustaining the consciousness that in the light of our history, South Africa needs to be boldly and fundamentally transformed so that all may lead decent, secure and fulfilling lives. It means continually igniting our imagination to conceive of creative new, just and humane ways of being and doing things. And it needs the constant desire to reconstruct, remake and develop our country in the interests of the many, not just the few.

This book aspires to contribute to the cultivation of such prophetic memory.

Acknowledgements

I am deeply grateful to all the scholars, friends and supporters who contributed to this publication.

My good friend Hoosen Bobat's recollections of the 1971 non-racial tennis tour of Europe on various occasions planted the seed of the idea to undertake research on the context and dynamics of the tour and to publish this book. He contributed his cuttings from Durban-based newspapers and photos of the tour, provided contact details for Oscar Woodman and Charmaine Williams, and assisted me at the Msunduzi Library on a few occasions.

The Dhiraj Squad members and their families all readily agreed to share information, old newspaper articles and photographs, and to be interviewed. They understood that this book was important for more reasons than reminiscence, and their support made research and writing infinitely easier.

My goddaughter, Che Ramsden, volunteered to undertake archival research in Britain to try to obtain the results of matches played by the Dhiraj Squad members during the 1971 tour. Her diligent search helped to fill in some gaps in the results.

Hearing one of Bobat's recollections, my close friend Professor Robert van Niekerk of the University of the Witwatersrand, implored me to undertake research and to write this book. He diligently read the final draft text and suggested useful revisions.

Despite his extensive research, writing and teaching commitments, Goolam Vahed, professor in the History Department at the University of KwaZulu-Natal was supportive throughout. He connected me with colleagues who facilitated my research, generously reviewed the final draft text, and provided valuable feedback. He alerted me to relevant newspaper articles, and pointed me to Thirunagaren Munsamy, senior librarian at the University of KwaZulu-Natal Gandhi-Luthuli Documentation Centre.

Professor Peter Alegi of the Department of History at Michigan State University readily critically reviewed the final draft text. Based on his extensive knowledge of South African sport history, he shared invaluable insights, asked probing questions, suggested additions to the text, and pointed me to various articles including some of his recent writings.

Lorna Rooy, wife of the late Alwyn Solomon who was a member of the 1971 tour, kindly provided articles on the tour from Cape-based newspapers, and shared photographs of Solomon. Together with the wider Solomon family, she responded admirably and fully to my interview questions.

Parvati Soma and her late husband Anthony Ellery from Pretoria kindly shared two files of newspaper clippings from old Transvaal-based newspapers and arranged their transport from Pretoria to Durban.

Independent Media and the African News Agency provided and permitted the use of various photos, and kindly waived any fees. My thanks specifically to Yogas Nair, Lance Witten, Shelley Kjonstad and David Ritchie.

Nirode Bramdaw kindly and readily gave permission to use photos from the 1971 editions of the *Leader* newspaper. I gratefully acknowledge the support of the Bramdaw Archive.

The British Lawn Tennis Association, and specifically Tara Granea, its customer support specialist, assisted with attempts to obtain results of 1971 United Kingdom tennis tournaments.

Nothe Masua of Bobat Wealth Solutions provided splendid assistance with scanning of newspaper articles and photographs.

Thirunagaren Munsamy efficiently assisted in searching for and scanning articles on the 1971 tour in the *Graphic* and *Leader* newspapers and directed me towards other archives.

Eshara Singh and her colleagues at the Msunduzi Library in Pietermaritzburg provided wonderful assistance and facilities for examining and scanning articles from various newspapers.

So did Chelsea O'Regan and her colleagues, Martin Brown, Shahiema Engelmann and Vela Huza at the Cape Town campus of the National Library of South Africa.

Yusuf Patel and his team at the Architects Collaborative generously scanned numerous photos used in the publication.

Viren Soma connected me with his father Hira Soma and uncle Jasmat Soma. Pauline Brown, Jasmat's wife, assisted with emailing me materials from Britain.

My good friend Ismail Asmal in Virginia, United States, provided me with Lorna Rooy's contact details.

Cornelius Thomas, head of the Cory Library at Rhodes University, enthusiastically supported publication of this book and provided invaluable advice on publishing.

Samiena Amien translated text from an Afrikaans newspaper into English and kindly considered copy editing the publication.

Farhana Paruk helped me to identify and scan relevant newspaper articles at the Msunduzi Library. She kindly transported Parvati Soma's files of newspaper clippings from Pretoria to Durban.

Yusuf Sayed, good friend, professor and South African research chair in Teacher Education at the Cape Peninsula University of Technology kindly fetched from, returned to, and delivered to me Lorna Rooy's files from Bellville, Cape Town.

Omar Badsha, director of South African History Online (SAHO) needed no persuasion to host the research materials that informed this publication on the outstanding SAHO website.

Various comrades, friends and colleagues had their ears bent about the publication during research and writing. My thanks to them all for listening and for their unfailing encouragement.

Abbreviations

ANC	African National Congress
BMSC	Bantu Men's Social Centre
BRGA	Bantu Recreational Grounds Association
CCIRS	Co-ordinating Committee for International Recognition in Sport
FC	football club
ILTF	International Lawn Tennis Federation
IOC	International Olympic Committee
ITF	International Tennis Federation
IUEF	International University Exchange Fund
KZN	KwaZulu-Natal
PNL	Polytechnic of North London
SACOS	South African Council on Sport
SAHO	South African History Online
SALTU	South African Lawn Tennis Union
SANLTU	South African National Lawn Tennis Union
SANROC	South African Non-Racial Olympic Committee
SASA	South African Sports Association
SATPA	South African Tennis Players Association
SATTB	South African Table Tennis Board
SnALTU	Southern Africa Lawn Tennis Union
SNLTU	Southern Natal Lawn Tennis Union
TASA	Tennis Association of South Africa
TCE	Transvaal College of Education
TRC	Truth and Reconciliation Commission
TSA	Tennis South Africa
UK	United Kingdom
UN	United Nations

US	United States
UWC	University of the Western Cape
YMCA	Young Men's Christian Association

1971 Tennis Tour Timeline

1970
December — Announcement of tour.

1971
10 April — Squad of Hira Dhiraj, Alwyn Solomon, Oscar Woodman, Hoosen Bobat and Cavan Bergman departs from the airport in Johannesburg.

11 April — Arrival in London. Hira is accommodated by the Bhanabhais at their home in Hornsey, London while the rest of the squad check into the nearby Hornsey YMCA hostel.

16 April — Jasmat Dhiraj, held up by a delay in the renewal of his passport, departs for London.

17 April — Jasmat accommodated by the Bhanabhais in Hornsey.

19–24 April — First UK tournament: Oxfordshire Junior Tournament, Norham Gardens, Oxford.

26 April–1 May — Second UK tournament: Rothmans Sutton Hard Court Championships, south London.

3–8 May — Third UK tournament: Rothmans Surrey Hard Court Championships, Guildford.

10–15 May — Fourth UK tournament: Bio-Strath London Hard Court Championships, Hurlingham.

17–22 May	Fifth UK tournament: Bio-Strath Droitwich Spa Tournament, Worcestershire.
21 May	Solomon returns to Cape Town for university exams.
24–29 May	Sixth UK tournament: Rothmans Surrey Grass Court Championships, Surbiton.
31 May–5 June	Seventh UK tournament: Rothmans Chichester Tennis Tournament, West Sussex.
7–12 June	Eighth UK tournament: Kent Championships, Beckenham Lawn Tennis Club – juniors.
7–12 June	Ninth UK tournament: Bio-Strath Wolver-hampton Tournament, West Midlands – seniors.
14–19 June	Tenth UK tournament: Rothmans South of England Open Championships, Eastbourne.
21 June–3 July	Wimbledon Championships.
early July	Bergman returns to Cape Town. Rest of the squad travel to play tournaments on the Continent.
early August	Tournament at Katwijk aan Zee, the Netherlands.
late August	Woodman and Bobat return to South Africa. Woodman later emigrates to Canada.
late August	Jasmat and Hira Dhiraj play in tournament at Mönchengladbach, Germany.
October	Jasmat Dhiraj remains in the UK in exile.
late 1971	Hira Dhiraj returns to Pretoria. In 1974, he emigrates to the UK.

Introduction

In 1971, the non-racial Southern Africa Lawn Tennis Union (SnALTU) sent its most promising young players on a four-month historic tour to play tournaments in Europe. The six-person team was known as the Dhiraj Squad, after national non-racial tennis champion Jasmat Dhiraj.

Apartheid South Africa in the 1970s was a racist and repressive society based on white supremacy and privilege, and black oppression and subordination. Laws, policies and practices either prohibited or strongly dissuaded contact between black and white persons beyond the workplace. Black tennis players were denied proper facilities, coaching and opportunities to excel, represent their country and play international tournaments; all those were the prerogative of whites. They could not belong to the same clubs as whites or compete in competitions with or against white players. Residential areas, education, health care, transport, worship, sport and other amenities were all racially segregated. Despite the barriers and constraints, many black sportspersons and sports administrators courageously and determinedly pursued anti-racism and non-racialism in sport and in wider society as a principle and ideal, often at great personal cost.

This book recalls the political, social and sporting conditions under which the 1971 non-racial tennis tour of Europe took place. It narrates the adventures of the talented young black tennis players who went on tour and its impact on them, both sporting-wise and personally, and the lessons that were learnt. It documents the shameful collusion of international tennis associations with the racist, whites-only South African tennis body of the apartheid era and their political machinations to prevent one of the Dhiraj Squad members, Hoosen Bobat, from playing in the Junior Wimbledon championships and becoming the first black South African to participate in that tournament. It contends that in post-1994 democratic South Africa, there has, paradoxically, been neither fitting recognition of, nor reparation for, outstanding apartheid-era black sportspersons such as those who toured in 1971, and that the apartheid legacy continues to impinge powerfully on tennis today.

It must be emphasised that this book is not intended to be a history of non-racial tennis in South Africa. Nor is its goal to address the important and vexed question of transformation in tennis after 1994, when South Africa became a democracy. Both are important issues that need to be assiduously researched, described and analysed in their own right. Hopefully, this book will be a catalyst for further historical and sociological research on non-racial tennis and tennis more generally in South Africa from the colonial period in the late 1800s, through to the 1910-1948 segregation and 1948-1994 apartheid periods and after 1994.

Here, mention must be made of the Non-Racial Sport History Project Gauteng. Initiated in 2015, this is a welcome project 'to record the histories of non-racial sport from the ground up – clubs and their administrators and players, provincial and then national, paying special attention to the role played by women'. It also seeks to co-ordinate efforts 'to record, preserve and publish the rich histories of non-racial sports to ensure their role in various facets of our history, including in the struggle against apartheid, is acknowledged'.[1]

The book draws on diverse sources of data. The principal source has been newspaper articles that reported on the 1971 tour or on matters pertinent to the themes of the book. The articles were sourced from the newspaper archives in the Msunduzi Library in Pietermaritzburg, the University of KwaZulu-Natal Gandhi-Luthuli Documentation Centre, Westville and the National Library in Cape Town, and from the personal collections of the players or their family members.

Numerous internet sites were used for contextual information, and for data on tournaments and players who were opponents of the Dhiraj Squad members. Interviews with the players and the wife of a deceased player were invaluable to illuminate various dynamics related to the tour and to pen biographies of the players. Very late in the research, a journal of letters to Hoosen Bobat while he was on tour, kept by his father, Ahmed Bobat, for the past 50 years came to light. Secondary sources in the form of books, book chapters and journal articles provided relevant data on sport under apartheid and the sports boycott of South Africa.

The interviews and letters represent the oral histories and neglected written materials whose use Alegi advocates as important antidotes to simple and unnuanced narratives. Those data sources are critical to ensure that all-too-often important, ignored, forgotten, neglected or marginalised social actors feature in historical accounts as makers of history. They also help to enlarge and reconstitute the archive, which is fundamental for decolonising histories of sport, for interrogating previous stories and narrating other and different stories, and for countering the '"big men" version of history'. The valuing, collection and preservation of more diverse voices of sportspersons and those associated with sport ensures that 'interviews are not about fact-checking information accumulated in written documents'. Instead, they become 'a discursive space in which non-elite actors have the power to show their scholarly interlocutors that local voices, experiences, and memories must take their rightful place in the larger historical narrative'.[2]

A comment on the nomenclature used in the book is necessary. Black refers collectively to African, coloured, and Indian South Africans who were racially oppressed, and denied the vote, citizenship and human rights under apartheid. The use of those terms, and white, does not imply acceptance of them. The ossification and deployment of these terms by chauvinists can have potentially dangerous consequences.

Hein Marais refers to the danger of recourse to 'rousing affirmations' about 'belonging' and identity that are 'inflected with racial and ethnic chauvinism' and to populist discourses of authenticity – of 'who constitutes a "true South African", who is a real African, who is black' – with ever more 'narrow exacting' interpretations.[3]

Marais' comments put into perspective the crass utterances on race some years ago of chief government communicator Mzwanele (Jimmy) Manyi and the repugnant tabloid chatter of Kuli Roberts on so-called coloureds. As Minister of Finance Trevor Manuel remarked, Manyi displayed 'the same mind that operated under apartheid' and did not appreciate that his 'utterances are both unconstitutional and morally reprehensible'.[4]

Given the apartheid legacy, there must be redress and social equity for economically and socially disadvantaged, impoverished, black and female South Africans. Judge Albie Sachs rightly notes that pervasive inequities 'cannot be wished away by invoking constitutional idealism'.

Still, we find ourselves in the grip of a profound paradox: the use of race to promote redress and to advance social equity. In Sachs' words, we are making 'conscious use of racial distinctions in order to create a non-racial society'.[5]

Such an approach, of course, has many dangers. For one, employing just race for redress purposes could benefit only or primarily black political and economic elites, and so simply reproduce the entrenched and acute class inequalities that exist in South Africa. For another, using race to advance redress and social equity could ossify racial categorisations and result in identities continuing to be constructed primarily along the lines of race.[6]

Yet, the goal and the strategies employed must surely be to erode and dissolve racial categorisation, and to ensure that identities instead are rich, multiple, fluid and dynamic rather than frozen along race lines. It is vitally important that we 'never lose sight of the fact that the goal is to establish a non-racial society in which social and cultural diversity is celebrated and seen as a source of vitality, and in which "race" as such ultimately has no political or economic significance'.[7]

In this regard, it becomes imperative to confront charlatans and chauvinists who stridently seek to give ever more 'narrow and exacting' answers to the questions of 'who is a real South African, who is a real African, who is black'. Self-serving answers to those questions could render millions of South Africans repressed subjects again. It could fertilise disgraceful manifestations of intolerance, hatred and genocide of the kinds that have resulted in the killing fields of My Lai, Sabra and Shatila, Srebrenica, Darfur, Rwanda and Gaza.

'Race' has no basis in biology, but is a social construct used historically to justify and implement economic, social and political arrangements to reproduce white domination and privilege and black subordination and disadvantage. That said, the use of racial categories is unavoidable in South Africa given the realities of race, racism and racial prejudice, and the need to measure the progress that is being made to overcome historical inequities.[8]

Furthermore, as Caroline Knowles argues:

> While racial categories are social and political constructs, they are also effective in the making of who we are in the world and

what we do in it. They operate in the manufacture of identities and in activities composing human agency . . . They don't have a force in human biology but that is a different point. They have a *meaning in social and political organisation and human action.*[9]

Part One

1

Fifty-Two Years Ago

The year 1971 saw the launch of the third Apollo mission to the moon. Given this book's subject and the Jim Crow laws, racism and oppression of blacks in the United States (US), it is important to recall the critical role three African American women mathematicians, Katherine Johnson, Mary Jackson and Dorothy Vaughan played in the success of the Apollo missions.[1] When Johnson was belatedly awarded the Presidential Medal of Freedom in 2015, it was noted that she 'refused to be limited by society's expectations of her gender and race while expanding the boundaries of humanity's reach'.[2]

On the technology front, in 1971 Intel released the 4004 CPU, the world's first microprocessor. In East Pakistan, a liberation war began that resulted in the independence of Bangladesh. The Pentagon Papers revealed the extent of US involvement in Vietnam and that the government had lied to its citizens about its imperialist embroilment.

In Detroit, on 21 May 1971, 'at the height of the Vietnam War', Motown singer Marvin Gaye released 'What's Going On', protesting about the war and drawing attention to the racism, poverty and inner-city destruction that afflicted the lives of black Americans. The 'album became a monster, spawning three hit singles on its way to becoming Motown's best-selling album to date' and 'many of the themes Gaye explores remain as relevant today as they were when he first wrote about them 50 years ago'. Indeed, in a country where black people must continue to mobilise against 'white supremacy, endless wars, environmental damage, police brutality and poverty, "What's Going On" remains as relevant as ever'. Some of the songs on the album spoke directly to the state of the world in the early 1970s. The 'title track, "war is not the answer, for only love can conquer hate"', condemned US repression in Vietnam. Gaye also highlighted environmental concerns, with '"Mercy Mercy Me (The

Ecology)" concluding with the refrain "How much more abuse from man can she [the earth] stand?"'[3]

On the US east coast, 'in New York, John Lennon sat down at a brown model Z upright piano and began to write what would become an inter-generational, transnational phenomenon – "Imagine"'. This, considered by *Rolling Stone* magazine to be the third greatest song of all time and Lennon's 'best-selling single of his solo career' held out the 'dream of real change in the world' and 'a vision of unity and of hope' that erased 'violence, hate, borders, poverty, greed, governments, religion, consumerism and capitalism'.[4]

In Paris meanwhile, Jim Morrison, co-founder and lead singer of the rock band The Doors and 'one of the most popular singer-songwriters and influential frontmen in rock history', was discovered dead in a bathtub. Associated with hits like 'Light My Fire', 'L.A. Woman' and 'Love Her Madly', he was just 27, joining others like Janis Joplin, Jimi Hendrix and Rolling Stones guitarist Brian Jones who all died between 1969 and 1971 aged 27.[5]

In 1971, too, the philosopher John Rawls published *A Theory of Justice*, which 'became an unlikely success, selling more than 300,000 copies in the US alone'. Rawls advanced 'a comprehensive philosophy of a free, fair society' that tried to reconcile 'freedom and equality', and democratic institutions and democracy with equity, inclusion and social justice as 'a consensual vision [and] aspiration for all liberal democracies'.[6]

The year 1971 was also the tenth anniversary of apartheid South Africa becoming a republic, following an all-white referendum in 1960. Black South Africans had nothing to celebrate; for them there was neither democracy, nor equality, nor social justice. Black inclusion in the economy and society was of a subordinate nature, with simultaneous exclusion from the fruits of their labour and equal citizenship and rights. Despite this, on Monday, 31 May 1971, while the Dhiraj Squad was on tour in the United Kingdom (UK), black South Africans were cajoled, bribed, bullied, pressurised and threatened to participate in imposed ceremonies that celebrated the anniversary of the white republic. Attendance alone was not enough: blacks also had to sing in Afrikaans the white national anthem, 'Die Stem van Suid Afrika'.

And they had to raise the white South African flag, the *Oranje, Blanje en Blou* (Orange, White, Blue). The Union Jack of the former colonial power, the UK, the flag of the old Afrikaner republic of the Orange Free State and the flag of the old Boer South African Republic all featured in the white centre panel of this flag of apartheid South Africa. (I recall, as a 13-year-old Grade 9 student, refusing, at the instigation of the Grade 12 students, to sing the anthem or observe the raising of the flag at my school in Greyville, Durban.)

Balthazar Johannes Vorster was prime minister, having succeeded apartheid architect Hendrik Verwoerd who was assassinated in 1966. For the small white minority, 17% of the overall South African population, in whose interests the apartheid regime ruled with an iron fist, 1971 was a time of political calm, prosperity and sharing in the economic boom of that time.[7] For black South Africans, the aftermath of the 1960 Sharpeville massacre was a period of intense oppression, extensive and stringent social control, fear and enforced acquiescence. The African National Congress (ANC), Pan Africanist Congress and other organisations were banned, and generalised repression intensified through the detention, banning, banishment and imprisonment of anti-apartheid political activists.

By 1971, however, there were political stirrings with the emergence of the Black Consciousness movement, catalysed by the formation in 1968 of the South African Students Organisation under the leadership of Bantu Stephen Biko. In 1971, there was a revival of the Natal Indian Congress and new beginnings in increasingly militant black worker organisation. Apartheid repression had decimated both during the 1960s.

On the sports front, in September 1970 there was a conference of various national anti-apartheid sports organisations in Durban. The conference committed itself to struggle for non-racial sports organisation, including school sport, to oppose and 'expose discrimination in sports and sports sponsorship', to mobilise appropriate sports facilities that were made open to all irrespective of race, and to 'form a national, non-racial sports organization'.[8]

At a subsequent gathering, the South African Council on Sport (SACOS) was launched on 17 March 1973.[9] It was considered the 'sports wing of the internal liberation movement in the 1970s and 1980s'. Its later slogan, 'No normal sport in an abnormal society', captured pithily the fundamental problem of playing sport in an authoritarian, racist and patriarchal society.[10] The slogan is credited to Hassan Howa, one of the founders of SACOS, its president between 1977 and 1981, and also the president of the South African Cricket Board of Control for many years. SACOS became a powerful force in mobilising and organising black sports organisations and sportspersons behind non-racial sport.[11]

While the Apollo mission was testing the frontiers of space and science, in South Africa another mission with more modest ambitions was quietly being stitched together. It was the first international tour by black South African players who played tennis under the SnALTU, which had been committed to non-racialism since its establishment in 1962, became a member of SACOS and adhered to SACOS philosophy.

The frontiers of black South African players were modest. They were to compete freely against tennis players irrespective of race, ethnicity and nationality; play in tournaments in Europe; improve their tennis; and be ambassadors for non-racial sport, upholding equality and human dignity in opposition to the pervasive racism and patriarchy in sport under colonialism and apartheid.

2

Sport and Social Justice

In the annals of non-racial sport under apartheid, a few black sportspersons achieved success and national and international public prominence despite the odds stacked against them, reflected in the absence of facilities, equipment and sponsorship, the lack of opportunities and coaching and the policies of a white minority regime that valued blacks only for their labour. The achievements of black sportspersons were significant, considering that they were excluded from competing on an equitable footing with white sportspersons and prevented from realising their promise at the highest level, with their ambitions thwarted, their aspirations unfulfilled, and their dreams shattered.

A year after the end of apartheid, Nelson Mandela observed in 1995 that 'we can now deal with our past, establish the truth which has so long been denied us, and lay the basis for genuine reconciliation. Only the truth can put the past to rest.'[1] However, among the many missed opportunities during the early years of post-1994 freedom was a Truth and Reconciliation Commission (TRC) on organised sport. Such a TRC would have laid bare the nature and range of apartheid crimes in the sports arena, its systemic underpinnings and manifestations, and the organisations and individuals that perpetrated the crimes.

It would have documented the impact on and consequences for black sportspersons and their organisations and the repression visited upon those who were committed to the cause of non-racial sport. A TRC on sport would have probed the role of big business in buttressing white domination in sport through generous sponsorship, and the involvement of the state and white-owned media, which devoted print copy and airtime principally to white sports. Indeed, sport journalism and sport journalists have much to answer for regarding the silences, elisions and exclusions that were characteristic of the apartheid era. Some contemporary sports journalists continue to reproduce those practices.

It would have recorded the shameful collusion of international sports bodies that condoned racism for decades, acting against apartheid South Africa only because of international solidarity campaigns to exclude the country from the international sports arena as part of the wider struggle against apartheid. And it would have heard, in contrast to the efforts of black (and a few white) sportspersons and administrators to advance non-racial sport, about black administrators and sportspersons who for a variety of motives – power, money, overseas travel, fame – accommodated racial segregation, collaborated with the apartheid state and were complicit in perpetuating black exclusion and subordination in sport.

Struggles for social justice are impelled by conditions of oppression, exploitation, repression, indignities and injustice of different kinds. First, there is injustice that has its roots in beliefs, prejudice, stereotypes, chauvinism, intolerance and fear of the 'other' – whether the other are people of different colour, races, social classes, sex, gender, sexual orientation, abilities, age, cultures, religions, languages, nationalities or from certain geographical areas. Racism, patriarchy, sexism, homophobia, xenophobia and the like entrench and reproduce social inclusion and exclusion, privilege and disadvantage, domination and subordination, and bountiful opportunity and lack of opportunity. While such beliefs and prejudices and the policies and practices associated with them benefit considerably some social groups and individuals, they simultaneously inflict great pain and suffering on other social groups and individuals.

Second, there is the largely ignored injustice that is deeply woven into and a key feature of contemporary social and economic structures and their underlying relations. These structures and relations, which have developed and ossified over a long period, are considered in some quarters to be natural, pre-ordained, even God-given. They are so entrenched in contemporary society that it is forgotten that they have been produced and reproduced by humans and are products of human thought and action. Of course, such forgetting is encouraged and aided by the rich and powerful and the institutions, organisations and spokespersons that they command.

Current structures and relations underpin the co-existence of unbridled wealth concentrated in the hands of a small minority and desperate and grinding poverty for millions; of enormous privileges for some social groups and tremendous deprivation for countless impoverished others; unbound economic and social opportunities for privileged classes and negligible opportunities for subaltern classes. Archbishop Oscar Romero of El Salvador, an outstanding humanitarian and fighter for social justice, who was tragically murdered while saying mass, observed that 'when the church hears the cry of the oppressed it cannot but denounce the social structures that give rise to and perpetuate the misery from which the cry arises'.[2]

Jody Kollapen, former chairperson of South Africa's Human Rights Commission, writes:

> The reality remains that for millions of people the promise of human rights and the vision of a just and caring world remains an illusion. Intolerance, war and impunity; starvation and greed; power and powerlessness all combine in a conspiracy of the powerful against the weak that invariably deepens the faultlines that exist in the world and within nations. These millions . . . see a world where disparities in wealth, resources and opportunities have grown, where human rights norms and values seem invariably to yield to the dictates of the rich and powerful; which expresses shock and outrage at arbitrary killing but at the same time is complicit in the killing of many more through hunger and disease – which could have been avoided.[3]

Romero and Kollapen draw attention to the injustice that is a consequence of how societies are organised economically and socially and conduct their affairs. It is not an accident of history that there are social groups that are wealthy and impoverished, privileged and disadvantaged, that possess and lack resources and opportunities, and that are powerful and powerless. These conditions are the outcome of contestation and struggle, conflict and co-operation – overt and hidden, dramatic and mundane, episodic and everyday – among and between social classes and groups in society.

South Africa made its transition to democracy in 1994 with an appalling economic and social legacy. Murray Leibbrandt notes:

> Colonialism and apartheid policy explicitly structured a fundamentally unequal South Africa. Spatially, they carved the

country into areas of commercial farming dominated by whites, impoverished Bantustans for Africans, and urban areas where white people had near-exclusive monopoly and controlled all location decisions. This spatial planning undergirded systemic inequalities in the allocation of education, health and all other services [including sport].[4]

Not surprisingly, South Africa entered a hoped-for more just post-apartheid future 'with a level of income inequality in competition with Brazil as the highest in the world. The inequality between racial groups was higher than anywhere else.'[5]

Despite some economic and social improvements in post-1994 South Africa, 29 years into democracy the cleavages of race, class, gender and geography persist. South Africa remains one of the most unequal and unjust societies on earth in terms of disparities in wealth, income, living conditions; and access and opportunities in relation to employment, education, housing, social services, health care – and sport. Indeed, 'income inequality has not changed much since 1994', and South Africa 'continues to generate extreme inequalities'. Today, 'The wealthiest 3 500 people own more than the most impoverished 32 million. Nowhere in the world is the documented gap between the wealthy and impoverished so vast. Nowhere else do so few own so much. And there are few other places where that privilege is protected at such costs.'[6] The degree of wealth inequality in South Africa is unparalleled as quantified by Imraan Valodia:

> The wealthiest 10% of the population owns 85% of all household wealth ... while the wealthiest 0.1% own 25% of it. Even further up the scale, the wealthiest 3 500 people – 0.01% of the adult population – own 15% of all household wealth in South Africa. And while the average net wealth of the top 1% is nearly R18 million, the liabilities of the bottom 50% exceed their assets. So, the most impoverished half of the population has a net worth of negative R16 000.[7]

Even though 'more people are better educated today' than before, 'children born today are more or less guaranteed to end up in the same position as their parents. In a country where nearly half the population are unable to escape poverty, that is a damning indictment.'[8]

Contemporary conditions mean that in South Africa:

> Only one in every four people are part of either the stable middle class or an elite. Half of the population lives in chronic, persistent poverty. In addition, about 11% can be classified as 'transient poor' and about 19% are part of a 'vulnerable middle class', people who are either in poverty or remain vulnerable to falling into poverty from one year to the next. This is a reality that dominates their daily lives.[9]

Race continues to be salient. The elite 'is almost three-quarters white, and more than 90% of white people are consistently "non-poor". By contrast, less than 10% of Africans are consistently "non-poor", and more than 60% are impoverished.'[10]

There is a third kind of injustice. It is rooted in the flagrant abuse and irresponsible exercise of power, or in ethical failures on the part of those who wield economic and political power and who are entrusted with governing, leading, managing and providing key public services such as education, health services and leisure activities, and with safeguarding the environment for future generations.

Those who are impoverished greatly depend on the effective provision of public services to secure their basic needs and improve their lives. Shortcomings and weaknesses in the provision of essential public services undermine their dignity, compromise the development of their potential and talent, thwart the realisation of constitutionally and legally enshrined social imperatives and goals, and violate their human and social rights. In short, they perpetrate grave injustices on the impoverished.

In this regard, Valodia correctly notes:

> Ultimately, inequality is about power . . . Inequality is, in essence, a maldistribution of power. It is about the conditions in a society that allow one group – whether based on race, gender, economic resources, age or sexual preferences – to dominate over another. It is, to use the words of Swedish sociologist Göran Therborn,

'a violation of human dignity: it is a denial of the possibility for everyone's capabilities to develop'.[11]

He adds, quoting economist Darrick Hamilton, that 'dramatic inequality is at least as much a problem of politics as it is of economics. It is time to go beyond the false narrative that attributes inequality to individual deficits, while largely ignoring the advantages of wealth.'[12] This question of human dignity being violated or affirmed and of everyone's capabilities being developed or thwarted is hugely important in relation to sport – and tennis during apartheid. Also pertinent is Hamilton's argument. Indeed, as will be seen, the tendency is to see talent and lack of capabilities largely in individual terms rather in relation to privilege and disadvantage. The notion of merit that is used to justify the persistence of inequitable conditions is seldom related to the advantages of wealth.

A final kind of injustice occurs when institutions and leaders refuse to acknowledge their crimes openly and truthfully, to confess their violations of human rights, to lay bare their misdemeanours, to apologise to their victims and survivors, and to institute meaningful redress and reparations for those who were or are repressed.

In the face of pervasive injustice, five comments are in order regarding the achievement of social justice in South Africa. First, colonialism and apartheid were predicated on a racially based system of inequality in which the majority black population in South Africa was denied equal access, opportunities and outcomes in sport, education and in various other areas. Post-1994, social policy has understandably been grounded on the principle of equality of provision, access, opportunity and outcomes.

Second, equality of treatment and opportunity is a necessary condition, but is not a sufficient condition to eliminate the systemic historical inequalities that black South Africans experienced under apartheid because they were subject to segregated, underdeveloped and unequal institutions and facilities. The inequalities – in sport and other arenas of life – continue into the present and cannot be undone or redressed by formal equality, for that ignores the inherited economic and social structures that sustain and reproduce inequalities. Formal equality must, therefore, be distinguished from equity. Whereas equality refers to the principle of sameness, and to uniformity and standardisation, equity is concerned with fair and just treatment. Equity is imperative if disadvantaged and marginalised social groups are to achieve substantive equality.

Third, meaningful redress requires political commitment on the part of the state, other institutions and key actors to institute purposeful measures to discriminate positively in favour of those who were and are disadvantaged. Redress measures in sport as well as in other social spheres are critical to ensure equity of access, opportunity and outcomes for disadvantaged and marginalised social groups. The measures must be substantive, backed by material resources, rather than purely symbolic.

Fourth, the widespread provision of sports facilities, equipment, coaching, playing opportunities and safe and secure environments, especially in impoverished communities and at schools in historically black areas, is critical for social justice in and through sports. It is a necessary condition to cultivate the sporting capabilities of all social groups and individuals, their development as lifelong sportspersons, their functioning as economically and socially productive people, and their ability to lead rich and rewarding lives.

Fifth, while such a social justice approach would be a significant advance on what existed in pre-1994 sport and apartheid society, it would represent a restricted, thin notion of social justice. Positive discrimination, in the form of affirmative action and similar measures, on its own and in the absence of far-reaching institutional transformation, leaves the status quo intact and unchanged. A substantive, and thick, idea of social justice must recognise the role that economic and social structures play in sustaining and reproducing inequalities and constraining equality, equity, redress and social justice in sport.

Therefore, in addition to measures of positive discrimination that operate essentially in terms of historical rectification and at the level of individuals, it is imperative to fundamentally recast social relations that ground inequality, privilege and disadvantage in sports and in the wider society and to undertake the institutional transformation of sports and economic and social structures.

To achieve transformation in sport entails advancing, creating and sustaining social justice. Transformation is part of a constellation of concepts associated with the idea and process of change – they include improvement, reform, reconstruction and development. These concepts must be carefully delineated, for their use 'interchangeably . . . [empties]

them of specific significance'.[13] While the change processes to which those concepts allude may be related, they differ with respect to the intent and nature of change. Improvement tends to be associated with limited or minor changes in existing organisation, policy or practice. Though the changes that constitute improvements could ameliorate social problems in sport, better facilitate the achievement of specific goals and have substantial impact, they usually involve marginal or limited change rather than substantive change in existing organisation, policy or practice.

Reform involves more substantial changes that have considerable, usually short-term, impact. The changes, however, remain circumscribed within the dominant social and power relations in sport and in the wider polity, economy and society. The changes undertaken could be far-reaching, could unwittingly create ferment and could foster conditions for more radical changes, but their intent is not to displace dominant social relations as much as to reproduce those in new ways and forms.

Transformation, by contrast, seeks to erode and dissolve existing and oppressive social relations and institutions, policies and practice, and to create and consolidate alternative and substantially new social relations, ways of being and doing things. The processes of dissolution and creation may, however, vary in pace and be uneven and may not result in the complete rupture or total and sweeping displacement of old structures, institutions and practices. One reason is that substantive change is always difficult to achieve and uncertain in nature. Another reason is that change is usually contested. Social forces with different economic, political and social interests and goals, even when they cooperate, also mobilise, organise and act to both bring about change as well as to resist change.

In South Africa, the discourse of transformation signalled the intent of ascendant democratic forces to pursue far-reaching and fundamental changes in sport and in other arenas in order to ensure a major rupture from the apartheid period and create a different kind of society after 1994. There has been belated acknowledgement of a few black sports notables who excelled in non-racial sport through induction into halls of fame and conferring colours and blazers and the like. However, there has been either insufficient recognition or total ignoring of most outstanding black sportspersons who could have achieved fame and fortune had it not been for the barriers imposed by apartheid.

There has been no restitution nor reparation, symbolic or material, individual or collective. Judging by the legends – erstwhile apartheid-era sportspersons like Gary Player and Ali Bacher – who regularly feature and are fawned over on radio and television and in newspapers and magazines, all it seems is to be glibly forgiven; worse forgotten. Never mind that those legends of the apartheid era were largely silent, or unabashedly condoned racism in sport, or actively undermined non-racial sport and in the process achieved glory, fame and riches while never testing themselves against black sportspersons.

The most widely known of the liberation movements, but by no means the only one, the ANC, campaigned for equality and equity in sport and the isolation of the apartheid regime and white South Africa from international sport. Through the Freedom Charter, adopted at the Congress of the People in Kliptown in 1955, the ANC proclaimed that 'the colour bar in cultural life, in sport and in education shall be abolished' and that a democratic 'government shall discover, develop and encourage national talent'. The commitment to an education that was 'free, compulsory, universal and equal for all children' implied new and expanded opportunities for black children and youth in the sports arena. Most important, the Freedom Charter located freedom and rights in sports within a wider set of human and social rights in a liberated South Africa.[14]

Alas, 29 years into democracy, sport under successive ANC governments reflects considerable continuity with the devastating imprint and scars of the apartheid past, with meaningful development, purposeful cultivation of talent and realisation of aspirations drowned on the altar of obsession largely with professional and commercialised sport, race quotas and the like.[15] A misguided glib rainbowism and banal declarations to forget the past and embrace the future has resulted in a convenient sweeping under the carpet of past reprehensible racist conduct in sport, part of an increasing amnesia about the effects of our violent and oppressive colonial and apartheid history.

But memories cannot be so easily blunted and must not be. William Faulkner writes: 'The past is never dead. It's not even past.'[16] Milan Kundera reminds us that 'the struggle of man against power is the struggle of memory against forgetting'.[17] And Primo Levi, a Holocaust survivor, urges that 'if it is impossible to understand, we ought to at least know. For what has happened once, can happen again.'[18]

Past and present are inextricably connected and inevitably shape the future. Mac Maharaj has rightly contended that 'to hide the horrors of the past in a collective amnesia [leaves] posterity with a legacy of festering . . . and unrelieved pain'.[19] James Baldwin, the African American writer and civil rights activist, reminds us that 'not everything that is faced can be changed, but nothing can be changed until it is faced'.[20] The late Eduardo Galeano, a South American journalist, novelist and acclaimed global football commentator, observed that 'if the past has nothing to say to the present, history may go on sleeping undisturbed in the closet where the system keeps its old disguises'.[21]

In our own context, the late, outstanding intellectual and liberation fighter Neville Alexander astutely observes that the key political question on the human condition in post-apartheid South Africa

> is how to move towards understanding without ever forgetting, but to remember without constantly rekindling the divisive passions of the past. Such an approach is the only one which would allow us to look down into the darkness of the well of the atrocities of the past and to speculate on their causes at the same time as we haul up the waters of hope for a future of dignity and equality.[22]

3

Reclaiming the Narrative on Tennis History

With reference to the sports arena, André Odendaal draws on Chinua Achebe who argued that '"in the colonial situation presence was the critical question, the crucial word. Its denial was the keynote of colonialist ideology."' Odendaal contends that 'the case of sport and sports history underlines Achebe's argument'.[1]

It is imagined, incorrectly, that black South Africans who were marginalised economically, politically and socially under colonialism and apartheid were absent from participating in, developing, organising and administering the game of tennis. As a result, writes Odendaal:

> Apartheid and exclusion became naturalised eventually, even amongst those who were themselves subjugated. These assumptions about the 'naturalness' of the 'culture' of sport continue to be reproduced in new guises without any great self-awareness by a historically illiterate media and sports constituency in the democratic era, reproducing and making acceptable past exclusions in sport in the process.[2]

He rightly contends:

> At the core of the project of decolonising South African sports history, therefore, is the effort to understand how the absences of the colonial subject in sport were engineered and how colonial narratives became fixed in the literature and minds of South Africans – and to attempt to redress this situation.[3]

What is required is more than mere marshalling of proof

> that black South Africans do indeed have a sports history, but rather a full-scale re-imagining and rewriting of the history of sport in this country. This rewriting must inevitably go with painstaking research and readings in still under-exploited archives and fields of enquiry despite the pressures of the post-modern digital age to produce instant outcomes.[4]

For tennis, as for other sports, some additional shifts are required. First, we need 'to go beyond existing colonial and apartheid narratives by integrating, from the beginning, at every stage and in every area, the experiences of hitherto excluded black [tennis players] in the country'.[5]

The standard narrative even today is exemplified by an article on the KZN Tennis Association website.[6] We are told that 'the history of Natal Tennis is the very history of South African tennis. The South African Lawn Tennis Union was founded in 1903.' That was a year after the founding of the Natal Tennis Association. This account admits that 'no one quite knows for sure how or exactly where the first game of tennis was played in Southern Africa, but there is a strong suggestion that the place was somewhere in Natal... The oldest club in the country is the Richmond Tennis Club', established the same year (1877) that the first Wimbledon tournament was held.

By the 1880s, tennis was a key 'feature of colonial life in Durban and Pietermaritzburg' and the first Natal championships were held in Pietermaritzburg in 1884. The old province of Natal (today KwaZulu-Natal) is credited with playing a key role in establishing tennis as one of the 'major sports in South Africa' due 'to the efforts of its many far-sighted officials'. They reportedly 'pressed for and established the South African senior inter-provincial tournaments and... South African junior championships'. Natal officials also instituted with the help of the South African sugar industry the tennis Sugar Circuit, which became the 'breeding ground for... world ranked players'. Of course, the Sugar Circuit was the exclusive playground of white South Africans.

While the KZN Tennis Association foregrounds the above narrative, its website includes another article. We are informed that it 'is based primarily on a missive from former tennis administrator, Mr E. Osman, and provides a brief, yet succinct account of tennis, as one of the sports of choice in the Black communities in KwaZulu-Natal'. It adds that 'due to a lack of documentation, much of the information is anecdotal and historical details cannot be verified'.[7] What this does is confer value on the archive as opposed to oral history, failing to recognise that there are also problems associated with archives.[8]

The ostensibly fact-based 'History of KZN Tennis' is an account entirely of tennis played by whites, with the staggering claim that it 'is the very history of South African tennis'. The claim is not mitigated by featuring an (ironically separate) article on black involvement in tennis.[9] There is some coverage of women's tennis. However, there is a silence on blacks playing tennis and their deliberate exclusion from the whites-only clubs and tournaments that were established in Natal and on the same pattern elsewhere. The legends of tennis mentioned are all entirely white.

Sight cannot be lost of the injustice that an industry – sugar – built originally on Indian indentured labour, and later black labour more generally, financed and cultivated leading white tennis players, but did little to support black players. Moreover, it condoned racial tennis, typical of corporate business under colonialism and apartheid.

Odendaal argues that tennis and other histories of sport cannot 'avoid dealing with the issue of gender. Next to deep-seated race and class discrimination, ingrained sexism has been at the core of the "traditions" and "culture"' of tennis and other sports. The 'power relations and socially constructed conventions' that made tennis and various sports white colonial games 'also reinforced patriarchal control over the female body, on and off the field'.[10]

Sadly, the non-racial sport movement, too, 'largely reflected the norms of South Africa's discriminatory patriarchal society. For example, it was only in the mid-1980s that sexism in sport became a debating issue within SACOS.' It is pertinent to note that in 1985 the non-racial tennis body, the Tennis Association of South Africa (TASA), 'was criticised for going ahead with the "presentation rituals" straight after the men's singles finals at its annual championships, even though the women's singles finals were still underway'.[11]

Farieda Khan writes that 'tennis in South Africa has a long history at both mainstream and township level, as well as a proud record of female participation dating back to the late nineteenth century'. Tennis is distinct 'from a male-dominated sport such as football' in that 'at a time when Victorian notions of passive femininity held sway, middle- and upper-class women enthusiastically became involved in playing social and competitive tennis from the earliest days of the sport in South Africa' in the late 1800s. Khan suggests that 'the participation of women in tennis was fairly remarkable during this era' because 'globally their participation in sport was commonly frowned upon, perceived as dangerous and as a potential obstacle to their ability to bear children'. However, 'it is likely that the acceptance of women in tennis was due to the fact that the game was perceived (like croquet), as an appropriate form of sport for women – i.e. not aggressive, overly strenuous or requiring physical contact – and thus not incompatible with the notion of being ladylike'.

While 'the formal and informal colour bar in operation' under colonialism would have meant that 'in all probability, membership of the early tennis clubs was exclusively White', black exposure to tennis 'would have occurred as part of the missionary school education (which included sport) then available to the elite'. As a result, 'they would then have formed

Black South Africans participated in organised tennis from the late nineteenth century (S. Mofokeng, *The Black Photo Album: Look at Me: 1890–1950*. Göttingen: Steidl, 2013).

separate clubs in urban areas where this was possible, as happened in Port Elizabeth . . . King Williamstown in the 1880s . . . Bloemfontein in 1893 and three in Kimberley in the 1890s'.

There 'is evidence that educated African women and girls did indeed participate in sport in general and tennis in particular. Further evidence is provided by the fact that in 1894, women were members of the three African tennis clubs then in existence in Kimberley and also played competitive tennis.' Khan writes that by the 1930s, middle-class African women 'utilised the facilities of the Bantu Social Club to play tennis' and 'many Johannesburg tennis teams, such as the Rosebuds and United Services included women, while there were also all-woman teams such as the Bloemfontein Ladies and the Johannesburg Ladies'.

She contends that 'while many women undoubtedly enjoyed the game, with some taking it fairly seriously, for others playing tennis was just a status symbol, an indicator that they were part of the leisured classes'. Status-seeking women 'featured in the social pages of the newspaper, *Bantu World*, having tennis parties in urban centres such as Bloemfontein and East London'.[12]

Peter Alegi, author of an authoritative book on soccer in South Africa, observes that 'sport seemed to hold a special place in the assimilationist dream of Africa's "citizens of empire" as it stoked the petite bourgeoisie's "deep desire for full cultural citizenship" in their communities'. Concomitantly, 'in the context of enduring colonialism and segregation, sport (to varying degrees) also influenced their growing political consciousness and demands for social justice'. Indeed, the 'black middle class's belief in and commitment to sport's universalism, fairness, equality, and merit – the "Games Ethic" – made sport relevant to broader struggles for civil rights and human rights'. While 'women were not absent from the story . . . in this early period they played mostly supportive roles; some did participate in cricket, athletics, tennis and other sports'. As Alegi indicates: 'More research is needed to document and understand how women's sports may have shaped Africans' assimilationist dream.'[13]

Khan notes that in Cape Town, among 'coloured communities, the development of tennis followed a similar pattern, with tennis being played on municipal courts by the business and professional elite during the 1930s'. With growing interest in tennis, 'a number of clubs were established which women eagerly joined . . . One such club was Wisteria, which was established in Salt River in 1934 by a group of Muslims (including women) many of whom were teachers.'

A non-racial junior tennis champion Lynnette (Thomas) Clarke 'who joined Progressive Tennis Club in Elsies River as a child of 11 in 1963, remembers tennis as a "family affair", which she greatly enjoyed as a tennis player'. Similarly, Avril Jansen, writes Khan,

> joined Athlone Tennis Club as a child of six in 1968 and by the age of 12 had already progressed to senior level. Subsequently she played in the top league and was good enough to represent Western Province at inter-provincial level. She remembers the 1970s and early 1980s as a time when tennis attracted the enthusiasm of the whole community. During matches there would be line of cars outside the courts, where there was a 'euphoric atmosphere' and 'the excitement was just magical'.[14]

Beyond Khan's important contribution, 'scholars are beginning to show that despite being pigeon-holed into gender roles, women have never been completely contained by Victorian and African patriarchal mindsets, and that substantial histories about their involvement in different sports are possible'.[15]

Goolam Vahed introduces the important dimension of the 'use of sport and recreation as instruments of social control'. He shows how, in the aftermath of mass popular protests in the late 1920s and the growth of the African population, the local state in Durban in the 1930s sought to control African leisure time and incorporate the African middle class. He writes:

> During the 1930s Europeans became aware of 'dangerous leisure' and missionaries, liberal humanitarians, administrators, and employers all had a deep interest in African 'free time'. It was believed that free time led to crime, drunkenness, illicit sexuality and riots, and that the leisure time activities of the working classes had to be controlled to produce a fit and competent workforce. Sport and recreation were used as an antidote to protest and militancy, and a means of instilling appropriate discipline amongst Africans.[16]

Chief Albert Luthuli (1898-1967), in 1960 the first African winner of the Nobel Peace Prize 'for his non-violent struggle against apartheid', played 'an occasional game of tennis for exercise' in his youth days in Natal and was involved for many years with soccer in Durban and nationally.[17] As a young man, he too

> internalized the liberal view that sport was a useful tool to 'moralize leisure time' of African youth. 'Games develop and call for the exercise of those qualities which contribute to the highest manhood,' Luthuli wrote in the Adams College publication *Iso Lomuzi*, 'and for most of us they help to keep us occupied in our leisure moments when otherwise the devil would be finding work for our idle hands.'

In due course, Luthuli 'came to appreciate the value of sport for black political mobilization'.[18] As Alegi notes:

> A quarter of a century before Dennis Brutus launched the first anti-apartheid sport organization (CCIRS, 1955), and nearly half a century prior to South Africa's expulsion from the Olympics (1970), Luthuli recognized the power of sport to build solidarity through sociability and to serve as a mobilizing force in the South African liberation struggle.[19]

In 1931, the Bantu Recreational Grounds Association (BRGA) was established in Durban to 'promote and foster knowledge' of various sports, including tennis. A tennis court was built in Somtseu Road in 1930 and the BRGA soon had four tennis courts under its control, more courts being built as the game became popular among the African middle class.[20] Clubs like the Star Lawn Tennis Club and Primrose Lawn Tennis Club emerged, with the latter wanting 'one court allotted for its exclusive use. Local clubs had "frequent friendly matches" between themselves, large crowds were in attendance and local players even entertained a visiting team from Richmond' in 1931.[21]

In 1933, modelled on one in existence in Johannesburg, the Bantu Men's Social Centre (BMSC) was established in Victoria Street, Durban. A state official hoped that it would '"have a great influence in restoring our prestige, would help in building up decent Native citizens, and would minimise the growing menace of disgruntled Natives"'.[22] The BMSC's membership was largely from prominent African elites. One of the bodies that used the BMSC was the Durban Bantu Lawn Tennis Association. An African Tennis Association was also in existence. In 1937, a gala held 'as part of the Coronation of King George VI' included a tennis tournament and 'by 1939 there was an annual tournament between Durban and Pietermaritzburg'.[23]

An official of the BRGA commented that 'tennis is to the "more enlightened Native as popular as Football is to his less enlightened brother"'. Bernard Magubane's take was that 'tennis was played by men of the "excuse me" class while "fit and strong" men, the authentic men, played football'.[24] Vahed observes that the idea that 'soccer was associated with ruggedness and tennis with mildness can be seen in the fact that soccer clubs had names such as "Wild Savages", "Assegais" and "Rebellious", while tennis clubs were named "Daffodils", "Morning Stars" and "Winter Roses"'.[25]

He makes two important arguments about the involvement of the local state in tennis, other sports, and leisure activities. First:

> An important feature of the emerging leisure activities was segregation along gender, class and, very important, racial lines. Africans spent virtually all their leisure time with other Africans, and males at that. The construction of parallel forms of sport and leisure structures meant that sport did not transcend the sectional divisions of Durban's social order. The rigid segregation between Whites, Indians and Africans had important consequences for identity and consciousness. Sport reinforced segregation rather than fostered assimilation.[26]

Much the same can be said about tennis and other sports in the rest of South Africa.

Second, 'the trend towards institutionalisation was another conspicuous feature of leisure in Durban'. Tennis became institutionalised, came under the control of the state, and part of the attempt to control blacks through regulation of their leisure activities.[27]

Odendaal argues that given the pervasive exclusion of black and women South Africans in sport, 'statistics are integral to the culture and romance of tennis and other sports. While 'statistics do not make for glamorous narratives, and they too are admittedly subjectively or socially constructed . . . they are indispensable in the attempt to make visible in professional, standardised ways the extent and depth of organisation and involvement of those excluded in the past'.[28]

Especially important, scholarship and histories of sports, including tennis, must go, according to Odendaal,

> beyond old sporting binaries – good/bad, apartheid/struggle, men/women, insiders/outsiders – to reveal something of the vibrancy, creativity, contradictions, joy and feelings which accompanied the playing of [tennis] in many different communities over many years: from the dreams and aspirations of individuals to the rich creativity and social tapestry found in team and club dynamics, to the determination and balletic skills of those who made it to the top.[29]

That is to say, sport histories must comprise 'multiperspectival approaches that explore and question rather than fix in simple terms the complex dynamics involved in the playing and organising of sport'. They must 'give insights into changing identities and the mindsets and motivations that were at play' among different groups in different places and spaces at different times and show that 'particular individuals and [tennis] communities had different views of themselves and different visions for the future'.[30]

In similar vein, Alegi calls for 'a new revisionist history' that goes beyond a '"master narrative" of South African sport history that privileges national redemption and patriotic heroism at the expense of more complex individual, local and global dynamics'. He advocates the use of oral histories and neglected written materials of grassroots social movements, organisations and coalitions as important antidotes to simple and unnuanced master narratives.[31] Those data sources are indispensable for reinserting into historical accounts important ignored, forgotten, neglected or marginalised social actors as makers of history.

Such wider sources help to expand and reconstitute the archive, which is fundamental to decolonising history, including histories of sport, for revisiting past stories and narrating alternative stories, and for decentring 'big men' as the sole or key actors. Valuing, gathering and preserving a much more diverse set of voices and memories of sportspersons, sports administrators, sports fans, activists, organisations and communities ensure that 'local voices, experiences, and memories... take their rightful place in the larger historical narrative'.[32]

On the one hand, making recourse to existing and new archives is about 'history and tradition, characters and experiences, which if not documented will leave future generations poorer'. But it is equally about history empowering 'people and communities written out of the past'.[33] However, it is not only methodology, the use of more diverse and neglected sources and decolonial approaches, that is important to advance sport history. Also necessary is 'to extend the history of sport beyond soccer, rugby, and cricket' – to sports like tennis as with this book, and to other sports.[34]

In so far as there is a '"master narrative" of South African sport history', it 'is a story told in three acts'. As Alegi describes:

> In the opening act, the consolidation of apartheid in the 1950s inspires sport activists to build an antiracist network seeking to racially integrate national teams, thereby casting sport in the political spotlight. The second act is set in the 1960s and 1970s as the sport boycott ostracizes white South Africa from the Olympic movement, world football, and nearly every other major sport – important symbolic victories in the larger quest for freedom. The third and final act unfolds against the backdrop of apartheid giving way to democracy in the early 1990s. Segregated sport federations merge into unified, nonracial institutions and South Africa's reentry into global sport is celebrated with home victories in the 1995 Rugby World Cup and 1996 African Cup of Nations, unleashing a wave of rainbow nationalist euphoria throughout the sports-mad nation.[35]

Alegi argues that 'like the Hollywood version in Clint Eastwood's film *Invictus* about the 1995 rugby triumph, this narrative of "victory, unity, and progress" is "based on a true story"'. However, while 'most critics warmly embraced the film', they neglected 'its factual inaccuracies and fictionalized embellishments, praising it as a stirring, uplifting story about how sporting events can unify people in racially divided nations'.³⁶ The problem is that the film's 'strategically selective, oversimplified version of the past conceals the complexities and contradictions of apartheid sport and the liberation struggle – "a world of moral ambivalence and ambiguity... in which people could be both resisters and collaborators at the same time"'.³⁷

Odendaal contends:

> The healthiest way to view the past non-racial sports struggles is by exploring and celebrating its diversity and contradictions, rather than producing nostalgic, uninterrogated narratives about a struggle of good over bad. In other word, a critical approach to storying the past is the best way to give it life and meaning in the present.

He argues that 'it was long established intellectual lineages and historical explanations germinating in the "struggle" (and outside the established universities) that ultimately intellectually subverted the master narratives of white domination, and contributed to the far-reaching reconstruction of South Africa over the past few decades'. Those 'intellectual lineages and traditions', therefore, 'have to be integrated more fully into the intellectual and academic narratives of South Africa in future. Not as own-affairs footnotes in a bigger story of academic history, but as part of the defining intellectual patterns in South Africa's development... The same applies to the sports struggle.'³⁸

Odendaal submits that 'the ideas that led to political mobilization and eventually democracy were also the ideas that guided the sports struggle' and that 'the struggle in sport, as in politics, was from the start opposed to racism and underpinned by ideas of equal opportunity'.³⁹

Far from, as suggested by the master narrative, the sports struggle beginning in the 1950s, the struggle against racism and for equity in sport in South Africa has a long and convoluted history. The approaches, strategies and tactics used to counter and defeat racism and advance equality and equity in sport and society changed and varied since the colonial period (1652–1910), through to the segregation period (1910–1948), the period of grand apartheid, the repressive reformism of the late 1970s and 1980s, and the transition to democracy (1990–1994).

However, the goals were, if not always identical, not dissimilar. The goals articulated and the strategies and tactics used at different times, in different places and spaces, and interpretation of them and their appropriateness and efficacy must be comprehended on the basis of values and principles for sure, but also with sensitivity to context.

As Philip Abrams argues:

> Doing justice to the reality of history is not a matter of noting the way in which the past provides a background to the present; it is a matter of treating what people do in the present as a struggle to create a future *out* of the past, of seeing that the past is not just the womb of the present but the only raw material out of which the present can be constructed.

Another reason is that 'what we choose to do and what we have to do are shaped by the historically given possibilities among which we find ourselves'.[40] Interpretation, then, cannot revolve purely around questions of the doctrines of organisations, the class and wider social locations of actors, their economic and political interests and the like; but must also consider the economic, social and political terrain on which sports organisations, groups and individuals operated, how they traversed this terrain, and their actual effects on this terrain.

Francis Piven and Richard Cloward put it well: 'What was won must be judged by what was possible.' To paraphrase them, the 'relevant question to ask is whether, on balance', non-racial sports movements, organisations, players and administrators 'made gains or lost ground'; whether they 'advanced the interests' of the dominated classes and social groups or 'set back those interests'.[41]

Lesley le Grange observes that a distinction is made between the ideas of '*blank spots* and *blind spots* . . . *blank spots* are what scientists know enough about to question but do not answer, and *blind spots* are what they don't know enough about or care about'. In these terms, black participation in tennis under colonialism and apartheid is a blank spot; 'indigenous sports/games were blind spots during the colonial period, and largely remain so in post-apartheid South Africa'.[42] Le Grange clarifies that 'decolonisation is the undoing of colonisation'. Whereas 'first-generation colonialism was the conquering of the physical spaces and bodies of the colonised', 'second-generation colonialism was the colonisation of people's minds' in which science, religion, education and sport played critical roles.⁴³ The end of colonialism was not necessarily the end of imperial domination. Previously colonised countries remained under the domination of their former colonisers through unequal economic relations and the dominance in the post-war period of international institutions such as the United Nations (UN) by the superpowers, especially the US.

Sport followed this trend, with international sports bodies often dominated by and directed at securing the sports interests of Western countries. The post-war era of independence of Global South countries such as India, however, also ushered in an agenda of decolonisation. In 1951, independent India hosted, for example, the first Asian Games to 'promote the feeling of unity and friendship between newly independent nations in the continent'.⁴⁴

Decolonising involves various processes and activities. One is deconstruction, which entails jettisoning narratives that wrongly portray, distort and denigrate the histories, cultures, experiences and abilities of black people. Second is 'rediscovery and recovery', which 'is the process whereby colonised peoples rediscover and recover their own history, culture, language and identity' and produce and disseminate their own stories of their past and present lives and existence.⁴⁵

Third is 'mourning', which laments 'the continued assault on the world's colonised/oppressed peoples' identities and social realities' and 'is an important part of healing and leads to dreaming'. Fourth is dreaming through which black and colonised people 'imagine alternative possibilities'.⁴⁶ In relation to the concerns of this book, dreaming would include the idea of redress for black people for past injustices in tennis and more generally, and an equitable future in which, irrespective of race, class, gender, income and geography, all people have meaningful opportunities to play tennis should they so wish.

At the same time, we would ask questions. Who actually plays tennis in South Africa and how does this square with the imperative of transformation? What opportunities exist at the school level? Who controls tennis in South Africa and internationally? Who controls sponsorship? We would also ask questions about the media and how it narrates tennis and its history.

Ultimately, '(re)telling South African black sport histories', including the history of tennis, would 'de-centre a white history', a predominantly male history, a 'big person' history and urban-centric history of sport; as part of epistemic justice, better scholarship and advancing the substantive transformation of tennis in South Africa. Le Grange notes that in post-1994, 'South Africa blacks are often told by whites to move on, to forget about apartheid. But mourning is an important ingredient in the healing process and a necessary step of decolonisation.' He contends correctly that 'the pain of historical exclusion in sport needs to be shared and felt – we have not had a Truth & Reconciliation process in Sport in South Africa'. He observes rightly that despite the illusions, 'on its own sport cannot' unite South Africans.[47]

The genuine unification of South Africans on and off the sports fields and arenas, as opposed to the current dubious and glib rainbowism, requires purposefully addressing the deeply entrenched inequalities in wealth, income and poverty bequeathed by colonialism and apartheid. Action on those fronts is a necessary condition for everyone to have meaningful opportunities to participate, flourish and excel in tennis and other sports.[48]

4

From Colonialism to Apartheid in Sport

Sport, like education, welfare, health and other activities in a society, is intimately connected with the ideological, economic and political conditions and practices in that society. Approaches to policy and practice on and related to sport are shaped by ideologies, political doctrines and economic and social (for example, cultural, educational and welfare) considerations. This means that there will inevitably be politics around sport, politics understood as struggles over existing relations, policies and practices in sport or around issues that have a bearing on sport, 'struggles that take as their *objective* the quantitative or qualitative change of those relations', policies and practices.[1]

Sport politics, then, has to do with contestations and struggles within the sport arena that have the aim of either preserving, modifying, eroding or transforming prevailing relations, policies and practices (questions such as the purpose and goals of sport, its role in society, its regulation, governance, organisation, financing, and so on). However, sport politics is not restricted solely to the sport arena but is also played out in other spheres like the state, other political institutions, the business sector, civil society and the media. It involves various actors, including the state at different levels, government, political parties, businesses, professional bodies, social movements, organisations and individuals.

How sport politics – contestations, struggles, collective mobilisation, organisation and action, and individual actions over sport and within sport and within and outside the sport arena – manifest themselves and what their outcomes are depends on: the nature of the sport arena as well as the nature of the state; the political terrain; society; and the authority, power and capacities of different actors and the resources available to them. Existing social structures, institutional arrangements, policies and practices condition the form and content of struggles, and their outcomes, in terms of achievements and failures.[2] However, although they condition struggles, they do not entirely constrain actions for change, thus rendering change impossible and guaranteeing the reproduction of the status quo. Struggles whether of a class, race, gender or popular nature in and beyond the sport arena can challenge, modify, erode and transform existing social structures, institutional arrangements, policies and practices.

This is because in South Africa, in the words of Harold Wolpe, the arenas and

> the apparatuses in and through which white domination [was] maintained may stand not only in a functional, complementary and supportive relationship to one another, but also in relations of contradiction and conflict . . . The possibility is opened up that, within certain apparatuses and institutions, white domination may continue to be reproduced, albeit in changing forms, while within others it becomes, at the same time, eroded.[3]

In other words, despite the generally authoritarian and repressive character of the apartheid state, its policies and institutions cannot be conceived as omnipotent, monolithic, homogeneous and entirely impermeable to political challenge and change.

The relationship between social action and existing structures must be 'understood as a matter of process in time'.[4] Thus, even if the activities of non-racial sport movements and organisations may not have been immediate and serious threats to apartheid domination, their struggles had the potential to weaken the pillars of such domination to the extent that the state was impelled to restructure the way it maintained domination. In this process, new conditions and a new and altered terrain of struggle could be established, which could be more favourable to the efforts of popular movements and organisations.

When the National Party came to power in 1948 on a programme of apartheid separate development, for some years there were no specific laws that prohibited black and white sportspersons from playing with or against each other.[5] Segregation in sports along the lines of race and ethnicity in fact predated apartheid: its roots lay in British colonial rule and was a social convention and practice.

Posel argues:

> Apartheid's principal imaginary was of a society in which every 'race' knew and observed its proper place – economically, politically and socially. Race was to be the critical and overriding faultline: the fundamental organising principle for the allocation of all resources and opportunities, the basis of all spatial demarcation, planning and development, the boundary for all social interaction, as well as the primary category in terms of which this social and moral order was described and defended.[6]

She notes that in apartheid South Africa 'life . . . was subject to powerful racial hierarchies' and that 'the apartheid government rapidly set out to assign every South African citizen a single racial classification, which would then become uniformly binding across all spheres of that person's experience'.[7] This occurred in terms of the Population Registration Act of 1950, which 'centralised population registration [and] was the bureaucratic cornerstone of the Apartheid state, the lynch-pin of the Group Areas Act, and of the Dompas (Reference Book)'. Classifying the population was critical to the legal foundations and working of apartheid and it 'was population registration that created the distinctive four-part racial order in South Africa – placing individuals into one of the basic categories' whose names changed over time and eventually came to be described as 'Coloured, Indian, White or Black'.[8]

What apartheid did was to further institutionalise and deepen an already existing system of racist hierarchies and conventions in sport. Douglas Booth writes:

> From 1948 the government gradually took control of sport until, by the early 1960's, any pretence of sports administrators being their own masters had vanished. Between 1962 and 1963 the Minister of the Interior, Jan De Klerk, outlined the government's policy on sport: each sport must have a separate controlling association for each population group; black associations should develop under the auspices of white associations with the latter acting as controlling bodies and providing representatives to

the corresponding world bodies; South Africa would not be represented by multiracial teams; and multiracial teams from abroad would not be issued with visas to play in South Africa. De Klerk repeatedly made reference to segregated sport as an 'old national custom' and this was used to justify government policy.[9]

The case of Indian South African golfer Sewsunker (Papwa) Sewgolum is poignantly illustrative.[10] In the late 1950s and early 1960s, Sewgolum played in and won the Dutch Open three times. However, he was not permitted to compete in professional tournaments within South Africa, which were exclusively for whites. With criticism and 'pressure, the authorities permitted Sewgolum to play in the Natal Open in 1963 at the famous Durban Country Club, after having been satisfied that apartheid laws would not be broken'.[11] Sewgolum won the Natal Open but 'to the eternal disgrace and shame of both the white golfing fraternity and government officials, [he] was not allowed to enter the Durban country club to receive his prize' as use of the clubhouse was for whites alone. How and where the trophy was handed to Sewgolum is a matter of contention, but not at issue is the fact that the prize-giving happened outside the whites-only club house.[12]

Sewgolum won the Natal Open again in 1965. In the process, he defeated Gary Player, an apartheid apologist at the top of his game. That day, Selvan Naidoo writes,

> saw all the caddies, waiters and factory workers standing slightly taller. This victory was far more symbolic than their hero winning a golf tournament. For the Black working class, this moment of pride was their fleeting victory against the evil system of apartheid that constantly denied them their place in the sun.[13]

Sewgolum's 1963 triumph 'embarrassed the Nationalists for he had beaten one of their own. They targeted him personally and banned mixed audiences so that Papwa's large throng of Indian supporters could not attend the South African Open in 1965.'[14]

In due course, Naidoo writes:

> The Apartheid regime had enough of Papwa embarrassing its white golfers and put an end to his career locally. In 1965, he received the fateful message from the Minister of Planning, Dr Carel de Wet, in response to an application for an open permit to play golf in white areas: 'I have to inform you by direction of the Minister that has already indicated the granting of a permit will be in conflict with government policy. In the circumstances the Minister does not see his way clear to approve the issue of a permit.'[15]

Sewgolum died in 1978 at the age of 49, 'penniless and a broken man because he was denied the opportunity to do what he loved most in life – play golf at the highest levels'.[16]

The privileged Gary Player by comparison had no impediments on his path, going 'on to become one of the greatest players the game has known, and a multi-millionaire'.[17] Player acknowledges that Sewgolum was 'very, very talented'. He is, however, begrudging about what the latter could have achieved; and he diminishes massively the full import of apartheid's destructive consequences for world class black sportspersons like Sewgolum by glibly stating that 'he came along at the wrong time, unfortunately'.[18] This observation of Player is unsurprising as he was an unequivocal supporter and apologist of apartheid in his heyday. This is abundantly clear from the following:

> I must say now, and clearly, that I am of the South Africa of Verwoerd and apartheid ... a nation which is the result of an African graft on European stock and which is the product of its instinct and ability to maintain civilised values and standards amongst the alien barbarians ... The African may well believe in witchcraft and primitive magic, practise ritual murder and polygamy; his wealth is in cattle ... A good deal of nonsense is talked of, and indeed thought about 'segregation'. Segregation of one kind or another is practised everywhere in the world ... We in South Africa ... believe that our races should develop separately, but in parallel.[19]

If racial segregation in sport was a matter of convention rather than strictly law, numerous laws still impeded the playing of sport without reference to race and strongly constrained non-racial sport.[20]

The 1950 Group Areas Act demarcated occupancy and residency according to race and in effect constrained social interaction between South Africans of different races. On 12 February 1965, a proclamation under the Group Areas Act prohibited blacks from various recreation places, including sporting events in areas reserved for whites. The Native (Urban Areas) Consolidation Act of 1945 and the Bantu Laws Amendment Act of 1963 prohibited non-Africans from entering areas reserved for Africans, while the 1957 Native Laws Amendment Act had provisions that could be used to preclude Africans from taking part in events held in areas inhabited by other race groups. The Reservation of Separate Amenities Act of 1953 restricted public facilities for the use of specific race groups.[21]

Racial segregation in sports as a matter of social practice did not lessen its devastating effects on black South Africans. 'Only whites could represent South Africa on international federations and only white players could earn Springbok honours in international competition.'[22] For white South Africans, segregated sport along racial lines reinforced and bolstered their already institutionalised privilege and advantage – it was a veritable programme of affirmative action for whites.

White sports administrators and sportspersons by and large supported the status quo and revelled in the benefits afforded them on and off the sportsfield by a racist government, for which many of them voted. Many of them were also racist, subscribing to notions of white superiority and the superiority of European economic systems, values, culture, languages and, of course, sport. This reflected the structural racism that permeated all areas of life under apartheid and which forcibly subordinated and disadvantaged black South Africans, especially women and those of working-class and rural origins.

A UN report on apartheid noted:

> The absence of direct legislation preventing mixed sport ideally suits the racist government. Special sports events for international consumption can then be staged by issuing permits or licences which normally expire about an hour after the termination of the

sports meeting. If there was direct legislation prohibiting mixed sport, South Africa would not be able to sugar-coat its policy of racial discrimination. It would not then be able to insert black puppets into its overseas delegations for parading at international congresses. The deliberate omission of this type of legislation is an essential ingredient in their plan to ward off total isolation.[23]

A commitment to non-racial sport among white South Africans was rare and the exception.

There was not 'a single case of a white organization defying the sports policy' of the apartheid government, though there were a few white individuals who participated in sports organised by black non-racial organisations.[24] Defiance of apartheid sports policy was led by and came from black advocates of non-racial sport.

In 1967, after asserting that notwithstanding the importance of international sports relations he would not compromise on racial segregation in sport, Prime Minister Vorster announced 'what was widely interpreted as a new concessionary sports policy' following South Africa's exclusion from the 1964 Tokyo Olympics and its suspension from international soccer and fencing.[25]

South Africa would field a 'multiracial team' for the Olympic Games, if there were 'any of our Coloureds or Bantu who were good enough to compete'; tennis teams could play against black teams within and outside South Africa, and other countries would be free to select whoever they wished when playing rugby and cricket against South Africa.[26] However, Vorster reaffirmed that 'no mixed sport between Whites and non-Whites will be practised locally', adding that 'in respect of this principle we are not prepared to compromise, we are not prepared to negotiate and we are not prepared to make any concessions'.[27]

In 1970, Vorster reiterated that 'South Africa will not give up its apartheid policy of racial segregation as the price for participating in world sport'. He stated that 'if the choice is between taking part in international sport and our way of life, which we have developed in this country over generations then naturally the majority of our people will say that we have no choice in the matter whatsoever'.[28] By 'majority of our people', Vorster, of course, meant white South Africans, since blacks were denied the vote and not considered citizens. It was a clear statement by the leader of white South Africa at the time that there would not be any forsaking of white minority *baaskap* and privilege in South Africa for the sake of playing international sport.

Vorster was speaking following criticism of the apartheid government's decision in January 1970 to refuse African American tennis champion Arthur Ashe a visa to play in South Africa and in the aftermath of the expulsion of South Africa from the International Olympic Committee (IOC) in May 1970. The previous year the growing international opposition to the apartheid government's racist policies increased when an all-white South African Davis Cup team played against Britain. They 'were greeted by the flour bombs of Peter Hain-led anti-apartheid demonstrators in Bristol'.[29]

By 1970, as Robin Kelley notes:

> The movement to isolate South Africa was in full swing. International action against South Africa included the cancellation of a West German hockey tour of South Africa; the suspension of South Africa from the International Amateur Athletic Federation; suspension from the International Amateur Wrestling Federation; and the refusal of the Jamaican government to allow white South African players and delegates to attend a world netball conference and tournament in Jamaica. Beyond the question of international diplomacy, the rising international consciousness of the realities of apartheid stimulated mass sports-related protests. 'Stop the 70s Tour', led by Hain in Britain, was able to mobilize 50,000 demonstrators against the Springbok cricket tour of England. In Dublin, Ireland alone, 10,000 people turned out to protest racist South Africa's participation.[30]

In the face of this determined and growing opposition, the apartheid regime dug in its heels. In 1971, Vorster clarified that while 'sport was important' it was 'not as important as many other things'.[31] Thus, 'participation in sport in South Africa should in the first place be seen against the background of the policy . . . of separate, distinctive development', which applied to whole of society.[32]

Piet Koornhof, the minister of sport and recreation, elucidated government policy on sport further: 'Separate participation in sport is a natural and obvious outcome of the government's policy of separate development.'[33] This statement demonstrates that ideological and political considerations weigh on and affect sport. Koornhof added that 'on club level... mixed teams will not or cannot exist. Precisely the same applies on the provincial level, and so, too, on the national level.'[34] Moreover, 'he would not allow social mixing to take place after racially mixed international sports meetings. Social events would have to be confined to the various races' "own areas".'[35]

At the same time, it was clarified that while there would be continuities in policy, there would also be 'adjustments, development and progress without sacrifice of principles' and 'a certain degree of elasticity' – essentially an adherence by the apartheid regime to key principles, with flexibility of tactics in accordance with changing international and local conditions. On occasion, 'a South African representative team, which consists of whites only' would be permitted to play against teams comprising solely of coloureds or Indians or Africans, with the last further restricted to team division along ethnic lines.[36]

Koornhof expounded:

> The multinational policy of the National Party means the following... A South African White team, consisting of whites only may play against a South African representative Coloured team consisting solely of Coloureds... If our policy is taken to its logical conclusion we will have a South African representative Zulu team and a South African representative Xhosa team.[37]

This was the advent of multinational sport, which paralleled apartheid separate development along racial and ethnic lines at the political level.

In 1959, the Promotion of Bantu Self-Government Act had been passed. Its 'immediate effect was to abolish the last vestiges of black representation in Parliament'.[38] It also unfolded, as part of a strategy of divide and rule, the programme of geographical segregation and consolidation of ethnically structured territorial units for Africans and of own-affairs bureaucracies for coloured and Indians. It was to these territorial units – the bantustans – that black African aspirations and demands for political rights were to be deflected as a way of preserving white minority rule over much of what would then become so-called white South Africa.

During the 1960s and 1970s, the apartheid regime made concerted attempts, through the inducements of supposed political power and material benefits, to entice and co-opt blacks to become junior partners in the administration of separate development. That eventually led between 1976 and 1981 to nominal independence for four bantustans – Transkei, Ciskei, Venda and Bophuthatswana. These initiatives were to culminate in the Koornhof Bills of 1982 and the tricameral parliament: racially segregated, supposed democracy for coloured and Indian South Africans; and so-called citizenship rights for Africans in the bantustans that would leave the white minority firmly in power. This proposed new dispensation was roundly rejected and saw the launch of mass-based anti-apartheid formations like the United Democratic Front and National Forum in 1983.

As noted, there was a similar state strategy in the sports arena. Generally, those black South Africans who collaborated with apartheid programmes and institutions economically and politically also did so in the cultural and sports arenas and vice versa. The policy of multinational sport 'reflected the National Party's belief that South Africa was a "confederation of nations" in which the identity of each individual nation was to be developed and preserved separately. The implementation of multinationalism represented the application of this ideology in a sporting context.'[39]

The key features in the early 1970s of multinational sport, which sought to stave off further international isolation and remain within the state policy of separate development, were the following. First:

> Teams representing South Africa's different racial groups (or 'nations') could compete against each other in certain sporting events, but no racial mixing of teams was permitted. Initially, such mixed competitions had to be deemed 'international' in stature to be considered within the multinational framework. Hence no mixing was permitted at club or provincial level.[40]

This meant that 'mixed teams from countries that had traditional links with South Africa (the United Kingdom, New Zealand, Australia, etc.) would be permitted to tour South Africa and to play, separately, against white teams and African, Indian and Coloured teams'.[41]

Second, black sportspersons who were 'affiliated to white federations would be permitted to take part, as individuals, in multi-national competitions; within South Africa these would be strictly national (race against race)'.[42] Third, the apartheid state continued to strongly regulate sport along race lines, 'instructed black and white sports people to form multinational sports confederations', and 'whites remained in charge of the new confederations'.[43]

Fourth, the status quo remained in that 'only whites could represent South Africa on international federations and only white players could earn national Springbok honours in international competition.' Fifth, multinationalism did not extend 'to club, or even provincial, competitions'; it was only applicable at the international and, at best, the national levels.[44]

In due course, as Venter notes:

> The policy evolved and expanded the definition of multi-nationalism on account of increased international pressure. Broadly speaking, this was an attempt to deflect this pressure by portraying progress through limited integration on the one hand, while still adhering to the central apartheid doctrine of separate development for all South Africa's race groups on the other.[45]

In Booth's view, the state's 'minimalist approach and badly managed reforms aggravated relations between non-racial and white sport'. Moreover, the white-controlled confederations maintained an attitude of *baaskap* and displayed no 'interest in negotiating democratic structures in sport'.[46] Given this situation, 'not surprisingly then, non-racial sports leaders rejected multinationalism. In 1972 they wrote to the IOC and denounced the new confederations as an attempt to deceive the world about integrated sport. Whites reject mixed sport and dialogue with them is "a waste of time", they added.'[47]

At the same time, multinational sport did represent a change in National Party thinking and state policy. It also created a new terrain of ideological and political contestation and struggle, on which democratic, non-racial sport formations had to intervene and to which they had to respond. After the 1976 student revolt, multinationalism permitted competition among 'professional clubs and, later, private schools'. Much as political activists critiqued and rejected separate development for falling far short of the demand for political and human rights within a common, unified South Africa, non-racial sports activists scorned multinationalism 'as Pretoria's attempt to globally project an image of substantive change while maintaining the architecture of apartheid intact'.[48]

Multinationalism's goals were threefold. One was to win the support of black sportspersons through co-optation into the structures of segregated sport. Simultaneously, a second goal was to divide black South African sportspersons and weaken non-racial sports and institutions. A third goal was to strengthen multinational sport and effectively ensure the domination of white sportspersons and sports bodies. The lure of multinational sports was the apartheid government and white sports administrators' promise to black sportspersons of better facilities, sponsorship and possible international competition. In turn, some black sports administrators and players permitted themselves to be used by the apartheid government and racist sports bodies as part of their propaganda to stave off the growing tide of isolation from international sports.

The apartheid state's sport policy was not only an affront to human dignity but also violated the first fundamental principle of the IOC's Olympic Charter, which in 1971 stated that 'no discrimination is allowed against any . . . person on grounds of race, religion or political affiliation'.[49] Despite this, Avery Brundage, the American president of the IOC between 1952 and 1972, 'told Lord Killanin, chairman of the IOC's commission of inquiry into South Africa, that apartheid was a government policy about which the IOC should not concern itself: "we must not become involved in political issues, nor permit the Olympic Games to be used for . . . extraneous causes"'.[50]

Seemingly, human rights and social justice were for Brundage extraneous causes. As Booth notes, 'the international sporting community showed little interest in South Africa's racial policies' and 'well into the 1960s white South African sports officials manipulated historical connections with international sport'.[51]

It was only with decolonisation and when newly independent Asian and African countries began to assert themselves with threats of boycotts that the IOC and other international sport bodies, whose weighted voting systems grossly favoured white as opposed to black countries, started to act against apartheid South Africa.[52]

5

Tennis under Apartheid

At the beginning of the 1960s there were four racially segregated national tennis bodies in South Africa. The South African Tennis Board operated in coloured communities and the South African Indian Lawn Tennis Association in Indian communities. The South African National Lawn Tennis Union (SANLTU) oversaw tennis in African communities. SANLTU, headed by Reggie Ngcobo, 'disbanded in Witbank in 1961 but was resuscitated' in 1962 despite some opposition from its affiliates.[1]

The fourth body was the exclusively white South African Lawn Tennis Union (SALTU), which subscribed to racial segregation and dutifully complied with the government's racist sports policy. Despite this, it enjoyed membership of the International Lawn Tennis Federation (ILTF) and was officially recognised as the controlling body for tennis in South Africa. It collaborated with the apartheid government to convene occasional carefully orchestrated multinational tournaments that included a few black players for international propaganda purposes.[2]

Unity talks among the black tennis bodies gave rise in 1962 to the SnALTU, which organised non-racial tennis between 1963 and 1978. However, it is contended that 'the first attempt at [black] unity with the formation of SnALTU in 1962 was not a great success'.[3] Regrettably, because of inducements and material rewards, SANLTU, which comprised only African players, continued to collaborate with the white only SALTU. Thus, in 1969 with the support of SALTU it received 'R2 000 in sponsorship for its championships [in] Kwa-Thema from a leading brewery'.[4]

Ebrahim Osman writes:

> The African component did not come in with full commitment. The [African] players participated in large numbers in [SnALTU]

events once or twice a year. But they continued with their separate leagues for the rest of the year. The [African] officials too did not come in wholeheartedly. What is more they continued to accept little cosmetic gestures from the white controlling body in the form of sponsorship, development clinics in the townships and some gifts of rackets and other equipment.[5]

A similar situation unfortunately pertained in soccer, where there was a separate league for Africans.

In 1971, SALTU conferred on SANLTU 'federal membership with full voting rights'.[6] In announcing the link-up between SANLTU and SALTU, Alf Chalmers, president of SALTU, dubiously contended that SANLTU was an organisation 'fully representing all Non-White groups in South Africa' and that it made SALTU 'fully representative of all races in South Africa'. It was observed that since 1964 both SANLTU and SnALTU had regularly turned down offers to affiliate to SALTU. SnALTU secretary Manikum Nadarajan (M.N.) Pather commented that unresolved matters were voting at SALTU, eligibility for the Davis Cup and, 'most important [blacks] would still be excluded from all White-run tournaments'.[7]

The SANLTU president, Reggie Ngcobo, said that he was promised eleven votes at SALTU meetings, 'international recognition' for SANLTU, participation in international tournaments with SANLTU players having as 'equal chance as Whites to play for South Africa', provision of coaching and financial support, and improved 'facilities for Non-Whites'. Ngcobo added that 'they were rejoicing at the opportunity of linking with the parent body controlling tennis in South Africa' and through the arrangement to 'future participation in South African and international tournaments'.[8]

Chalmers' claims about the representativeness of SANLTU and, therefore, of SALTU were demolished. It was pointed out that there was no evidence that SALTU had government permission for blacks to play for South Africa locally or overseas. The new arrangement meant that the all-white SALTU remained dominant. In according SALTU parent body status, Ngcobo shamefully colluded in accepting SANLTU's own subordinate status. The opportunistic motive informing the new arrangement was blatant: SALTU was 'looking to the future of South

Africa's position in world tennis. And once the non-Whites are allowed to participate in South African competitions they hope the doors will open for South Africa's return to the ILTF.'[9]

Alegi points out that this affiliation process took place in various sports, including soccer.[10] He rightly notes that 'the interesting question is why were African bodies willing to accept this crude co-optation'. He suggests:

> One important factor ... has to do with the restriction/prohibition on African land ownership in urban areas, which made Africans almost completely dependent on white authorities for access to playing spaces. In the late 1970s it became a major bone of contention within SACOS after the adoption of the double standards resolution. This inequality (among other factors, including political differences, state repression, commercial incentives, etc.) may also help to explain why SACOS had a notoriously difficult time recruiting African members into its ranks.[11]

Following the death of the SANLTU president, in the late 1970s a 'new President, Don Kali, withdrew SANLTU's subservient affiliation to the white' SALTU, and SANLTU and the non-racial SnALTU came together in 1979 in Benoni to form the non-racial TASA.[12]

Those black sports administrators and players who participated in multinational sport and tournaments were considered by anti-apartheid organisations and activists as collaborators with apartheid, as sell-outs or, in the derogatory terminology of the Black Consciousness movement, as non-whites. In some communities, they were ostracised and boycotted socially. The strength of opposition to multinational sport is evident in the statement below of the SACOS president, Frank van der Horst. Observing 'the most crippling and devastating obstructions of Apartheid in sport, education and society', he said:

> Our organisations have refused to collaborate with racist multinational sport. The powerful weapon of the Double Standards Resolution was used to cleanse our sports bodies from

traitors and defectors who were corrupted by racist sport. We resolutely opposed all tours to South Africa while the oppressive laws of Apartheid enslave an entire people.[13]

Concomitantly, the 'struggle for non-racial sport' was linked to 'a democratic and liberated society' and required 'non-racial players and administrators [to] display their strength of character and determination'. They had to 'resolutely and aggressively oppose the evils of the system' to 'bring about fundamental change in sport and society'.[14]

In 1972, when some African and coloured players participated in the SALTU-organised South African Open, Jasmat Dhiraj accused them of stabbing non-racial players 'in the back' and as being 'selfish' people 'who think only of themselves'. He noted that 'according to white standards it is progress', but for blacks 'it is practically nothing'. In order to participate, those who played would have had to affiliate to the SANLTU, which had subordinate affiliate status with SALTU. He insisted that tennis had to be integrated 'from club level upwards'.[15]

Peter Lamb was one of the players who initially played tennis under SnALTU and SACOS, but was seduced by multinational sport and its associated economic benefits. He 'was selected for the national Davis Cup team in 1978, probably mostly to appease protesters' against apartheid, and was the first black player to represent South Africa in tennis.[16] The author, representing Natal, played Lamb, representing the Cape Province, at the 1973 South African Senior Schools Sports Association interprovincial tennis tournament in Durban. Confession: the author was soundly beaten by Lamb in straight sets, having no effective response to his powerful ground strokes.

Long-time non-racial tennis administrator Ebrahim Osman observes:

All the inequalities of the Apartheid system impacted on sport – nonexistent or poor facilities, virtually no sponsorship, no development or coaching programmes at school and junior level, no incentive to strive for excellence since people of colour were barred from open national and international competition [and] blatant discrimination in the provision of funds and resources by local and government authorities.[17]

Moreover, 'apartheid saw to it with a host of legislative, physical and logistical restrictions that Africans, Coloureds and Indians, not only played their sport separately from the white community but also from each other'.[18]

A tongue-in-cheek article by The Fakir (one Ranji Nowbath) when white South African women won the Federation Cup in 1971, highlighted additional home truths about tennis under apartheid using familiar tropes and stereotypes. To begin with The Fakir addresses the white women formally rather than by their first names. This is because although the well-known white tennis commentator Charles Fortune could call them by their first names, 'the likes of me cannot get down to this kind of familiarity with persons who are their superiors'. He acknowledges that 'some think we suffer from an inferiority complex'.[19]

The Fakir observes that 'the "glory"' of the Federation Cup victory 'is heightened by the fact that the burden of achieving world fame for our country has to be borne by a small [white] minority of our people'. Since this 'must be a great strain' on the white community, their 'sacrifices are greatly appreciated'. He goes on that the women 'will be surprised to learn that some of us would like very much to assist you in your tasks. It is not fair that so much should have to be done by so few on behalf of so many.' He was 'an avid tennis fan' who enjoyed tennis from a young age and was 'lucky' to attend 'a school which had a tennis court'.[20]

He even had 'visions of representing' South Africa but 'was too lazy and failed to take advantage of the many facilities provided to me' – like the single tennis court for 800 boys, which 'was paid for by the Indian community'. After school, The Fakir says he 'lost interest in the game and like others of the Indian community became indolent'. Actually, he 'had to scheme and use all sorts of tricks to join a tennis club and this involved too much effort'. His article points out that in Durban over a ten-year period in the 1960s the Durban City Council spent R9 million on sporting facilities for whites. The amount spent on the much larger Indian community was R300 000. Spending on other black communities was negligible.[21]

Alegi points out that 'taxpayer-funded recreational amenities for the white minority and ramshackle facilities for the black majority became the norm everywhere in apartheid South Africa', while Christopher

Merrett 'shows how this process worked in painstaking detail, providing valuable evidence of its enduring legacy for sport and society today'.[22]

The Fakir gives 'thanks' to the all-white City Council for the 'bountiful favours which are bestowed upon us by our City Fathers. They look after our interests even though we do not bother to vote for any of them in the Municipal elections.'[23] Blacks, of course, did not have the vote.

The looking after, though, did not yield 'a single public tennis court' for blacks. In contrast, 'Whites take the trouble to elect our City Fathers to office and that is why they have several dozen public tennis courts provided by the Council' – the connection being made clearly between political power and material benefits. The Fakir usefully highlights class differences in the black community related to playing tennis. He notes that the best players 'come from wealthy homes as their parents can provide the courts and pay for their coaching'. Moreover, wealthier Indians are too mean to 'provide sufficient tennis courts for their people. They expect the City Council to give them everything on a plate.'[24]

In the face of the inequities and disparities, it was necessary to forge unity in and outside sport of the oppressed black community and to wage the struggle for equality, equity and social justice in tennis and in wider society.

6

International Collusion with Apartheid Sport

As noted, despite its principle of non-discrimination, the IOC shamefully permitted South Africa (white South Africans) to participate in the Olympic Games from 1904 onwards. It was suspended only in 1964 from the Tokyo Olympics and in 1968 from the Mexico Olympics and eventually expelled in 1970, owing to mobilisation and threats of boycotts by African and Asian countries, and other countries linked to the Soviet Union.[1]

Remarkably, the IOC 'sent a delegation to South Africa in 1967 that issued an extraordinary report that there was no racial discrimination in South African sport. As a result, the IOC invited South Africa to Mexico City. Outrage followed and the IOC backtracked, withdrawing the invitation at the last minute.'[2] The expulsion was a victory of international solidarity, which opposed tours by South African teams, protested against them, and mobilised boycotts of events that featured them.[3]

Ultimately, the 1968 exclusion was the fear of 'a boycott by dozens of countries and hundreds of athletes. It helped that African American track-and-field athletes from the Olympic Project for Human Rights, the group behind the famous "silent gesture" protests of Tommie Smith, Lee Evans and John Carlos, had joined the African coalition in support of sanctions against South Africa.'[4] The 1968 victory and eventual expulsion of South Africa from the Olympic Games occurred on the bedrock of pan-African and global anti-racist struggles. The sport boycott shone a spotlight on apartheid, sensitised sportsmen and sportswomen to racism in South Africa, popularised the anti-apartheid movement, and denied whites international competition and white supremacists the use of sport for self-glorification. It also pressured white sport bodies to explore alternatives to racist sport, heightened international solidarity with the South African liberation struggle, and inspired hope that apartheid could be eroded and dismantled.

Many of South Africa's 'all-white sports federations had not only established firm links with national sports organizations of other countries, but had also managed to get into executive positions of many international federations'.[5]

Despite regular submissions by non-racial sports organisations to international sports associations to act against racist sports bodies in South Africa, these efforts found unsympathetic ears and initially bore no fruit. For example, the 'International Lawn Tennis Federation (ILTF) . . . rejected proposals since 1965 for the exclusion of the white SALTU'. One impediment was the ILTF's 'weighted voting system . . . Two European countries, Britain and France, [had] more votes than the whole of Africa put together.'[6]

The ILTF was created in 1913, with fifteen countries as inaugural members. In 1924, it was officially recognised to exercise authority over

Tommie Smith and John Carlos with anti-racist Australian white athlete Peter Norman at the Mexico City Olympic Games, 1968 (*Griot*, 2015).

tennis worldwide. By 1939, there were 59 affiliated countries and the ILTF offices were based in London. In 1963, 'the ILTF celebrated its 50th anniversary by launching the Federation Cup, an international women's team competition designed to match the men's equivalent, Davis Cup, which had been in existence since 1900, but not under the auspices of the ILTF'.[7] The ILTF ignored applications for membership from the non-racial SnALTU. Despite its constitution containing a clause against racism, which was patently flouted by SALTU, no action was taken against SALTU for a long time.

Alegi points out that 'white South Africa was significantly assisted in world tennis by the fact that it was one of the founding members of ILTF, playing its first Davis Cup in 1913. This strengthened the hand of elitist white European and American men in charge of international tennis, most of whom were unsympathetic to apartheid's critics.' Moreover, 'tennis was not an Olympic sport from 1928 to 1988, which bought ILTF some time and space to deflect growing pressure to exclude white South Africa from its ranks'.[8]

In 1969, the English secretary of the ILTF, Basil Reay, visited South Africa. It was reported that 'in an astonishing meeting here this week, Mr Basil Reay . . . tried to persuade the non-racial Southern Africa Lawn Tennis Union to affiliate to the country's White tennis union'. Reay proposed that SnALTU should accept affiliation similar to the provincial tennis bodies and would thus have four delegates out of a possible 48 delegates to SALTU meetings. He conceded that the offer 'was not attractive and not in accordance with international tennis laws', but suggested that it was best in the circumstances. The response that 'he got was the same that the White South African Lawn Tennis Union has been getting for years: a firm no'. M.N. Pather retorted that 'the offer is simply not acceptable . . . It's not administration we're after – we want to play with them.'[9]

Osman recalls that 'at the end of the "fact finding" visit' Reay travelled 'to Durban to meet Mr M.N. Pather and myself. He came with return air tickets for us to go to Johannesburg to sign a "unity agreement" on the humiliating terms proposed by the white body. We listened to Mr Reay for 10 minutes and then showed him the door.'[10] The non-racial SnALTU rightly refused to accept any subordinate status and affiliate to SALTU. At a council meeting in January 1970 in Port Elizabeth,

SnALTU 'again rejected any form of subservient affiliation to the all-White SALTU'.[11] Pather reiterated the position that 'we accept nothing that makes us subservient to another body. We are a non-racial body and believe that merit only should count.'[12]

Pather, or MN as he was generally known, was an estate agent by profession but devoted much of 'his time, energy and money to furthering non-racialism in sport' and the isolation of South Africa from international competition. Educated at Sastri School in Durban and taking up tennis in the 1940s, Pather 'became the record clerk for the Clairwood Lawn Tennis Club'. In due course, he became associated with various sports, and was secretary of SnALTU as well as of SACOS.[13] Like other non-racial sports activists, he and his family experienced state harassment. He was posthumously awarded the Steve Tshwete Sports Award in 2006.[14]

Not only did the Reay proposal not address racial segregation in tennis, it also displayed an all-too-familiar and offensive colonial mentality: SALTU would remain the parent body to which the other bodies would affiliate in a subordinate relationship.

Enuga Sreenivasulu (E.S.) Reddy, who was director of the United Nations Centre Against Apartheid, noted that 'South Africa remained a member of many international sports federations with the help of its Western friends who enjoyed weighted voting in several codes of sport like tennis'.[15] White sports bodies went to great lengths to maintain their international affiliations and recognition in the wake of increasing efforts by non-racial sports bodies and international allies to secure their expulsion.

A brochure of the white SALTU exemplified its desperation and deviousness. It displayed 'numerous pictures showing mixed sport in South Africa – no doubt, all of the photographs taken' at the occasional multinational tournaments mounted for international appeasement. Brazenly, and without permission, the whites-only SALTU recorded the non-racial SnALTU as the co-publisher of its brochure, malfeasance that SnALTU exposed and for which it demanded and received an apology. However, the SALTU ploy worked: its 'publication did impress many west Europeans and South Africa managed to escape expulsion from international tennis'.[16]

In April 1971, Vorster made the bizarre proposal 'that the time had come' for blacks 'to form their own international sporting ties' and that the white minority government would provide 'all possible encouragement'. This made sense only in the context, of course, of the apartheid regime's pursuit of the policy of multinationalism in sport and its separate development and bantustan policies. Since each country could affiliate to an international sports body only through a single national body, M.N. Pather remarked that Vorster was 'virtually asking the world bodies to amend their constitutions to suit South African sports policies' – founded on racism.[17]

Even more ludicrous were the statements of Frank Waring, the apartheid minister of sport. He stated that he 'could see no difficulty' in black South African sports bodies 'inviting overseas White teams to the country'. However, competitions with international white teams had to be played in black areas and had to be for black audiences only. Waring conceded that he 'could not see any team coming to South Africa to play' black teams, 'as the project would be a financial flop since black sports bodies did not possess the facilities to hold such competitions'. Pather wryly observed that Waring's proposition was akin to 'presenting a loaf of bread to a patient who's being fed intravenously'.[18]

To acquire greater international legitimacy, white sports bodies promoted multinational and multiracial sport under their direction (as distinct from non-racial sport) and instituted superficial development programmes along racial and ethnic lines aimed at cultivating black sportspersons. Desai alludes to such development programmes concerning cricket and the person of Ali Bacher. He notes that development and money allocated to it were not directed and controlled by the non-racial cricket body, but rather by the white cricket body and Bacher specifically. By positioning 'himself as the champion of black cricket development, with a stratum of paid officials in the townships', Bacher sought to promote alternative voices and give credence to his 'own centrality to development'.[19]

In 'mirroring the apartheid state's strategy of the time, Bacher wanted to break the back of non-racial cricket while creating a web of patronage under his control'. He also disingenuously linked rogue international tours to South Africa with the development of black cricket. Such tours were said to benefit black cricket development in various ways with those opposing them not having development at heart – a 'classic attempt to divide and prevail'. Bacher and similar white sports administrators' approaches not only sought to efface the efforts of non-racial sports bodies and their long histories of developing black sport. Development programmes under white direction were also presented as 'benign missionary adventure[s]. Apartheid would be mitigated by white paternalism from above, not black struggle from below. Lurking behind the argument was the old imperial assumption that blacks were not capable of governing themselves.'[20]

With their long-standing connections with white sports bodies and sports administrators, international sports bodies were generally part of the problem. An observation about the cricket publication *Wisden* applies to it too. *Wisden* 'was on the wrong side ... It believed that visiting cricketers, repositories of enlightenment [sic], could bring illumination to that benighted land. Phooey! *Wisden*'s line ... was misconceived. Apartheid in South Africa couldn't be tempered; it had to be dismantled.'[21]

Despite the general collusion of international sports bodies with apartheid, it was not all defeat. On the international front, the first significant victory for non-racial sport came in 1956. The racist whites-only South African Table Tennis Union was expelled from the International Table Tennis Federation and the non-racial South African Table Tennis Board (SATTB) was accepted as a member.[22] Contributing to this victory was the Co-ordinating Committee for International Recognition in Sport (CCIRS), formed in 1955 in Durban to fight racism in sport and secure the affiliation of non-racial sports bodies to international sports federations. It 'was disbanded in 1956 due to police harassment'.[23]

In 1958, the South African Sports Association (SASA) 'emerged out of that first organized attempt at sport boycott politics'.[24] It was, in turn, replaced in 1962 by the South African Non-Racial Olympic Committee (SANROC).[25] SASA is credited as playing 'a very important role' in advancing non-racial sport and sport administration among black South Africans.[26] It is stated that SASA 'by constant negotiation eliminated many of the racial barriers among [black] South African sports bodies so that in most sports it became normal for Africans, Indians and Coloured to play together and to share the administration'. By helping to create 'a unified [black] front against white sport participation and administration the foundations were laid' to strengthen non-racial sport and eventually isolate white South Africa through an international sports boycott campaign, which 'amounted . . . to the most prominent, extended antiracist campaign in the history of world sports'.[27]

Associated with SASA as its secretary and with SANROC as its president respectively was University of Fort Hare graduate, athlete, educator and poet, Dennis Brutus. Brutus, 'the preeminent sports boycott figure for more than two decades', is an excellent example of the repression experienced at the hands of the apartheid state by non-racial sports administrators and sportspersons identified as a threat to white South Africans' enjoyment of international sport.[28] Brutus 'played an instrumental role in the cancellation of the West Indies cricket team's

Dennis Brutus (*Post*, 20 January 1963).

proposed tour of South Africa in 1959'.[29] In Brutus' view, that victory 'cemented the S.A.S.A.'s role as the "campaigning body on racism in sports"'.[30]

Mary Corrigall writes that Brutus 'was closely watched by the security police. In 1960, when a state of emergency was declared following the Sharpeville killings, security officials raided the homes of SASA officials and took away all the documents they could find. None were returned.'[31] In 1961, Brutus was served 'a banning order that forbade him to write. This was followed, in 1963, with a second ban prohibiting him from belonging to any organization, teaching, or attending any gathering of more than two people, including any sports event.'[32] The statements and writing of banned persons could not be published or disseminated. Not being able to teach meant that Brutus could not earn an income and this had consequences for his livelihood.

In 1963, when Brutus and some colleagues met 'a Swiss journalist visiting South Africa, who intended to report his findings to the IOC', security police arrested him 'allegedly for violating the terms of his banning order by attending a gathering of more than two persons'.[33] An IOC meeting scheduled for Germany in 1963 was to debate the matter of South Africa and its participation in the Tokyo Olympics of 1964. Brutus was determined to testify at the meeting and broke his bail conditions in order to travel to Germany. However, he

> was detained by the Portuguese security police in Mozambique and secretly handed over to the South African Government. When outside Johannesburg police headquarters, he attempted to escape in order to draw attention to his whereabouts. He feared for his life if the world at large did not know of his arrest and detention. At point-blank range a police officer shot him in the stomach in a busy Johannesburg street.[34]

Spending time recovering partially in a prison hospital, Brutus received an eighteen-month prison sentence 'for contravening the terms of his banning order', fifteen months of which was spent on Robben Island.[35] Prison guards assaulted and abused Brutus, most likely because of his role in keeping South Africa out of the 1964 Tokyo Olympics.[36] On his release from prison, he left South Africa on an exit permit, which precluded his return to the country.

Dennis Brutus (*Post*, 15 December 1968).

In exile in the UK, along with fellow exiles Chris de Broglio and Reg Hlongwane, Brutus helped to reconstitute SANROC in 1966. Following the SANROC victory of South Africa's suspension from the 1964 Tokyo Olympics (expulsion was in 1970), the apartheid state hit back: SANROC's leaders found themselves 'in prison, under house arrest, in exile, or underground', and in 1965 SANROC was outlawed.[37]

In 1970, South Africa was excluded from the Davis Cup 'on the grounds that the Springboks' entry was likely to disrupt the tournament'.[38] A year later there were moves to exclude white South African women from the Federation Cup. Chalmers and past SALTU president Ben Franklin travelled to Europe to stave off the new attempt. In trying to secure the hosting of the Federation Cup in South Africa in 1972, SALTU vice-president Francis promised the ILTF that it would host the 'world tournament without any signs of racial discrimination' and that there would be 'visas and venues regardless of race or political views'.[39] SALTU succeeded in the short term and hosted and won the 1972 Federation Cup in South Africa, but in 1977 South Africa was excluded.[40]

To give a semblance of authenticity to merit selection, rather than selection on the basis of colour, trials were held for the Federation Cup team. Four African women were chosen for trials that, according to Norman Middleton, chair of an ad-hoc committee on non-racial sport, were a farce. They occurred in secrecy at a private court from which the public was excluded, and the four handpicked trialists were not the strongest black players in South Africa. The four African players were 'chosen as guinea pigs', and it was 'a foregone conclusion that the South African team will be all White'.[41] Other stronger black players were overlooked because they were part of the non-racial tennis body. M.K. Naidoo, president of the SnALTU, said players from his body were snubbed because they 'would match the Whites'.[42]

Chalmers was of the view that the apartheid state's new multinational sport policy was an 'advancement' and believed rather naively that 'it will be very difficult for the rest of the world to find fault with us'. He pinned his hope on SALTU's standing in the ILTF improving 'following the rapid progress in the SALTU's Non-White "federal body"'. He expressed disappointment 'to hear from the ILTF secretary, Mr. Basil Reay' that Jasmat Dhiraj was critical of the essentially African SANLTU. He opined that 'we have extended the hand of friendship to Dhiraj' and advised 'him to join the SANLTU, which is becoming increasingly representative of all our Non-White players, though it has recently been a predominantly African body'.[43] Chalmers' insistence that Jasmat had 'to join a union affiliated to' SALTU demonstrated great arrogance and a mindset that typified naturalised white superiority.[44] His demand in effect was for Jasmat to join the exclusively African SANLTU.

M.N. Pather observed that if Jasmat did join SANLTU, he would have to 'forego his principles and live in isolation for the rest of his career'.[45] However, Jasmat 'put his honour before the chance of a lifetime. He believed in non-racial sport. Never mind the personal cost.'[46] Pather was adamant that the white 'SALTU should have accepted the entry of Jasmat Dhiraj and let the authorities act afterwards. In failing to do so, it missed an opportunity to promote tennis for all players in the country.' Pather pointed out that black players like Arthur Ashe and Australian Evonne Goolagong were permitted to play in the South African Open, but local black players like Jasmat were excluded. He argued that if the likes of Ashe were eligible to play because their own tennis associations were members of the ILTF, then logically Jasmat too was eligible because he belonged to a 'London club affiliated to the world body'.[47]

A brief detour around the Goolagong and Ashe visits is in order. Despite anger among non-racial sports organisations and Aborigine activists at Goolagong's participation in the South African Open, her visits to South Africa did not generate great controversy as with the case of Ashe. Perhaps it had to do with her being, in the words of a *New York Times* reporter, 'an uncomplicated, innocent, very happy girl who is still unaware that problems of race and politics do intrude into sport'.[48] The Aborigines Advancement League's John Newfong counselled Goolagong not to play in South Africa, saying that while she was 'entitled to the prestige, honor and glory she will accumulate', she had 'no moral right to allow this prestige to be used against our interests'. He considered her being accorded the status of honorary white 'an insult . . . to her, to her people at home, and to black people everywhere'.[49]

Honorary white was a peculiar apartheid-era designation deployed by the government for pragmatic or opportunist reasons to sidestep its own strict classification of the population into different race and ethnic-based groups. The innovation of honorary white indicates that, when necessary, the apartheid government was malleable at the margins in order to preserve white domination and minority rule. The status 'honorary white conferred on individuals and groups, who otherwise would have been designated non-white', all or most of the privileges and rights that were reserved for whites and denied to blacks.[50] The action of the apartheid government underlines that the designation of social groups and people is 'a historically specific social construct, inextricable from prevailing power relations'.[51] The pressure on the apartheid state to create the status of honorary white arose from economic, trade and diplomatic imperatives (as in the case of Japanese and Taiwanese) or from the growing international cultural and sport boycott after the 1960s (as in the case of foreign celebrities, artists, sports teams and individual sportspersons).[52]

The initial denial of visas to African American Arthur Ashe by the apartheid government, beginning in 1969, and his subsequent award of visas and four visits between 1973 and 1977 generated considerable controversy on various fronts. This played out on a global stage: 'Tennis was, more so than many other sports, transnational in its dimensions. Tennis players traveled most of the year to play in tournaments in dozens of nations throughout the world. In this way, the tennis community was particularly globalized.'[53]

For one, initially the apartheid government denied Ashe visas to play in the South African Open, which was establishing itself as a major tournament with considerable prize money, for being outspoken about racism and social justice. Certainly, Ashe was conscious about apartheid and had expressed solidarity with the black American athletes prepared to boycott the 1968 Olympic Games in protest at South Africa's participation. For another, when eventually granted a visa in 1973, seemingly on his own terms, his visits were to the consternation of key activists like Dennis Brutus. Brutus sought to debate with Ashe his position on engagement with the apartheid state and his insistence on visiting South Africa, despite the anti-apartheid movement promoting the 'complete isolation of the segregated nation, including in the arena of sport'.[54] For Brutus, Ashe's 1973 visit 'had done more to legitimize apartheid than to dismantle it'. On his departure, Winnie Mandela advised Ashe that the 'best thing you can do is ask the South Africans what you can do to help in their struggle'.[55]

It was the likes of Trevor Huddleston, John Collins and Ambrose Reeves who together with 'a variety of groups and individuals drawn from political and trade union circles, South African exiles and black anti-colonial activists' who had pioneered the UK anti-apartheid movement and specifically the boycott campaign in 1959.[56] In 1954, it was Huddleston who

> issued the first call for an international cultural boycott of South Africa in the London *Observer*, writing 'I am pleading for a cultural boycott of South Africa. I am asking those who believe racialism to be sinful or wrong . . . to refuse to encourage it by accepting any engagement to act, to perform as a musical artist or as a ballet dancer – in short, to engage in any contracts which would provide entertainment for any one section of the community.'[57]

By 'any one section of the community' Huddleston meant that international artists should refuse to perform, as some did, for exclusively white audiences but his call also extended to not playing for racially segregated audiences. Huddleston contended that fundamental change in South Africa

> could only come about through the efforts of the 'Christian conscience' which, he argued, 'should be so aroused as to find expression in the isolation of South Africa – until she repents'. This was the key to Huddleston's argument. It was not only that a conversion of white South Africa was required, but also that action – in the form of an international campaign to isolate South Africa – was required in order to bring it about.[58]

Huddleston 'did not hit upon the idea of a boycott at random, but drew on the repertoire of a range of South African movements. A key weapon for anti-colonial campaigners, the boycott had come increasingly to the fore as a strategy of protest by the late 1950s.'[59]

At best, Ashe's actions raised the question of and took a position on 'how best to confront apartheid, through engagement or disengagement'.[60] At worst, his insistence on engagement was congruent with the US government policy of constructive engagement as a means of influencing the apartheid state to change its policies, although there was also blatant support for the regime for strategic Cold War reasons. Overall, it appears that there were various motives, not all entirely virtuous, that underlay Ashe's insistence on playing in South Africa. One gets the impression that there was also a measure of arrogance, individualism and naiveté on the part of Ashe. A reviewer of Ashe's biography writes that he 'trivializes the destructiveness of apartheid by ridiculing it and not raging against it', and fails to use his status to put 'tremendous pressure on United States-South African tennis policies to the benefit of black South Africans'. Moreover, he 'instead ... spreads the mythology of tennis officialdom and the United States corporations that promote "constructive engagement" with the apartheid state and express sanctimonious statements like "sport and politics don't mix"'.[61]

To return to the matter of black players not being able to play in premier tournaments in South Africa, it was sheer fabrication on

Chalmers' part that SANLTU was becoming representative of black South African tennis players. That Jasmat could not play in the South African Open was blamed on the non-racial SnALTU not affiliating to SALTU, Chalmers remaining adamant 'that players will have to belong to an affiliated association in order to qualify'.[62]

In April 1972, Jasmat, working with SANROC, travelled from exile in London to Copenhagen to present a memorandum to a special committee sitting on 'whether or not to allow South Africa to play in the 1972 Davis Cup competition'.[63] Chalmers was infuriated by Jasmat's presence in Copenhagen, petulantly claiming that 'he had no right to be there. They virtually turned it into a public meeting.'[64] Conrad Johnson, who had played under SnALTU, gave evidence to prevent South Africa's expulsion. In 1969, he led a 'Sunrise Squad from Western province [that had] campaigned abroad' and was 'expelled by the Western Province Tennis Board for accepting R850 from the Coloured Affairs Department, thus violating the Board's resolution'.[65] In response, Jasmat accused Johnson of 'just trying to stab us in the back' and noted further that Johnson had been 'suspended for life' by SnALTU. While Jasmat played a key role in South Africa's exclusion from the 1972 Davis Cup, he observed that 'he was not alone' in efforts to 'crush racialism in tennis' and that 'it was the South African Nonracial Committee for Olympic Sport who planned it all'.[66] South Africa was permitted to participate again in the Davis Cup from 1973 when in 1972 'at a special committee meeting in Helsinki, delegates voted 5-2 to readmit [it] . . . with only the Soviet and Indian delegates opposing readmittance'.[67]

South Africa was, however,

> placed in the Americas Zone instead of the Europe Zone where other African countries played. It won the 1974 Davis Cup after India refused to travel to South Africa for the final. There were protests at its matches in the United States in 1977 and 1978. In 1977 several countries threatened to withdraw, and in 1978 several did withdraw in protest. In 1979 South Africa was banned again.[68]

For the 1973 Davis Cup, SALTU's Chalmers gave 'an assurance that there will be mixed trials to select the Springbok team'. He reiterated that while 'every non-White who deserves a chance to play for South Africa will get it' they had to 'be affiliated to the S.A.L.T.U. through their own bodies. Those belonging to splinter groups will not be considered' – a clear reference to the non-racial SnALTU.[69]

Chalmers' deceit and twisting of facts in the service of his agenda to legitimate apartheid is revealed in his churlish questioning of Jasmat's status as the best black South African player at the time. He contended that 'I was told in Cape Town that he has never played against Coloured or Africans and thus he cannot claim that distinction'.[70] This was a blatant lie. Chalmers not only peddled lies about Jasmat's status and fraudulently used SnALTU's name on a SALTU brochure; he also exemplified the arrogance of many whites that they alone were ordained by virtue of their skin colour to govern and dictate the course of tennis in South Africa. This behaviour was buttressed by the collusion of the ILTF and its recognition of a racist body as the sole representative of tennis in South Africa.

Ultimately, it was white minority political domination and international collusion that established the whites-only SALTU as the supreme authority for tennis in South Africa, in contrast to SnALTU which upheld non-racialism in sport and was an inclusive organisation, but which ironically was considered a splinter by SALTU. Today, fortunately, the IOC seems to understand that 'the goal of Olympism' is to preserve 'human dignity'. 'Sport is a human right' and there cannot be 'discrimination of any kind, such as race, colour, sex, sexual orientation, language, religion, political or other opinion, national or social origin, property, birth or other status'.[71]

7

The Historic 1971 Tour

The preceding chapters have provided an account of the racism, collusion and deceitful intrigue that characterised South African sport under colonialism and apartheid. They have also considered its international dimensions, as well as the struggles to oppose such racism and exclusion in sport generally and in tennis specifically. It is against this backdrop of racism and apartheid inequities that the full significance of the first-ever international tour by black tennis players under the banner of the non-racial SnALTU, which was planned and undertaken with some secrecy, needs to be appreciated.

Understandably, there was fear that the apartheid government would refuse passports to the non-racial players if they discovered the preparations. More so, given that in 1957 a non-racial table tennis delegation participated in the World championships in Stockholm. After that, the apartheid government vindictively prohibited future overseas contingents by denying team members passports. The SATTB consequently 'resolved not to participate in internationals until there [was] complete nonracialism in South Africa'.[1]

Hoosen Bobat recalls that the memory of the 1957 non-racial table tennis players being denied passports meant that the 1971 non-racial tennis team generally 'kept a very low profile in the press and media before our departure'. The SnALTU strategy

> was that our team members would meet in Johannesburg on the day of our departure. All our tickets had been bought individually as though we were going on a holiday to the UK and Europe. It was only when we were all on the plane that we were relieved that we are now on the tour as the first ever official non-racial South African tennis squad.[2]

On the eve of the tour, SnALTU secretary M.N. Pather was interrogated by security police. He was one of the key organisers of a 1970 conference that brought together black and white sports administrators to explore the creation of unified non-racial bodies in different sports. As Booth records:

> This emphasises that alongside advocating the boycott of apartheid South Africa, SACOS initially ... also pursued negotiation with white sport. In 1970 the conference of national non-racial sports organisations unanimously accepted a resolution that national bodies maintain 'dialogue with all racial and other bodies.' Despite the experiences of its predecessors, SASA and SAN-ROC, which had unsuccessfully pursued negotiation, several SACOS affiliates wrote to their white counterparts, urging them to unite – in the interests of sport.[3]

The state's response was 'a visit from the Security Police and the threat that some sort of action may be taken against the man who tries to promote non-racial sport'. Pather was told that 'investigations concerning your activities have been completed and certain recommendations are on their way to Pretoria' and warned that '"restrictions could be placed on him"'.[4] SnALTU convened a special national meeting to 'discuss the unwarranted intimidation and interrogation' of Pather. It condemned the police actions and pledged to stand 'four-square behind' Pather and 'support him in his endeavours to promote the game of tennis'.[5]

Despite the attempt to maintain a level of secrecy about the tour, in early 1970 a newspaper article noted the decision of the SnALTU council meeting in Port Elizabeth to send a four-person squad to play in overseas tournaments for four months.[6] Pather stated that apart from Jasmat, three of the squad, yet to be chosen, would be 'juniors from Western Province'. He expressed confidence that Jasmat 'will not let us down' as 'he has everything on his side, height, youth and all the fitness that make a champion player'. In something of a flourish, reporter Farook Khan wrote about Jasmat not only playing the European circuit but also, if he did very well, in the US Open at Forest Hills.[7] The US tour, unfortunately, did not materialise.

Then, in December 1970, the president of SnALTU, Ebrahim Osman, looking ahead to activities in 1971, mentioned SnALTU's hope

Veteran non-racial tennis administrator Ebrahim Osman (*Leader*, 25 December 1970).

'to send a junior squad under national champion Jasmat Dhiraj early next year to take part in several European tournaments'. He indicated that some Natal juniors, including Bobat, were 'strongly favoured to win places in the team'.[8]

Adding momentum, in February 1971 Osman referred to the 'climate [being] better now than it has ever been' for black tennis 'to break on to the world scene'. He indicated that SnALTU had taken 'bold steps', including the selection of a six-person team to take part in tournaments in Europe.[9] Osman's publicity for the tour is curious; given the intensification of repression under Vorster, his public statements could have attracted the attention of the security police. Perhaps, the media had got wind of the tour or maybe Osman's public remarks about the international were emboldened by the IOC expulsion of South Africa in May 1970.[10]

Sending a team to tour Europe was an expensive undertaking. It was reported that SnALTU required R6 000 – in today's terms about R416 000 – and it was hoped that 'business organisations and lovers of sport will come forward to assist' and that 'players and officials will make a concerted effort' to raise funds.[11] SnALTU administrators, clubs, players parents, family and friends and small black businesses chipped in to sponsor the team. Families and friends provided money for personal expenses. Bobat recalls that in addition to his father, a fellow tennis player provided him with money prior to his departure. His father sent additional money through associates who travelled to Britain. In London, Bobat occasionally stayed with his uncle and aunt, Ahmed (Gino/Stretch) and June Jeenah, which helped save on expenses. His uncle also hosted the squad for meals.[12]

At that time, the major local and foreign multinational companies like the South African Sugar Association, South African Breweries, Colgate-Palmolive and Peugeot-Citroen largely toed the government line, and supported white and multinational tennis but contributed nothing or little to non-racial tennis. This was the case with non-racial sport in general and highlights the role of business in buttressing privilege and subordination in sport under apartheid. When SnALTU approached some of the companies – and others like Rothmans, Stellenbosch Wineries and BP – to support its tournaments, their usual response was that their sports sponsorship budgets were already committed.

Nonetheless on 10 April 1971, 'the first ever tennis squad of colour left the shores of South Africa to play tournaments in Europe'. The team under the banner of the national SnALTU came to be known as the Dhiraj Squad – a term that seems to have been coined by Osman. From Gauteng (then Transvaal) the squad comprised Jasmat Dhiraj and his brother Hiralal Dhiraj, 'both national champions and among the best players of colour produced in the country'. Oscar Woodman, Alwyn Solomon and Cavan Bergman, a secondary school student and the youngest team member, were squad members who hailed from the Western Cape; and Hoosen Bobat joined the team from KwaZulu-Natal (then known as Natal).[13]

Regarding the composition of the tour squad, five comments are in order. First, in terms of race, three of the six players were coloured and three were Indian. In the language of the Black Consciousness movement, they were part of the oppressed majority and therefore black South Africans. This political definition of the Black Consciousness movement stressed a shared social and political experience of racism and apartheid exclusion as the primary factor unifying blacks and as the deciding factor for blackness, regardless of cultural roots or skin complexion. The definition rightly and unequivocally rejected the official apartheid government term non-white, as it by implication offensively upheld whiteness as the standard.

There were no African South African players in the squad. There were certainly African players who were members of clubs that were affiliated to the provincial and regional bodies of SnALTU. Unfortunately, none of these players in that era were ranked highly or were greatly successful in national tournaments. This reflected the particularly severe obstacles and debilitations that many meritorious African players encountered in the context of apartheid exclusion. The inclusion of promising African players, even if not highly ranked at that time, would have been symbolically important in the context of the wider objectives of non-racial sport. It is possible that SnALTU was imprisoned by an absolutist discourse of merit – as we will note later, there was reference to it believing 'that merit only should count'.[14]

Yet, as SnALTU itself was all-too-aware, tennis in South Africa was not played on a level playing field. Opportunities were profoundly shaped by an unequal social structure of class, racism, patriarchy and other social fractures. The idea of merit when decontextualised does not help to erode or eliminate structural inequalities. Harvard philosopher Michael Sandel contends that ideas of merit and rewards through 'dint of effort, talent, hard work' is part of the 'rhetoric of rising', which has become 'an article of faith, a seemingly uncontroversial trope' on the part of liberals.[15]

Alegi comments that problematic ideas related to merit were 'also deeply embedded in the core ethos of sports. Even radical activists like Brutus bought into the Victorian ideology of sport as a space of merit, fairness, and equality.' He suggests that 'in part this was due to their educational background', but it may have also been 'a political calculation'. At the same time, Brutus and radical anti-apartheid sports activists understood well 'sport as a mobilizing force and as cultural terrain for contesting power'. Yet, 'the fabled "level playing field" remains a chimera', opportunities are unevenly distributed and those who don't succeed are condemned to 'carry the burden of their own failure'.[16] A glib notion of merit 'deepens divides and corrodes solidarity'.[17]

A more diverse squad would have been ideal. The fact that the team was not fully representative demographically does not in any way detract, however, from it being a non-racial squad. Non-racialism was consistently upheld as a principle and ideal but its desired implementation and practice was constrained by both the structural realities of colonialism and apartheid and by material conditions.

For example, the Black Consciousness movement was exclusively black but it was profoundly anti-racist and committed to non-racialism and a non-racial unitary South Africa. It accepted that 'South Africa is a country in which both black and white live and shall continue to live together'.[18] As trenchantly explained by Steve Biko, the goal was a

> completely non-racial society [without] . . . guarantees for minority rights, because guaranteeing minority rights implies the recognition of portions of the community on a race basis. We believe that in our country there shall be no minority; just the people. And those people will have the same status before the law and they will have the same political rights.[19]

However, in a context where colonialism and apartheid made black people 'foreigner[s] in the country of [their] birth and reduce[d] [their] basic dignity', exclusive black organisation was seen as a necessary strategy.[20] 'It's a question of the oppressor and the oppressed, so we had to galvanise ourselves, and that's where we came with the concept of black solidarity: to bargain from a position of strength.'[21] This was further underscored by the South African Students Organisation's policy manifesto, which spoke of an open society. The realisation of such an open society was viewed as depending, ultimately, on the independent efforts of blacks and therefore necessitated an initial withdrawal on their part in order to first establish black solidarity and unity.

Second, the first non-racial SnALTU squad to tour overseas was an exclusively male affair. It is not self-evident why this should have been the case. Women tennis players were well-established in some of the SnALTU regions and there were local and national tournaments. As we shall see, Charmaine Williams happened to be touring the UK and joined the squad but was not officially part of the tour. Apart from her, there were other promising junior and established women players who could have benefited from such a tour and given tennis among women and non-racial tennis a fillip.

Perhaps the national SnALTU officials who decided on the tour were not convinced of the value of including women on the tour; in this regard they imbibed and manifested the damaging and exclusionary patriarchal attitudes that were dominant at the time. As Alegi notes, sadly such attitudes 'endure to this day (in spite of inclusive rhetoric by sport administrators and corporate sponsors, as well as some positive changes in elite performance sports)'.[22] Cost was a constant issue of concern and SnALTU had to mobilise considerable funds to support the tour. However, the matter of cost does not justify only non-racial male tennis players being sent on tour and women players being excluded. Here, there is a link with the concern of diversity raised earlier as this relates not only to the absence of African players in the team, but also women.

Third, all six players were South Africans. This may seem a trite point, but nothing precluded those who were foreign nationals from surrounding countries or elsewhere from playing tennis under SnALTU and being part of the squad. Indeed, players from neighbouring countries such as Rhodesia (Zimbabwe) and South West Africa (Namibia) participated in SnALTU tournaments.

Fourth, all the squad members were from major metropolitan areas – three were from Cape Town, two from Pretoria and one from Durban. This draws attention to the predominance and relative privileging of urban-based players in tennis generally and SnALTU specifically, with a consequent and relative neglect of the development of the sport in rural areas.

Fifth, the six Dhiraj Squad members were all from essentially middle-class backgrounds. This suggests that apart from being a largely urban-based sport, tennis was primarily a sport played by the black middle classes and draws attention to class and socio-economic stratification in black communities.

Departing from Jan Smuts (today OR Tambo) airport in Johannesburg, the intention was for the squad to spend almost four months on tour and compete in tournaments in the UK and, finances permitting, on the European continent. The Dhiraj brothers, Solomon and Woodman, were to play senior tournaments, the other players in both junior and senior competitions. Darroll Carolissen of the Western Cape travelled with the team to undergo training in tennis coaching.

Charmaine Williams, from Stellenbosch has joined the South Africa non-White tennis squad on their tour of British and Continental tournaments. The ambitious twenty-year-old school-teacher came over to Britain in December using her own resources on a see-play-and-learn-programme. Charmaine's comment on the standard of the game here and her opponents is interesting. "I find I am playing tennis against people who do nothing but play tennis. At home I played for two hours each day after school and for a bit longer at week-ends. Some of the women players here have stronger back-

Charmaine Williams (*Leader*, 4 June 1971).

Charmaine Williams, a twenty-year-old school teacher from the Western Cape, used her own resources to travel to the UK in December 1970 on a 'see-play-and-learn programme'.[23] She linked up with the squad and played some tournaments. The case of Williams perhaps underlines the contention earlier about tennis being largely an urban middle-class black sport. In 1968, Williams won the under-19 women's championships at the Southern Africa Open held at the Green Point Track tennis courts in Cape Town when she defeated Amy Gelderbloem of Eastern Province 6-3, 6-2.[24]

Jasmat, the captain of the tour squad, was not able to travel with the other members when they departed on 10 April. A travel agent was tardy in renewing his expired passport and he was only able to depart on

15 April. He had, however, feared that the state could withhold his passport for two reasons. The first was for 'playing with Cliff Drysdale and then applying to play in the S.A. White Open. They tried to dissuade me.' The second reason was that he refused to be a stooge and join a club affiliated to the African tennis union, which had a subservient connection with the white tennis association.[25]

On his departure, Jasmat 'was dressed in Springbok colours, wearing a plain gold shirt under a green blazer'. He 'chuckled' wryly that 'I'm a South African so I felt that I should wear the country's colours when I arrive overseas'.[26] Historically, Springbok colours (green and gold blazers) were awarded from 1906 to individuals and teams that represented South Africa in international sport competitions. Under colonialism and apartheid, these sportspersons were white South Africans.

In 1963, the South African Rugby Board copyrighted 'the Springbok emblem and Springbok colours as a badge under the Heraldry Act to pre-empt any other sporting body copyrighting it' and stated that they would 'share the Springbok colours providing that they were only awarded to white amateur sportspeople representing South Africa internationally'. Later, by law only 'white South Africans could be awarded Springbok colours', though a few honorary whites were also awarded colours. Not surprisingly, the Springbok colours came to be viewed as a symbol of white supremacy.[27] After 1994, the Protea became the national sporting emblem, although the national rugby team continued to embrace the Springbok emblem and colours. Alegi draws attention to 'the controversy over the Springbok name, logo, and colours that erupted after Madiba's endorsement in 1994-95' and that 'the cricket Proteas have also been criticized for the apartheid origins of the term'.[28]

Given this context, Jasmat's sporting of the green and gold could have been viewed mistakenly by some in non-racial sports circles as embracing a racist emblem and generated controversy, though it does not seem there was any. His action can be seen as a powerful and subversive symbolic challenge to a racist code and as an exercise in prophecy – the proposition that alternative frameworks of meaning, in contrast to those that are dominant, are possible.[29] Interpreted in this way his adorning, as a black sportsperson, of the green and gold colours highlighted the absurdity of national colours being restricted to white South Africans and, as a form of prophecy, projected a future in which colours and emblems

80 Tennis, Apartheid and Social Justice

Jasmat Dhiraj at Jan Smuts airport
(*Pretoria News*, 14 April 1971).

Jasmat Dhiraj collecting his passport from a state official (*Pretoria News*, 14 April 1971).

(whatever they would be) would not be proscribed and prescribed along the lines of race.

Denied good facilities, professional coaching, regular high-level competition, sponsorship, the undeniable inducement of representing one's country, and given the new challenge of playing on grass courts, M.N. Pather observed that 'it's hard to say how our boys will fare, although we know they will try their best'. Pather had no unrealistic or outlandish ambitions for the squad. His approach was laudably developmental. He said there was no expectation that the players would 'produce miracles after only one trip' and that SnALTU hoped to send the same team and other promising players again in 1972. The pioneering 1971 trip would 'enable these players to get more experience and grounding, which would be an asset to them when they return next year'.[30]

On tour when in London, the Dhiraj brothers shared a room at the home of the Bhanabhai family in Hornsey, north London. The other players lived in a YMCA youth hostel a short distance and walk from the Bhanabhai family home. While playing tournaments they lived in

Oscar Woodman, Cavan Bergman, Jasmat Dhiraj and Hira Dhiraj with the Bhanabhai family, 4 Palace Road, Hornsey, north London.

The Dhiraj Squad with the Bhanabhai family, north London.

affordable accommodation such as YMCA hostels, bed and breakfast establishments and sometimes with local families.

To expedite travel, the squad bought a cheap second-hand green Ford Thames van. Woodman remembers helping Carolissen overhaul the engine in the Bhanabhai family's front yard, while Hira recollects that they 'bought a couple of mattresses to sit on at the back of the van' and 'some camping equipment in case we needed to camp out'.[31] They also used public transport in the form of trains and buses and, in London, the underground. Before the advent of Thatcher's Britain in the late 1970s, the UK had a welfare state that tried to promote the public good, like accessible and inexpensive mass transport, for ordinary citizens. Bobat remembers that to 'some tournaments, like Eastbourne we travelled by train. The UK transport system was very efficient, so we were able to get by.'[32]

Food on the tour 'was not ideal' but the team members 'had to adapt quickly and move on'.[33] Food was bought at cheap cafés and from Wimpy fast-food outlets, their mixed grill being a favourite. Solomon mentions eating fish and chips regularly.[34] The players had to do their own washing of clothes, which Hira doubts any of them did back home.

For tennis practice, they secured temporary membership at the Coolhurst Tennis and Squash Club in Crouch End, north London.[35] When not playing tournaments, most mornings were devoted to four hours of practice and training with an additional hour in the late afternoon.

In South Africa, the squad members would have played largely on medium-paced hard cement courts or medium-to-slow paced bitumen courts. Occasionally, they may have played on slow-paced sand courts. They had no experience playing on fast-paced grass courts or indoor wood courts. On the tour, they had to adapt to all the different kinds of courts: slow clay, medium hard courts, and fast grass and indoor wood courts. Indeed, those who played in the first Oxford tournament began their matches on slow clay courts and had to play their final rounds on indoor wood courts because of inclement weather.

Whether a court surface is fast or slow depends on

> the friction between the court and the ball. If the court is a high friction surface (grainy, sand, clay, brand new hard courts, maybe rough grass) this makes for a high coefficient of friction between the ball and the court. This decreases the pace on the ball after the bounce, but this energy must go somewhere. It is not totally lost, as energy is conserved. This energy contributes to a higher bounce of the ball instead. This is a slow court.[36]

By contrast,

> if the court surface is smooth and fast (old hard courts, smooth courts, carpet, slick grass, etc.), the coefficient of friction between the ball and the court is much lower. The allows the ball to maintain more of its original pace after the bounce. The trade-off is that the bounce will not be as high. This is a fast court.[37]

The various

> types of tennis court surfaces are constructed in different ways and using different materials. Their different construction and composition affect several aspects of a tennis match, including

the velocity of the shots, the ball bounce, and the players' capacity of moving around. Some players, like Roger Federer, adapt better to courts with faster surfaces, while others like Rafael Nadal perform better on slower and bouncier courts.[38]

Grass courts, which are rare today and only used at Wimbledon

> tend to allow the ball to slide when it bounces, which makes the overall game a lot faster. In addition, the ball tends to stay low and close to the ground, which means that shots with slice are usually more effective than shots with topspin. Players who hit flat shots, big servers, and good volleyers are usually very successful on grass courts.

In contrast, the way clay courts, such as at Roland Garros, home of the French Open, are constructed 'makes them slow and bouncy, which makes it great for strong baseliners and players who use a lot of topspin in their shots'. Moreover, 'players are able to slide around the court'. Hard courts, such as those used at the Australian Open and the US Open and for most of the major professional tournaments have surfaces that are 'usually considered medium, medium-fast, or fast'.[39]

In so far as the playing qualities and styles of the different tour players are concerned, Jasmat considered his game to comprise a 'very good service, a very good forehand, a very good sliced backhand that was later supported by a topspin backhand and a very good net game'. He preferred playing attacking tennis, which was 'a very successful way to win matches and a relative novelty' in non-racial tennis.[40] Hira says:

> Jasmat was a natural with a lot of talent. Already at eighteen years old, he possessed every stroke and consistency. He worked very hard at his game and developed a strong serve and a powerful forehand. He also had a deadly drop volley. What he lacked was pace in his strokes. His greatest asset was that he hated losing, especially when he became number one in South Africa and did not lose to anyone in any competition for almost four years.[41]

In Bobat's view, Jasmat was the 'undisputed king of non-racial tennis in the late 1960s and early 1970s, taking over the mantle from the legend of non-racial tennis – maestro David Samaai'. Jasmat was 'tall, lean and athletic', with an 'excellent all-court game, solid serves and a top-class second serve' – the 'hallmark of a champ'. His 'main weapon was his excellent forehand, which he used to great effect'. He was skilled at getting to the net and could make use of 'well-placed volleys and overhead smashes. He had a magical "dink" or drop volley.' Jasmat possessed an 'amazing fierce concentration and a will to win'. He was able to 'adapt his game to suit the conditions and the approach of his opponent, and he was comfortable on the baseline or being at the net'. He had no real weaknesses in his game, but Bobat says that a top international coach, of the kind not available to him in South Africa, could have helped Jasmat to add more power and weight to his first serve and his backhand.[42]

Hira, according to Jasmat, had 'a very good service, excellent sliced backhand with a strong flat forehand, which was at times inconsistent and an aggressive net game with very good smashes and volleys'.[43] Hira says that he 'developed a strong backhand' that was 'better than Jasmat's good steady slice'. He 'practised with Jasmat on most days after work and never ever beat him or took a set off him'. Only later, in the UK did he get to beat Jasmat and after his first victory he beat his brother often. He adds that he 'was also very consistent but did not have the pace to overpower Jasmat, whose big serve and big forehand was the difference. He also developed a winning drop volley when he made his way to the net.' Hira considered his strength to be his fitness, being 'quick around the court and going to the net at every opportunity'. Paradoxically, despite being very fit, his 'Achilles heel was cramps', because, he says, 'I perspired more than anybody I know and that led to cramps. Also, in those days we were discouraged to have too much liquid – so I dehydrated and that resulted to cramps.' Both Dhiraj brothers were coached by D.D. Patel.[44]

Bobat observes that Hira was 'a great personality, superb athlete, fit and fast around the court'. He was 'a late starter in tennis, as his teen years were dominated by top level soccer'. However, 'once he concentrated on tennis, he moved quickly up the ranks', having a 'solid all-round game with top serves and volleys. He had the ability to play serve and volley or play on the baseline.' Bobat confirms Hira's own critical self-assessment by noting that Hira 'sometimes battled severe cramps, not through lack of fitness but because he perspired profusely'.[45]

Alwyn Solomon was 'a really warm and friendly personality', who 'had an excellent all- court game' and 'was very quick around the court'. Indeed, 'on his day, no player could match his blistering ground strokes'. Solomon 'preferred playing from the baseline but was very adept at the net with solid volleys and smash'. If there was a weakness, it was that Solomon 'sometimes lacked self-belief' and was vulnerable to mind games.[46]

Oscar Woodman is described as 'a truly colourful character' who possessed an 'excellent physique', was 'superbly conditioned' and 'had textbook style strokes'. He had 'one of the best backhands at the time of the tour, which he could hit flat or with underspin'. He also had a 'great net game, with solid volleys and a dependable overhead'. He was 'comfortable both on the baseline' or going 'to the net'. One area that Woodman needed to work on was greater consistency 'with his first serves'.[47]

Hoosen Bobat was selected to tour because he was the top-ranked junior in South Africa at the time, having won the Western Province, Natal and national under-19 titles. Bobat was both physically fit and mentally tough, with a solid all-court game. He had arguably one of the best backhands at the time – ranging from his favorite underspin stroke to flat or topspin strokes – which he used to great effect to dominate matches. His volleys were excellent and complemented by a consistent smash. His serves, however, needed work: they were well placed but lacked punch. Hoosen was coached by his father, Ahmed Bobat, and as Ken Rosewall grew in tennis stature he moulded his game on that of Rosewall. Early on his idol and mentor was David Samaai; later Jasmat Dhiraj had a tremendous impact on him, both as a player and on his personal political development regarding non-racial sport.

Cavan Bergman 'was selected as a junior in the squad because of his undoubted talent and athleticism'. He had a 'solid all-round game with a top-class forehand and strong serves and volleys. Early in his career, his backhand was not as strong as the rest of his game.'[48] Bergman himself states that 'on the tour I had no idea what game style I had. I just played and tried to make less mistakes than the opponent.' His 'strength then was to try as hard as possible and to never give up'.[49] His 'backhand was always a weakness because of an incorrect grip'. He had been coached holding the racket only with 'a continental grip which was very restricted'.

The Historic 1971 Tour 87

Hira and Jasmat Dhiraj practising at Coolhurst Tennis and Squash Club, north London.

In later years, he developed 'a serve and volley game' because he 'strongly believed that the best form of defence is attack'. For Bergman, his 'physical fitness was a huge strength'. His mental and psychological approach was also 'a strength because of my ability to analyse my opponents and come up with a winning game plan like plan A or plan B and, if necessary, to interchange as the match progressed'.[50]

8

UK Tournaments
April to June 1971

The squad members were scheduled to play various tournaments, beginning in Sutton, Surrey on 26 April 1971 and ending in Eastbourne on 19 June 1971. In the process, it was hoped that team members could become eligible for the Wimbledon qualifying rounds in mid-June.

Locations of tournaments in the UK, 1971

1. Oxfordshire Junior Tournament, Norham Gardens, Oxford (19–24 April)
2. Rothmans Sutton Hard Court Championships, south London (26 April–1 May)
3. Rothmans Surrey Hard Court Championships, Guildford (3–8 May)
4. Bio-Strath London Hard Court Championships, Hurlingham (10–15 May)
5. Bio-Strath Droitwich Spa Tournament, Worcestershire (17–22 May)
6. Rothmans Surrey Grass Court Championships, Surbiton (24–29 May)
7. Rothmans Chichester Tennis Tournament, West Sussex (31 May–5 June)
8. Kent Championships, Beckenham Lawn Tennis Club (7–12 June) – juniors
9. Bio-Strath Wolverhampton Tournament, West Midlands (7–12 June) – seniors
10. Rothmans South of England Open Championships, Eastbourne (14–19 June)

With two weeks to get acclimatised to the UK, the first scheduled tournament was the Rothmans Sutton Hard Court Championships in south London between 26 April and 1 May. However, as a departure from the schedule, an opportunity arose to participate in the under-21 Oxfordshire Junior Tournament in Norham Gardens, Oxford between 19 and 24 April. The juniors arrived in Oxford a day late, but officials accommodated them. They made the best of their good fortune, sweeping into all the finals. Woodman and Solomon played each other in the singles final, with Solomon winning 6-3, 6-2. In the run-up to the finals, Woodman beat the reigning champion, Chris Ronaldson, 5-7, 8-6, 6-1. Ronaldson had beaten Bergman in the quarter-finals.[1] Bobat and Bergman shared the honours in the doubles final when rain prevented play; and Bergman and a British partner, Lyn Maxwell, shared the mixed doubles prize when rain also washed out their final.[2]

Results from a newspaper article (*Leader*, 30 April 1971).

Jasmat observed that the juniors had a 'good chance of doing well in major junior tournaments. The hard courts suit the style of the players.' But he cautioned that 'when we start on grass the story might be different'. SnALTU secretary M.N. Pather was 'a happy man' because of the juniors' triumphs in their opening tournament. He commented that their performance demonstrated 'that if our players are given the opportunity they would prove themselves'.[3]

The first scheduled event in which the squad played was the Rothmans Sutton Hard Court Championships in south London between 26 April and 1 May.

Also playing in this tournament was the Australian First Nation tennis player Evonne Goolagong, then a nineteen-year-old rising star, who won the women's singles final.[4] Goolagong won the Rothmans Surrey Hard Court Championships in Guildford that followed and in which the Dhiraj Squad also took part. Soon after, she won the French Open in Paris and then Wimbledon for the first time, beating fellow countrywoman Margaret Court.[5] As we saw, in the early 1970s Goolagong violated the sports boycott of South Africa and won the South African Open in Johannesburg in 1972, playing as an honorary white.

The squad did not have a good showing in Sutton, but Jasmat was not disappointed. He noted that 'it was bitterly cold, the boys were not used to the slow surface, and they found it tough getting used to the conditions'. He didn't mind the players losing as 'we are here to learn'.[6] In first-round defeats, Solomon 'was hammered 6-0, 6-0 by Geoff Notman

Left to right: Hira Dhiraj, Jasmet Dhiraj, Alwyn Solomon, Charmaine Williams, Hoosen Bobat, Darroll Carolissen, Oscar Woodman and Cavan Bergman (*Cape Herald*, 8 May 1971).

of Britain and Woodman lost 6-3, 6-1 against Australian Geoff Perkins'.[7] Hira 'dropped the first set 4-6 against his British opponent J. Hill, but then gained control of his game and took the next two sets 6-3, 6-3'.[8] He then lost to Adi Kourim of Australia 6-2, 7-5.[9] Carolissen, suffering from 'fibrositis in his back', lost 1-6, 0-6 to A. Hammond, ruefully complaining that 'this cold bites through your bones'. Bergman lost to J.P. Malvin 6-8, 2-6. Charmaine Williams, described as 'the Cape Coloured girl from Stellenbosch', lost 1-6, 1-6 to UK player Lesley Charles.[10] The reporting by one Justin Dowling exemplified the racialised mindset of many white journalists. The race of the white South African players was never mentioned; Jasmat was, however, referred to as a 'non-White' and Williams as 'Cape Coloured'! 'On a court made tortoise slow by heavy rain' and 'in a temperature just above zero', Jasmat beat UK player Owen Hanson 6-1, 6-1 in the first round.[11] In the second round, he went 'down to the top South African and Junior Wimbledon champion Byron Bertram, who eventually won the Sutton tournament'.[12]

Jasmat described his 2-6, 1-6 loss to Bertram as a 'bitter disappointment'. He understood that the contest 'between White hope, Bertram', and him as the 'Black hope' was 'not only a match but a measure of the struggle' between the racist white sport establishment and the forces of black non-racial sport. Jasmat observed that the white tennis establishment sought to exploit his loss to Bertram to justify their racist exclusion of black tennis players from tournaments in South Africa.[13] He was contrite that he did not beat Bertram, or at least extend him as black sportspersons had hoped. He was not pleased with his form: 'I am not playing well.' He was finding the courts 'very slow and slippery' and experiencing 'difficulty with the bounce of the ball'.[14]

The reality was that it was early in the tour. Jasmat complained that 'I do not feel tennis. I will in the next few weeks. I must first accustom myself to the tennis rat race, and overcome the inhibitions and complexes that I have developed in South Africa.'[15] The inhibitions and complexes to which Jasmat referred were real enough. Asked about any especial challenges that were experienced on tour, Bobat comments that 'also initially we had to overcome the so-called inferiority complex of playing against white tennis players'.[16]

Some reflection on the meaning of these personal observations and experiences of black non-racial sports players in the wider context of the struggle against white racism in sport is necessary. Franz Fanon writes

Jasmat Dhiraj and Byron Bertram (*Star*, 28 April 1971).

about the psychopolitics of the effects of the colonial encounter and racism on not just black bodies but also, and perhaps especially, on the black psyche. Psychopolitics alerts us to 'the role that political factors (i.e. relations of power) play within the domain of the psychological' and 'how politics impacts upon the psychological, and how personal psychology may be the level at which politics is internalised, individually entrenched'.[17]

Neuroses, unconscious inferiority complexes and the like are not purely individual, but an 'explicitly social psychological phenomenon, rooted in the specific historical and political contexts of colonisation' and its concomitant racism, oppression and violence. They are 'an outcome of a specific configuration of power, of real material, economic, cultural and sociopolitical conditions that continually celebrate and empower the white subject and continually denigrate and dispossess the black man or woman'. They 'are ultimately derived from inequalities present in wider social structures and cannot as such be reduced to the internal psychical workings of individual subjects'.[18] Apart from violence and the threat of violence, as Fanon writes, 'books, newspapers, schools and their texts, advertisements, films, radio' and their messages of white superiority and black inferiority insidiously 'work their way into one's mind' and affect the actions of black people.[19]

Bobat recounts that at one tournament a man unknown to any of the squad members came over to them. He said that he had been observing them and was puzzled why they seemed to battle against the white, and especially white South African, players. In his view, they, the squad members, were the better players. The man asked whether it had to do with racism and the notion of white superiority in South Africa and their effect on the psychology of black South Africans. The squad members had not considered this but were conscious that they entered matches, especially against white South Africans, with some anxiety and self-doubt. Being made conscious of the probable reason for their understandable self-doubt was invaluable. Now, they could mentally confront the problem.

It is instructive here to consider the thinking of liberation movement intellectual and fighter Bantu Stephen Biko and the Black Consciousness movement that arose in South Africa after 1968. They posed the tasks of the 'liberation of the Black man, first from psychological oppression by themselves through inferiority complex, and secondly from the physical one accruing out of living in a White racist society'.[20] The key themes of Black Consciousness as a doctrine of self-discovery and self-realisation included 'liberation from psychological oppression, the building of a new awareness, the establishment of a new basic dignity, the framing of a new attitude of mind, a rediscovery of the history of the people, and a cultural revival'.[21] The Black Consciousness movement stressed the need for blacks to develop their own value systems and to define themselves, rather than be defined by others. The emphasis was on self-reliance: on, as Biko put it, blacks doing 'things for themselves and all by themselves'.[22]

Following his defeat by Bertram, Jasmat was confident that he could 'do better'; and the best way to do better was through 'competition – international competition – not for one month but for ten to twelve months'. He did not mind losing, as through defeat and failure he would 'improve'. He assured those following the tennis tour that the squad would get stronger and that they planned 'to eat, drink and sleep tennis'.[23]

Jasmat took issue with Justin Dowling and Dennis Done, two foreign correspondents of South African newspapers that served a white readership, for their 'unbalanced reporting on the performances of the six-man SALTU squad campaigning on the British circuit'. He was irked by their drawing unwarranted 'disparaging conclusions about the standard' of non-racial tennis in South Africa because of his loss to Bertram. He rightly pointed out that the correspondents had no appreciation of the effects on black players of the absence of 'first class competition . . . proper coaching and pitifully inadequate facilities', and of playing for the first time against opponents 'who enjoy international competition for nine to ten months of the year'.[24]

Especially insidious was the news blackout and silence of the correspondents on the good performances of squad members against ranked players. Hira Dhiraj had defeated a top South African junior, Frank Briscoe, 6-4, 3-6, 6-2 before falling to top Rhodesian Hank Irvine 5-7, 0-6. Bobat had extended highly rated Australian Geoff Masters before succumbing 7-9, 3-6. In the later Guildford tournament, Bobat narrowly lost to the top American junior D. Crawford 8-6, 3-6, 7-9, after leading 5-2 in the final set. Bobat and Woodman reached the quarter-finals of the A-level singles of the London Hard Court Championships at Hurlingham. Jasmat and Hira had a strong showing against Hank Irvine and Andrew Pattison, quoted as being 'one of the best doubles combinations in Southern Africa', losing 2-6, 4-6.[25]

Jasmat also tackled white South African tennis players. Based on his contact with some of them on the tour, he acknowledged that many of them were 'great chaps' but urged them to move from 'just the voicing of sympathy' to refusing, 'as a form of passive resistance', to participate in 'segregated tournaments in South Africa'.[26] He took aim at the system whereby Frank Briscoe, whom Hira had beaten, could participate in Wimbledon because he belonged to a union that was recognised internationally, despite its racist adherence to segregated sport. Hira, however, tragically could not take part in Wimbledon – because he belonged to a union that upheld the principle of non-racial sport. And, of course, Hira could not play Briscoe in tournaments in South Africa because of segregation.

In the second scheduled tournament of the tour, the Rothmans Surrey Hard Court Championships in Guildford from 3 to 8 May 1971, Hira came up in the second round against fellow South African Bertram and lost 2-6, 3-6; a slightly better performance than brother Jasmat who had lost to Bertram the week before. Jasmat lost in the second round to Australian Adi Kourim 2-6, 4-6.[27]

As noted, in a close fought match, Bobat was beaten by the American junior Doug Crawford 8-6, 3-6, 7-9. Bobat noted that 'the players are doing their best to get accustomed to playing in cold drizzly weather on slow damp courts'.[28] He pointed out that 'service is one of the most important aspects of play in overseas tournaments'. The players were 'learning fast'.[29] The squad members were said to be 'thoroughly enjoying the challenge and putting in a lot of practice in difficult conditions'.[30]

Between 10 and 15 May, the squad played their third tournament, the Bio-Strath London Hard Court Championships at Hurlingham on the banks of the River Thames. In the first round, Hira beat white South African Frank Briscoe, 6-4, 3-6, 6-2. Down in the first set, it was felt that Hira 'would face a disappointing defeat. But it was not to be. After losing the second set, Hira came back strongly in the third set to lead 4-2 and then take the set 6-3.' He fell in the second round to top Rhodesian Hank Irvine 5-7, 0-6. Jasmat commented that Hira's was an 'encouraging win and should definitely boost the morale of the squad'.[31]

Jasmat lost to Patricio Cornejo, ranked number two in Chile, 2-6, 5-7. As noted, in the doubles, Jasmat and Hira lost to the Rhodesian pair Irvine and Pattison, 2-6, 4-6.[32] Putting up a great display in the first set against the rated Australian Geoff Masters, Bobat lost 7-9, 3-6.[33] Woodman and Bobat reached the quarter-finals of the A-level singles at Hurlingham. Bergman contends that Bobat achieved a lot in the way he stretched Masters, as the Australian was a strong player who went on to win many double titles, including some Grand Slam tournaments, in the following decade.[34]

On 21 May 1971, Solomon returned to Cape Town. He was a second year B. Com. student at the University of the Western Cape and had to sit for his mid-year examinations.[35] It appears that the SnALTU were in the dark about Solomon's early return home. M.N. Pather expressed concern. He said that SnALTU should have been advised about any planned early return as it meant that Solomon competed in only four tournaments. He suggested that another player could have been provided the opportunity given the expense involved. Pather indicates that Jasmat had also 'expressed deep disappointment' at Solomon's return home.[36]

The rest of the squad proceeded to the Bio-Strath Droitwich Spa Tournament, 200 kilometres north-west of London at the historic spa town near Worcester, held between 17 and 22 May. Woodman 'provided the match of the day when he had [Paul] Kronk struggling for survival', making his opponent 'battle every inch of the way for his narrow 9-8, 5-7,

6-3 victory'.[37] (Some tournaments, including Wimbledon in 1971, used the best-of-12-point tiebreaker at 8-8 instead of 6-6, as it does currently.)[38] Jasmat exacted revenge on Kronk, scoring 'one of his best victories in England ... when he beat the top Australian player ... 5-7, 9-8, 6-3 ... In a thrilling match, [he] fought back from a deficit in each set to clinch the match.' This was despite a two-hour delay in the final set, when Kronk 'walked off the court because the public address system on an adjoining court irritated him'.[39] In subsequent years, Kronk reached three Grand Slam doubles finals and won six international doubles competitions.[40] Jasmat eventually lost to the Pakistan number three seed, Saeed Meer, 9-8, 6-8, 2-6 after a close-fought 'ding-dong match'.[41] In a second-round match, Hira beat J. Coe 6-2, 6-0. Bobat lost to the Rhodesian player, Sheridan Towers 6-0, 6-1 and Bergman 'lost to Mandelstrom 6-0, 6-1'. However, in a 'three-set tussle', Bobat and Bergman had 'a good doubles win over Woodman and Rana' winning 5-7, 8-6, 6-3.[42]

Next, the squad headed back south, to the Rothmans Surrey Grass Court Championships at Surbiton, south-west of London, held between 24 and 29 May 1971. At Surbiton, Jasmat lost in the first round to South African Derek Schroeder, ranked number 3 among whites in South Africa, 5-7, 6-4, 4-6.[43] The loss was disappointing because he had 'led 3-0 in the final set'. In Carolissen's view, Jasmat 'did not have the big match temperament to pull it off', a somewhat condescending remark given that Jasmat had won numerous titles and was the SnALTU senior champion. Schroeder commented that Jasmat 'played solidly' but would 'do well if he learns to hustle a little more'. Hira lost to the British player, Philip Siviter, 3-6, 2-6.[44]

On 30 May 1971, the squad members participated in a round-robin doubles tournament. The Dhiraj brothers had a good run. They beat R. Lucas and T. Billington 6-8, 6-3, 6-3 and defeated P. Warren and P. Redman 6-3, 11-9, but eventually lost 3-6, 5-7 to T. Billington and A. Gibson. Woodman and Bobat lost all their doubles matches, going down to T. Billington and A. Gibson 3-6, 3-6, to R. Lucas and T. Billington 1-6, 5-7, and P. Warren and P. Redman 1-6, 5-7. So did Bergman and Carolissen, who fell to T. Billington and A. Gibson 3-6, 5-7, to R. Lucas and T. Billington 1-6, 2-6, and to P. Warren and P. Redman 5-7, 0-6.[45]

The squad then made its way south to the cathedral city of Chichester, 130 kilometres south-west of London in West Sussex for the

Rothmans Chichester Tennis Tournament between 31 May and 5 June. In the second round, Bobat beat D.J. Mercer 6-2, 6-1 but then lost to the seasoned 31-year-old South African, Derek Schroeder 6-0, 6-0. Bergman beat A.J. Cottis 6-3, 6-8, 6-3, while Woodman lost to Philip Siviter, 4-6, 6-8.[46]

The next tournament, in which only the juniors participated, was the Kent Championships, held at the Beckenham Lawn Tennis Club, 16 kilometres from London, from 7 to 12 June. Bobat narrowly lost in the singles to R. Andrews, 4-6, 6-8. Woodman lost to C. Russell 1-6, 6-4 and Bergman lost to the number one seed, US player Erik van Dillen 6-1, 6-1.[47] In the doubles tournament, Bobat and Bergman were defeated by Americans Stan Smith and Van Dillen 6-1, 6-1.[48]

Losing to the Americans was no disgrace. The South African juniors were rubbing shoulders with international players at the top of their game. In 1971, the 24-year-old Smith lost to Australian John Newcombe in the Wimbledon singles final in five sets and then defeated Jan Kodeš to win the US Open final. In 1972, Smith beat Ilie Năstase in the Wimbledon singles final. In 1971, the pairing of Smith and Van Dillen lost in the US Open doubles final to John Newcombe and Roger Taylor and in 1972 they were defeated by the top South African duo of Bob Hewitt and Frew McMillan in the doubles final at Wimbledon.[49]

The seniors moved on to their penultimate tournament in the UK from 7 to 12 June 1971, the Bio-Strath Wolverhampton Tournament in the West Midlands, 210 kilometres north-west of London. The regional press reported that in a match played on the new 'centre court at the Wolverhampton tennis club', the number one seed and 'British Davis Cup player Stanley Matthews . . . unexpectedly dropped the opening set 6-4 in a first-round clash against Hiralal Dhiraj (South Africa)'. It went on that 'but any hopes the South African may have harboured of providing a major surprise on the first day of the tournament were quickly quashed'. Upping his game, and putting Hira under 'relentless pressure', Matthews took the next two sets 6-0, 6-0. Jasmat beat a local player, A. Pinson, 6-0, 6-0 in the first round but fell in the second round to Rhodesian Andrew Pattison, 6-1 6-2.[50]

The Wimbledon qualifying rounds were scheduled for 14 to 19 June 1971, leading up to the Wimbledon championships between 21 June and 3 July 1971. Unfortunately, none of the squad qualified for the Wimbledon championships. In the case of the Wimbledon qualifying rounds, the team members either did not apply or qualify; or, as in the case of Jasmat and Hira, refused to play the qualifying rounds. Hira says that 'Jasmat and I were offered a chance to play in the qualifying event, but we refused as we had applied to play in the main event on the grounds that we were the top two players' in SnALTU. He observed that 'the two top white guys got straight into the draw because in those days the two top players from any country would get straight in. So, on those grounds we stood firm and accused the committee of being biased.[51]

The Bobat affair: Junior Wimbledon and apartheid abroad

A major controversy erupted when Bobat was denied entry into the Wimbledon junior championships.[52] He recalls that a representative of the tennis racket and ball manufacturer Dunlop provided a delivery service for letters and telegrams to the team members and remembers the thrill of receiving the telegram that informed him he had been accepted to play at Wimbledon! Bobat would have become the first black South African to play at the Wimbledon junior championships.[53] However, unknown to him, roadblocks would be placed in the way to thwart his dreams.

Bobat turned down

LONDON

HOOSAIN BOBAT'S application to represent South Africa in the Junior Wimbledon has been turned down because the association to which he belongs, the South African Lawn Tennis Union, is not recognised in Britain.

This is the disappointing news which followed on the defeats suffered by all the members of the squad in Beckenham and Wolverhampton last week.

After defeating a local player 6—0, 6—0, in the first round of the sixth leg of the Bio-Strath circuit at Wolverhampton, the South African champion, Jasmet Dhiraj was beaten by the Rhodesian Andrew Pattison, 6—1, 6—2.

WON FIRST SET

His brother, Hiralal, won his first set against Stanley Matthews in the first round 6—4, but lost the next two 0—6, 0—6.

The three younger players in the South African squad all went out in the first round of the under-21 tournament at Beckenham.

Oscar Woodman lost to C. Russell 6—1, 6—4. Cavan Bergman lost to the No. 1 seed Van Dillon 6—1, 6—1. Hoosain Bobat lost to R. Andrews 6—4, 8—6, 8—6.

The manager of the squad, Mr. Darroll Carolissen, spent the week on a tennis coaching course in Berkshire.

Next week the squad moves on to Eastbourne.

Bobat's application to represent South Africa is turned down (*Cape Herald*, 19 June 1971).

Stalwart SNLTU sports administrator Ebrahim Osman has written that 'Bobat's entry to Junior Wimbledon was accepted on the basis of his undoubted talent and potential. But it was not to be.' The white union 'through its president Alf Chalmers objected to the entry because it was not "official" and Hoosen Bobat's name was removed from the Draw from Junior Wimbledon . . . another sporting victim of apartheid'.[54]

'Not official' referred to Bobat not belonging to a recognised South African body, such as the racist white SALTU.[55] A stormy meeting ensued with Chalmers and Reay in London. Jasmat accompanied Bobat and challenged Chalmers (whom he provocatively referred to as 'Baas Chalmers') to tell Reay whether Bobat could play for a club affiliated to SALTU. Chalmers sat silently and smirked in a corner of the room. Reay showed no interest in Chalmers' response.[56] The South African players 'argued that they were members of an English club which meant that they were recognised by the British Lawn Tennis Association which is affiliated to the International Lawn Tennis Federation' – a reference to the Coolhurst Tennis and Squash Club that they had joined in order to practise.[57] This contention fell on deaf ears.

Jasmat was furious that Bobat was denied the opportunity to play and the blatant collusion between the whites-only SALTU and the ILTF. He was dumbstruck by Reay's contention that 'there is nothing I can do' and says that he carried those words around with him during the Wimbledon championships.[58] Dhiraj noted that there was much talk about not mixing sport with politics. Yet when they were mixed and resulted in racial injustice, tennis players and administrators remained silent instead of attacking and sanctioning SALTU for condoning racism. By supporting and participating in tournaments that excluded black players from tournaments in South Africa and not speaking out, they effectively colluded with racism.

Moreover, they were complicit in thwarting and denying black tennis players the opportunities to realise their potential and talents. 'How many players,' Jasmat asked, 'have been wasted, are in the process of being wasted or will be wasted and frustrated in the future?' It was ironic for the likes of Reay, other white administrators and white South African players to tell black players to 'go overseas' to play and develop, when they were prohibited from playing in their own country. Yet others, including foreign black players, were made honorary whites and permitted to play.[59]

SALTU president 'Baas' Alf Chalmers and ILTF secretary Basil Reay.

SALTU negotiated with the government for international black tennis players – like Arthur Ashe and Evonne Goolagong – to play tournaments in South Africa but, hypocritically, made no such efforts when it came to local black South African players.[60]

Jasmat pulled no punches. He argued that black players were degraded by being denied their sporting rights and human rights to play tennis freely. In the process, those who kept quiet or supported the white SALTU and its racism in tennis also degraded themselves. He made an impassioned appeal to administrators and players: 'Why don't you support me? Why don't you stop supporting the other side and help me to win back my human dignity and my rights as a tennis player? Give us a chance.'[61]

9

The Rest of the Tour

Not able to participate in the qualifying rounds for Wimbledon, the squad participated in their final UK tournament, the Rothmans South of England Open Championships at Eastbourne, 117 kilometres south of London on the Sussex coast, from 14 to 19 June 1971.

Jasmat says that they played well on grass courts and that he won the singles, doubles and mixed doubles titles. Officially, 'Bobat and P. Orchard and P. Orchard's sister and I shared the doubles. The younger Orchard sister did not want to share the title' and proposed that they travel to their local club 'and play the final there'. They did that – Jasmat and the younger Orchard sister won, making her 'very happy'.[1]

The Wimbledon tournament was a highlight on the tour but, not surprisingly, getting tickets to matches was a struggle and not everyone succeeded. Jasmat we know attended Wimbledon because there is a photo of him there with Arthur Ashe. Bobat was fortunate to secure an invite from a junior woman player whom he had met on tour to accompany her on the first day of Wimbledon. On some days, he used media entrance passes from Paulin Rai Bramdaw, who was brother of the publisher of the Durban-based *Leader* newspaper. Paulin was 'an international correspondent to many publications, mainly in India, but also on occasion submitted articles to *The Leader*'.[2] Bobat carried a video camera to impress officials and give weight to his media 'credentials'.

Bergman cannot remember precisely how he attended Wimbledon. He watched the first- round match on Centre Court between the reigning champion John Newcombe and South African Bob Hewitt, which Newcombe easily won 6-4, 6-3, 7-5.[3] Hira does not recall attending Wimbledon and watching any live tennis matches. He thinks that some of them 'watched it all on TV; there was no TV in South Africa at that time and so we enjoyed the tennis on TV'. He remembers seeing in action 'some of the players who we played against or who played in the tournaments we took part in'.[4]

At the end of the UK schedule in July, Bergman returned to South Africa. The remaining squad members – the Dhiraj brothers, Woodman and Bobat – took their Ford van on the ferry across the English Channel to Belgium, intending to play in tournaments in the Netherlands, Germany, Switzerland, Monaco and Sweden.[5] Finances, however, stymied such an extended tour and the squad members were able to play only in the Netherlands.

Having crossed the Channel, one of the cylinders of the Ford Thames van blew on the outskirts of Brussels, requiring a visit to a garage. The garage was, however, shut until the following Tuesday because of a long weekend. Being able to drive only very slowly, the squad checked into a camping resort for the weekend. Fortunately, at the outset of the trip they had wisely equipped their van with basic camping gear and there were mattresses in the van on which they could sleep. To cook they needed paraffin for their primus stove, but a new problem arose: they were clueless about the Dutch, French, German or Flemish word for paraffin. Eventually, after many attempts, they secured fuel for the primus stove and were able to cook meals.

At a loose end for the weekend, they walked around the camping site and 'came across a tennis centre with four beautiful courts'. They asked a security guard if they could play a little; he said why not, play as long as you wish, the courts were to be demolished after the weekend! They played for many hours and on the Tuesday morning made their way to the garage to effect the necessary repairs to the van. A new problem arose: the van needed new pistons but they would take at least a week, possibly longer, to arrive. The mechanic, however, worked his magic on the engine so that it would function on three cylinders and assured them that it would get them around Europe with just a little loss of power. And work it did: according to Hira, 'it never gave us any problems and at the end of the tour it was still going'.[6]

That same day they got to Katwijk aan Zee, a small coastal town on the North Sea west of Leiden and set up camp again. The next day, they found a tennis club nearby. A helpful official not only permitted them to practise but, observing their standard of play, organised a tournament by summoning local Dutch players. During the tournament, he arranged for the squad to have free evening meals at a local hotel.

Hira Dhiraj and his South African friend, Vinoo Manga, with the famous green tour van in the Netherlands, 1971.

Jasmat reached the singles finals, losing 'to a very good Dutch player' and the Dhiraj brothers were beaten in the semi-finals of the doubles competition. Their performances made them 'very popular in the town', and they featured in the local newspaper alongside their van that sported 'The first Southern Africa Lawn Tennis Union Non-racial Squad' on one side.[7] The squad and Charmaine Williams rented a beach hut and on their first morning had breakfast at a café on the beach. The owner of the café generously invited them to breakfast at her hut every morning and served them no matter what time they rose. She and her family, the De Leeuws, became lifelong friends of Hira, and Hira's family regularly spent Easter weekends with them at their home in Katwijk aan Zee.

Dhiraj Squad members sightseeing in Delft, 1971.

Hira Dhiraj, American Jared Florian (right) and a Dutch acquaintance, the Netherlands, 1971.

In the Netherlands, Jasmat and Hira linked up with some Americans, including Jared Florian, Steve Messmer and Bill Drake, whom they had met previously in the UK. Drake was head coach at the University of Minnesota, and they enquired about the possibility of Bobat obtaining a tennis scholarship to Minnesota. Drake had a look at Bobat and was impressed. Subsequently, there was correspondence with Bobat, with Drake very keen to have him join the University of Minnesota. Bobat's father was not in favour of Bobat junior taking up the scholarship offer and the opportunity passed.

After arriving back in London, Jasmat took the Americans sightseeing. Florian could not believe that three years previously, in 1968, London Bridge had been sold to an 'American oil tycoon for a cool $2,460,000 ... subsequently dismantled and shipped over to lake Havasu in Arizona, where it was reassembled and still stands today'.[8] Later, Jasmat took up an invitation to the US from Florian and stayed with him. In turn, on a tennis tour to England, Florian and Messmer stayed with Jasmat. Florian and Jasmat still correspond to this day.

While in the Netherlands, a Dutch coach advised Jasmat to talk to the Dutch Lawn Tennis Association and lent him his car to visit their offices. The association helped to enter him and Hira in tournaments in Germany and Belgium. In late August, Woodman and Bobat travelled back to London and returned to South Africa. The Dhiraj brothers continued to Germany with the intention of returning to South Africa in time for the non-racial national championships in December 1971.

The brothers took a train to Cologne, having entered a tournament in a small town near the city. Arriving at the tournament, they noticed what seemed to be many juniors practising. Only when the matches were announced did it dawn on them that it was an under-18 tournament! They immediately informed officials of their mistake in registering for the tournament. Possibly because of their youthful looks, and being the only players of colour, the officials begged them to stay and play. Hira easily beat a seventeen-year-old from Switzerland in the first round but told Jasmat that they could not continue. They informed the officials and planned to return to London the same day.

The officials pleaded with them to stay a while so that they could make some calls to try to enter them in other tournaments. The wait paid dividends. They secured entry to a senior tournament, with full hospitality, which began a few days later in Mönchengladbach, a short train journey away. Short of money, they roughed it out in Cologne by spending the night at a café and on benches along the River Rhine and then proceeded to Mönchengladbach.

They both lost in the first round of what Hira describes as 'a very high-quality tournament'.[9] The top seed was Wilhelm Bungert, who had reached the 1967 Wimbledon singles final and was a member of the 1970 German Davis Cup squad that lost to the US in the finals. In the doubles competition, they played a 'good match' but lost against the Chileans Patricio Cornejo and Jaime Fillol.[10]

In a small town on the border of the Netherlands and Belgium that housed families of employees of the Philips Electrical Company, they played in a tournament for visiting players. Two players represented their countries and played opponents from other countries in singles and doubles. South Africa (the Dhiraj brothers) played India, represented by the Amritraj brothers, Vijay and Anand, in the first round. They played well, but Jasmat lost in the singles to Anand Amritraj and they lost the doubles as well. Vijay Amritraj began playing the Grand Prix professional tennis circuit in 1970; and just three years later he reached the quarter-finals of Wimbledon and the US Open. In 1974, he beat Björn Borg in the US Open before losing in the quarter-finals to Ken Rosewall.

In 1974, the Amritraj brothers were members of the Indian team that reached the finals of the Davis Cup, on the way triumphing over Australia and the Soviet Union. In the finals they were scheduled to play South Africa in Johannesburg. The Indians refused to play South Africa, in opposition to the regime's apartheid policies. South Africa was awarded

Top Indian players Anand Amritraj (centre left) and Vijay (centre right) (*Leader*, 9 July 1971).

the match and the Davis Cup, becoming only the fifth country to secure it, but it was a hollow victory.[11] Jasmat subsequently met Vijay Amritraj at Wimbledon on two occasions when Vijay was a tennis commentator and describes him as a friendly, down-to-earth character.[12]

10

Lighter Moments and Tour Lessons

It was not all about tournament tennis matches, training and preparations on the tour. The players squeezed in as much sightseeing as possible during the limited time available, especially when they were in London. This was Bobat's first overseas foray. He was for the 'very first time exposed to TV' and 'watched many shows, movies, documentaries and live music performances'. He also saw 'many movies, especially those that were banned in South Africa', and attended a 'live performance of the musical *Hair* and of Shirley Bassey live at the Royal Albert Hall'. Bergman also recalls going to the Shirley Bassey performance and attending a Miriam Makeba show.[1]

Hira recounts that on their 1969 short tour they experienced disaster when they visited a launderette. They followed the instructions carefully, only to be greeted with multicoloured clothing because they 'just threw the "whites" and coloured clothing together'.[2] Fortunately, one Billy

Fred Perry tennis tops were popular in the 1970s.

Woodgate, associated with the Fred Perry tennis apparel company, took sympathy on them and sponsored two sets of white tennis outfits.

Perry was a former world number one player who won eight Grand Slam tournaments, and the first to win a career Grand Slam (all four titles), which he did in 1935 at the age of 26.[3] In time, the Dhiraj brothers learned to 'fold the clothing immediately they came out of the dryer, thus saving [them] the trouble of ironing'.[4]

Bobat shares that one evening he and Woodman visited a club. There, they ran into a group of young women sporting badges reading 'Liberate South Africa', who they discovered were Scandinavians. Woodman went over to the women and introduced himself, saying that he liked their badges and that he was South African. Woodman being fair-skinned raised doubt that he was indeed a black South African. He summoned Bobat to vouch for his nationality. Bobat mischievously told the women Woodman was fibbing, but that he, as should be obvious from his complexion, was South African and part of the oppressed majority in South Africa.

Bergman recollects that they 'used to train every morning'. On one occasion, John Lloyd, who later became a British Davis Cup player, winner of three mixed doubles Grand Slam titles, and first husband of tennis star Chris Evert, asked rather condescendingly, 'Can Africans play soccer' and challenged them to a soccer match.[5] Lloyd, says Bergman, 'seemed to still be on a "high" from England's 1966 World Cup triumph. Hira and Oscar were very good footballers, Alwyn was pretty good and I was decent. The poorest player was Bobat and so we stuck him in goal.' They 'thrashed Lloyd and his English mates. After that, he changed his tune and insisted on mixing the teams!'[6]

In Katwijk aan Zee two Dutch teenage girls came up to Jasmat and asked if they could scratch his arms. He told them to go ahead. They did so and asked why the brown tan on his arms did not come off. When he replied that it was permanent, they were both surprised and envious; they had to spend hours in the sun to get a tan! In the Netherlands, too, Jasmat remembers some women on a train gossiping about him and Hira in a generally complimentary and positive way about what they liked about them. Drawing on their Afrikaans, they understood enough of the women's comments. When they left the train they told the women 'ons het alles verstaaan', and they all shared a good laugh.

For Jasmat, the 1971 tour provided many lessons. One was that planning was vital. He feels that it would have helped to consult someone with experience of tours and if there had been a tour manager.[7] Bobat, likewise, comments that 'it would've been good to have had an experienced European coach/manager attached to the team'.[8] Another lesson was that adequate funding was important as they had to struggle moneywise. Indeed, finances were a struggle throughout the tour and Carolissen warned SnALTU in early June that 'unless the union [was] prepared to give them further financial backing' the players would have to return by mid-July. He added that 'we have come over for experience and are certainly getting it' and was of the view 'that the group would benefit tremendously if we could stay longer'.[9]

Linked to Jasmat's comment on planning, Carolissen acknowledged that he had made a mistake in purchasing excursion tickets lasting only 90 days and that it meant that each of the group would have to spend an extra R102: 'Some of the players [did] not have this type of money.'[10] On his early return from the tour in late May, Solomon confirmed that the squad was 'having to watch the financial position very carefully'. His departure meant that their funds could go a bit further. The Western Province Tennis Board added R250 to its original contribution of R800 towards the squad's expenses and a further R30 per month for Woodman for two months.[11]

Jasmat was of the view that wealthy members of the Indian community could have been tapped for greater financial support, but he was mindful that some in that community unfortunately held prejudices that stood in the way of support for non-racial sport.[12] The *Cape Herald* suggested that it was necessary 'for tennis enthusiasts to dig into their pockets to assist the team to stay in top tennis company'.[13] Jasmat was being honest about the schisms within the Indian community. While there were progressive sections committed to non-racial sport and aligned to the anti-apartheid liberation movement, there were also conservative and reactionary sections (as there were in other black communities) that were racist and colluded with the apartheid state and its policy of separate development.

A third lesson was that intensive training, constant practice and a high level of fitness were important for success in international tournaments. Jasmat was impressed by the extent of training and practice undertaken by the players who regularly played tournaments.

Earlier, we noted that in 1971 John Rawls published his important book, A *Theory of Justice*. The same Rawls makes the trite but important point that in tennis 'time never runs out, as it does in basketball and soccer' and in other sports. This not only 'means that there is always time for the losing side to make a comeback', but it also means that stamina and fitness and the ability to endure long games, sets and matches are critical to success in tennis'.[14]

Jasmat's view was that black players had to begin to 'think of themselves as professionals and not as part-timers if they are to progress in world tennis'. They had to 'travel overseas every year, as do the white juniors, and play in as many tournaments as possible'. Back home, the tennis 'circuit [was] too limited' and only when playing overseas did one come to realise 'how many good players there are' even in tournaments in which the world's leading players did not participate.[15]

On his return to South Africa in late August 1971, Bobat expressed the view that unless black players could play in the main tournaments in South Africa that were restricted to whites, they could not reach the top. He pleaded, 'give us a chance here and we can prove our worth'. Bobat contended that 'going overseas for three months of the year and taking on seasoned campaigners who play in top-class championships for eight to nine months puts us at a great disadvantage'. SnALTU could not 'afford to send [players] overseas regularly'.[16] Williams observed that 'I am finding that I am playing tennis against people who do nothing but play tennis. At home I played for two hours each day after school and for a bit longer over weekends.' In that context, she was 'not too disappointed with my showing so far. I am learning'.[17]

Jasmat's view was 'that our hope lies in our juniors', who had to become 'dedicated' and 'find a new approach, discipline themselves and make a career out of the game'. This meant being 'prepared to stay away from home about eight months of the year'. He was confident that they 'could attain a standard to make a reasonable living'.[18] There was also the matter of having good players against whom to practise. Jasmat reported during the tour that 'we are getting desperate. We cannot get anyone to practise with.' Carolissen concurred that the squad needed 'stiff opposition in practice. It is useless us practising together as we have been doing. We can do that at home.' Securing new players against whom to practise was not easy. Jasmat observed that 'all the players on the circuit

The Dhiraj Squad being coached by the head coach of Finchley Manor Tennis Club (*Post*, 25 July 1971).

are old friends and have been coming here for years. It is only natural that they fix up practice sessions among themselves.'[19]

During the tour, the squad underwent a coaching session conducted by one C. Georgeson, the coach of Finchley Manor Tennis Club. He considered the squad members 'attractive and very good stroke players' but there was 'scope for improvement in services and overhead shots'. Moreover, the 'consistency was not good enough during match practice' and the players had to develop the correct 'mental temperament' as it was critical for success. Above all, the players needed 'more competition'.[20] Only 'match play in major tournaments' could 'sharpen up some aspects of their play'.[21]

Bobat was of the view that tournaments were 'better organised on the Continent than in Britain'. They were 'treated better on the Continent and received free accommodation and pocket money in Holland'.[22] He contended that 'the White S.A. body still has some powerful friends in England', who placed impediments on their path.[23]

Jasmat was convinced of collusion between international tennis bodies and racist white SALTU and of their active marginalisation of the non-racial tennis movement. The excuse was that non-racial tennis players were not ranked in South Africa, when it was common knowledge that racism and apartheid precluded black tennis players from equitable opportunities and participating in tournaments.

An unnamed observer opined that the 1971 tour 'was not properly planned and was, to a certain extent, a good deal of wasted effort'. From the perspective of benefits for the black players, the contention that the tour was wasted effort is dubious. What was true was that 'future tours needed more planning from the England end, especially regarding tournaments and events' as was the concern that the squad members were not 'given sufficient help from experts in England'.[24]

Tony Mottram, a former British number one and Davis Cup player, and chief coach of the Lawn Tennis Association, agreed to run a coaching session for the squad but given his busy schedule that did not materialise. Mottram subsequently became the national coach of Great Britain and was known for demanding total dedication from his charges.[25]

One person who did step up to provide support through a useful teach-in session at Hurlingham was Angela Buxton. Buxton was ranked number five in the world and had a great year in 1956 when, at the age of 22, she was Wimbledon singles runner-up and won the doubles titles at the French Open and Wimbledon with Althea Gibson, the first African American champion. Sadly, the following year Buxton was forced to retire because of tenosynovitis, a serious hand condition. She had an affinity with the black South African squad. Being Jewish, she experienced severe discrimination in the UK, struggled to find training facilities, and was turned down for membership by various clubs, including the All-England Club, despite numerous applications.[26]

11

Conclusion

The second part of this book presents biographies of each of the six black tennis players who participated in the first, historic, non-racial tennis tour of Europe of 1971. Here, the preceding analysis of the tour is drawn together, with brief comments on the squad members following their return from the tour; together with observations on questions of recognition, restitution and transformation in tennis post-1994.

The 1971 Dhiraj Squad tour was a farsighted, bold and commendable initiative of the SnALTU. A communal effort of committed non-racial administrators, players, their families, friends and well-wishers, the tour offered six of South Africa's most promising male black players the opportunity to test themselves against the world's best players in new places, settings and, in some cases, on hitherto unfamiliar court surfaces.

Given the lack of facilities, professional coaching and the absence of high-level and regular match play for black players in apartheid South Africa, there were no outlandish expectations regarding the players' performances and achievements. The tour was intended to be a pilot and developmental. It was an opportunity for the players to participate over four months in tournaments, experience the rigours of regular competition and to play on and adapt to different court surfaces. It would provide the squad exposure to the world's leading players on court and in training; permit them to obtain advice and perhaps some coaching; cultivate further their tennis capabilities; and allow them to return home more knowledgeable, skilled and experienced and to share the lessons learnt on tour with other players.

For the Dhiraj brothers from Gauteng, it was their third overseas foray, the previous trips in 1968 and 1969 being undertaken with the support of local clubs and provincial bodies. For Solomon and Woodman, it was their second time in Europe, both having taken part in the Western Province sanctioned Sunshine Tour of 1969. For the two youngest players, the eighteen-year-old Bobat from Durban and the seventeen-year-old Bergman, in transition from Cape Town to Johannesburg, it was their first overseas adventure.

The players' pride in being selected to tour overseas and represent SnALTU was obvious. From the outset, it was prominently emblazoned on the side of the second-hand Ford Thames that they purchased for travel between tournaments. Members of a racially oppressed majority, they represented the noble non-racial ideal and the non-racial and democratic South Africa to which they and their tennis association were committed. Given the repressive conditions at that time in South Africa, the team was counselled to concentrate on tennis and avoid making public political statements and stirring controversy.

The Dhiraj Squad, it was hoped, would be the forerunner of more and larger squads in future years because in South Africa, as Bobat noted, there was insufficient competition, the players did not compete in testing enough tournaments and the standard of tennis was lower than that overseas.[1] In the face of the indignities and injustices black players experienced in South Africa, it was, however, nigh impossible to remain entirely silent and there were occasions that necessitated honest and forthright public comment. Jasmat Dhiraj, the oldest member, captain of the squad and a natural leader, was the courageous and outspoken interlocutor.

Described by Bobat as 'a real-life hero', as a 'truly amazing, strongly principled person', from whom he 'quickly learnt a lot about life and the real world', Jasmat was warned of the likelihood of state repression on his return to South Africa. He 'sacrificed his whole life because he was not able to return to South Africa', which was a great setback not only for him personally, but also because his 'not being able to come back to South Africa to share his vast skills as a player and champion [was] the biggest blow for South African tennis'.[2]

Indeed, Jasmat not returning to South Africa for fear of repression was a great loss for non-racial tennis at many levels. On the court, he was at his peak, unbeaten for many years; and his character and competitiveness would have been an inspiration to contemporary and future black tennis players. As undisputed champion, the efforts of competitors to dethrone him would have raised the overall standard of tennis. Very likely, he would have moved into coaching and drawn on his abundant knowledge, expertise and experience to nurture future generations of outstanding non-racial tennis players. But it was equally off the court that Jasmat's exile from his homeland was a tragedy. Non-racial tennis locally lost an intelligent, principled, committed, determined, passionate and articulate champion of non-racial tennis and sport. In due course, he would probably have ventured into administration in the service of non-racial tennis and sport more generally and ably advanced the causes of non-racial sport and a non-racial, non-sexist and democratic society. Fortunately, he was able to continue contributing through SANROC in the UK to the international campaigns to defeat apartheid South Africa through the sports and cultural boycotts, disinvestment and sanctions.

Overall, despite some organisational shortcomings and the lack of adequate funding, the 1971 tour offered invaluable lessons for possible future tours and, as was noted earlier, had many positives for the players and non-racial tennis. Bergman comments in 1971, 'I was not a good tennis player.' The tour was the catalyst that made him a better player: 'My whole tennis life was developed by the tour. It whet my appetite to be a better player.'[3] In the immediate aftermath of the tour, there was a visible improvement in the performances of the players who toured and in the following decades Solomon and Bergman especially came to dominate the local scene. The tour also emboldened the SnALTU, which sought more international competition for its players and regular overseas tours.

The *Post* newspaper commented that the '"experiment" in sending a six-member team abroad last year was a great success. This was proved at the national championships that ended in Kimberley recently.'[4] It pointed to Solomon winning the 1971–1972 singles title by overcoming Andre Jansen from Colesberg, Bergman triumphing over Claude Moonieyan in the under-19 tournament, Hira Dhiraj and his partner, Chota Vawda, winning the doubles title, Woodman and his partner Arnie Poole being losing double finalists, and Bobat losing in the quarter-finals to Hermie Abrahams. It could also have pointed to Solomon reaching the semi-finals of the 1971 Western Province Open, where he lost to Poole, and to Woodman reaching the finals and succumbing in three sets, also to Poole.[5]

The tour squad players' successes continued in 1972 and 1973. In 1972, Solomon won the Boland Open, beating Petersen in the final 5-7,

6-2, 8-6, 4-6, 6-4. He was then losing finalist at the 1972-1973 national championships against Poole, but won the doubles title with Petersen.[6] In 1973-1974, Solomon regained his national singles title, defeating Poole 7-5, 5-7, 6-3, 3-6, 6-1 at Bellville South, and retained his national doubles title with Petersen.[7]

Hira Dhiraj won the 1972 Western Province Open, defeating fellow tourer Woodman 7-5, 9-7, who beat Bobat 6-2, 7-9, 6-4 en route to the final. Hira and Bergman won the Western Province Open doubles title against Trevor and Quentin Lawrence 6-3, 6-0. In 1973, Hira beat nineteen-year-old Bergman in four sets in the Transvaal Open championships at the Newlands courts to retain his title. It was said that Hira 'belongs to the David Samaai-Jasmet [sic] Dhiraj-Herman Abrahams school. They believe in a positive approach which means serve and volley.'[8]

Woodman either captured titles or was in the running. In the 1972-1973 national championships he and Charmaine Williams won the mixed doubles title, which the pair retained over the following two years.[9] In 1972-1973, he was losing semi-finalist in the men's singles to Solomon. It was noted about the Solomon-Woodman semi-final that it 'provided spectators with the proof of what overseas visits had done to improve the play' of the two players.[10] Also in 1972-1973, Woodman and partner Poole lost in the men's doubles semi-finals to the Samaai brothers, and the following year the same pair lost again in a five-setter in the doubles final to Solomon and Petersen.[11]

Bobat, too, had credible performances, despite injury troubles. In 1972, he won the Natal Open and was losing semi-finalist to Woodman in the Western Province tournament. In the 1973 Natal Open he lost in the final to Poole 1-6, 7-5, 6-2, 6-3 and, partnering Ismail Asmal, lost to Poole and Hira in the doubles final 6-4, 6-4, 3-6, 6-2.

The tour did a 'world of good' for Charmaine Williams.[12] Three months after her return from overseas, she won the 1971 Western Province Open singles, doubles and mixed doubles titles.[13] She then proceeded to win both the 1971-1972 women's singles title and the doubles championship with Alfreda Abrahamse at the national tournament in Kimberley.[14] In 1973, she won the Natal Open women's singles title.

The 1971-1972 national champs, Solomon and Williams, were both 21-year-olds. Eddie Fortuin, the SnALTU national vice-president, spoke about a new era in non-racial tennis. The *Cape Herald* commented that 'their victories provide justification for the continuation of the . . . policy of sending young players overseas, for both spent some months in England and on the Continent early in 1971'.[15]

Williams, as noted, 'was not part of the official party, but went at her own expense and joined up' with the squad 'to gain experience'.[16] Her success should have obliged a rethink about sending only promising male players on overseas tours, but judging by the reference below to a 'six-man squad' being sent in 1972, sadly it does not appear to have done so. A Natal official, A.M. Bobat (Hoosen's father), was reported as saying that a six-man squad would tour again in 1972 as 'our players badly need top class competition for at least 10 months of the year'. Learning from the 1971 tour, the squad would 'be drilled by a top class coach' as 'the squad that went overseas last year sadly lacked a coach'. Bobat said that Jasmat was 'likely to join the squad' and that he wanted the players to 'eat, drink and sleep tennis'. He observed that 'it's going to cost a fortune but the money will be well spent'.[17] Despite an obvious keenness to send more squads overseas, lack of finance was a major constraint. It was decided to postpone the planned 1972 tour until 1973 in order to raise the funds needed.[18] Unfortunately, no further tours of non-racial squads materialised.

A decade later, the lack of sponsorship continued to bedevil the development of non-racial tennis at all levels. Veteran *Cape Herald* journalist Barry Hopwood graphically set out the problems and challenges faced by non-racial tennis players and administrators. Writing in the immediate aftermath of the 1981–1982 national tournament, Hopwood observed that 'the standard of play at the Tennis Association of South Africa has reached a level where its members can hold their own in amateur competition in most parts of the world'.[19] Indeed, the top players could all compete internationally.[20] He emphasised that this was not morale building but a statement of fact and was acknowledged by an ITF delegation a few years previously.

Hopwood pointed to positive features. One was the determination of Cavan Bergman who lost in the Southern African Open but determinedly came back to defeat his vanquisher a few months later in the Natal Open. Another was the hard work of Raymond Anthony, who persevered to defeat Bergman after many losses to him. A third was seventeen-year-old Charmaine Carolissen, who played eighteen days out of 22 and 31 matches that included three national finals in a single day.

He also pointed to other realities. It took great commitment to be involved in playing three major tournaments, including the national open in a three-week builder's holiday period during late December and early January. Players and families made considerable financial and other sacrifices to travel long distances for tournaments without sponsorship. Hopwood drew attention to the cost of equipment for playing tennis and observed that 'it must cost each player a small fortune in travelling and board and lodging expenses'.[21]

The lack of sponsorship meant that players from working-class backgrounds were unable to take leave for any extended period and could not compete regularly; the travails of promising Pascalina Katu from Lesotho were cited as an example. It also affected the proper organisation of national and interprovincial competitions: the duration of the national tournament was too short; and too many senior and junior tournaments were played simultaneously or over a short three-week period.[22]

The only sponsorship in the early 1980s was R13 000 by Coca Cola for a national junior tournament. The premier national event was 'particularly unsuccessful' in obtaining sponsorship, but not for lack of trying. Twenty businesses were approached, including South African Breweries, Old Mutual, Toyota, Philips SA, Barclays Bank, Pick n Pay, McCarthy and Telefunken, but all declined to sponsor. Other companies such as BP, Rothmans, United Tobacco and Jet Stores did not bother to respond. Instead, 'business houses, and especially those that are white controlled, tend to associate themselves with Government-recognised codes, which also obtain television coverage.' Hopwood noted that 'big business houses are prepared to back the white South African Tennis Union to the hilt. One sponsor alone gave them R352 000 for this year's circuit. But they are not prepared to help non-racial sport.' Given the circumstances in which tennis was played in apartheid South Africa, Hopwood rightly paid tribute to the 'hardy lot', whose sacrifices demonstrated great solidarity to uphold and play non-racial tennis and to convey 'the true message of non-racial sport'.[23]

Five of the six players from the 1971 tour are still alive. Solomon tragically passed away in 1999, at the much-too-early age of 49. In 1971, all the touring players lived in South Africa; a decade after the tour three had emigrated. Jasmat Dhiraj, as noted, did not return from the 1971 tour and thus joined the legions of South Africans who were forced into exile or emigrated for political reasons related to apartheid. In 1973, Jasmat became the UK's first officially qualified and recognised black professional tennis coach. Hira Dhiraj decided that he would have a better future elsewhere and immediately began to gather resources for a return to the UK.[24] He left South Africa in 1974 and joined brother Jasmat in London. Both have lived there ever since, Jasmat working as a schoolteacher and Hira as a tennis coach. They continued to play tennis with considerable success in various senior tournaments. The tour revealed to Oscar Woodman the possibility of a different world 'with endless opportunity' and reinforced his commitment 'to getting the hell out of South Africa'. He emigrated to Canada in 1999 and still resides there.[25]

Alwyn Solomon, Hoosen Bobat and Cavan Bergman remained in South Africa. The 1971 tour was a brief six-week affair for Solomon, given that he had to return to write university exams. Following the tour, he had a distinguished career in the ranks of non-racial tennis, winning numerous provincial and national tennis tournaments. He qualified as a tennis coach and in the late 1990s was associated with the junior Western Province team dubbed the 'dream team'.

Unable for family reasons to take up a tennis scholarship at a US university that would have provided him the opportunities of dedicated coaching and college and other overseas competition, Bobat became demotivated. The episode 'killed his competitive edge' as 'here I was, one minute on top of the world . . . and the next I was offered a scholarship to the US and couldn't go'.[26] Affected by a shoulder injury, he continued to play at the highest levels only until his mid-20s in the late 1970s. He, however, spent many years coaching and cultivating young black tennis players in Durban.

Like Solomon, Bergman, the youngest of the tour members, had a highly successful career in non-racial tennis during the late 1970s and 1980s, winning numerous national and other championships. In 1984, he was TASA sportsperson of the year, acknowledged for among other things his unwavering commitment to non-racialism. He trained as a professional tennis coach and in 2001 was associated with the South African Davis Cup team.[27]

The harsh reality is that if any of the tour squad members had sought to play competitive tennis internationally and at the highest levels, they would have had either to go into exile or emigrate; or compromise their principles and affiliate to the white SALTU and play multinational sport. None of them were prepared to betray their profound commitment to non-racialism with the result that they became casualties of the institutionalised system of racial domination, their promise not fully fulfilled, their dreams and aspirations frustrated. It is a salutary reminder that apartheid was a killing field of the talent and ambitions of countless black South Africans, who were denied the opportunity and support to play tennis and succeed at the highest levels of the game. Who knows what the Dhiraj Squad members and others may have achieved, given the opportunities?

In contrast, white players of their age and of that time faced no systemic impediments. They were free to pursue their ambitions locally and internationally and some went on to achieve considerable success. In doing so, most looked away, accommodated the system and demonstrated neither substantive opposition to racism in tennis or society, nor solidarity with their fellow black players. They remained 'confined within apartheid borders of thought and experience', in which many whites continue to remain trapped even today.[28]

Both the tour and the general climate around the time of the tour revealed starkly the hypocrisy, arrogance and dishonesty of white sport administrators, especially 'Baas' Chalmers. Desperate to keep alive international tennis competition for South Africa, Chalmers went to great lengths to denigrate the non-racial tennis fraternity and to make scurrilous comments about its outstanding representative, Jasmat Dhiraj. Racism in tennis in South Africa was for a long time abetted strongly by the international tennis governing body. Like many other international sports bodies, it ignored, indeed whitewashed, the racist foundations of colonialism and apartheid and its necessary consequences for tennis.

There was shameful and shocking collusion until the mid-1970s between the ILTF and its white administrators and the exclusively white SALTU and its white administrators. ILTF secretary Basil Reay personified the collusion, and the colonial mentality and arrogance, by insisting that the non-racial SnALTU accept second-class affiliate status with SALTU. He was entirely oblivious of the indignity and submission to the racist status quo that this would have represented.

The historian Eric Hobsbawm cautions that 'political pressures on history... are greater than ever before... More history than ever is today being revised or invented by people who do not want the real past, but only a past that suits their purpose.'[29] He usefully warns about histories and biographies sanitised of complicity with oppression and exploitation; the kinds that make one wonder how colonialism and apartheid were able to survive so long if prior to 1994 there were no supporters of apartheid, no opponents of freedom, equality, justice and democracy.

This is also a warning against selective recall and amnesia about our history and an injunction to ensure that we assiduously recover and cultivate an understanding of the past, as this is the only basis upon which a democratic South Africa can build its future. Documenting the systemic violation of human rights is vital, both in the struggle against amnesia about the crimes and injustices of apartheid and in defending, asserting and promoting the human rights and social justice that democratic South Africa's Constitution and Bill of Rights proclaim.

If 'the archive becomes the official repository of memory... it is simultaneously a crucial site in the process of forgetting'.[30] Regrettably, the TRC gave no attention to sport and the effects of racism in sport on black South Africans. To the extent that its records become the official repository of information on the horrors of apartheid, this has the danger of obscuring practices such as racism in sport and the gross denial of opportunities to black South Africans to realise their talents in sport.

Since 1994, South Africa has embraced global capitalist sport, has seemingly prioritised the staging of global sports spectacles in which massive public investment arguably yields more in private returns than public goods, and has 'successfully hosted the rugby, cricket, and football World Cup tournaments'. Despite the deracialisation of sport administration and although

> many national teams are now more accurately representative of the country's racial demographics sport has experienced limited 'transformation', the South African term for the policy of reversing the massive inequality separating elite performance sport and proletarian sport. This inequality bequeathed by apartheid and worsened by more recent developments [such as state capture

and the looting of public funds by corrupt politicians and state officials] affects every sport.³¹

There is a gaping 'imbalance in the allocation of resources between elite and mass-based sport'.³² What Dale McKinley writes about soccer may in large part be true for tennis:

> The 'people's' sport was effectively privatised. Decrepit soccer infrastructure at municipal level and public schools could not be adequately addressed, training programmes for community and school coaches were left in the hands of volunteers, and the provision of basic soccer equipment and grassroots development programmes for the legions of township and school-going youth players had to rely, for the most part, on individuals, sympathetic community groups and hoped-for support from the private sector.³³

Impoverishment in South Africa still follows the contour of race and blacks predominantly constitute 'the more than 40 per cent of the population that struggle to meet their basic needs', meaning that 'most township residents and the poor in general lack access to basic sporting facilities, proper equipment, adequate coaching or career opportunities in sport'.³⁴

The legacy of racism in tennis and in the wider society continues to impact on tennis post-1994. Veteran non-racial tennis administrator Ebrahim Osman observes about the period 1994 to 2004 that 'it was a decade when tennis lurched from one crisis to the next with a lack of vision, little or no progress in grassroots development or transformation, little or no inspired leadership and many personal agendas'.³⁵

Farieda Khan contends that in tennis:

> The standard of competition and level of public interest has declined considerably since the heyday of mainstream tennis during the apartheid era. While many private club and municipal facilities with top-class facilities in former White areas are still in operation, the standard of tennis generally has declined. Further, since South Africa seldom holds international competitions

which would attract top-ranked players, this means that serious competitors have to train and compete abroad.[36]

Osman, an immensely selfless, committed, honest and considered administrator who played and served non-racial tennis for 60 years, soberly, and somewhat depressingly, concluded that by 2014, there was

> no real transformation, internationally we are in the doldrums; there is no real game sponsorship . . . The fact that over the 20 years of the new era we have not produced a single player of colour to remotely reach international level . . . says it all. Tennis in my view remains the most untransformed sport in the new South Africa and tennisites of colour are in no way near enjoying the fruits of liberation democracy.[37]

Robbie Naidoo, a former KwaZulu-Natal tennis champion of the late 1980s and 1990s and a qualified tennis coach who nurtured many promising black juniors concurs that there has been a disappointing lack of transformation. He is of the view that there has been little progress especially in black working-class areas and that non-racial tennis was stronger prior to 1994 than today.[38]

The emphasis is said, as in other sport, to be on mainly very talented tennis players, an approach that 'does not address the needs of ordinary communities at school and club level' and which 'will not contribute to the resurgence and re-establishment of tennis as a major sport in South Africa'. Moreover, 'the financial and infrastructural inadequacies in the tennis sector have contributed to a general decline in the levels of interest and participation in the sport among black communities'.[39]

Of the 1971 tour squad members, Cavan Bergman continued playing non-racial tennis the longest, won numerous senior championships and became one of South Africa's most qualified and experienced tennis coaches. After 1994, he became assistant to South African Davis Cup squad captain Kevin Curren. He has witnessed the continuities and discontinuities in tennis close up. Bergman concurs that there has been little substantive transformation in terms of who plays tennis, the provision of facilities, equipment and opportunities, and coaching in disadvantaged schools and areas.[40] In 2012, of the 18 000 registered players in South Africa, just 40% were black – this in a society in which 91% were black.⁴¹

He feels that those non-racial tennis administrators who kept a distance from the discussions in the late 1980s and early 1990s on uniting tennis under a single new body made a blunder. Old-style racial and ethnic thinking also bedevilled the forging of a genuinely new dispensation in tennis. Regarding the former issue, Booth contends that instead of being a tactic,

> The sports boycott became a strategy against apartheid per se. But SACOS assumed too much of the sports boycott; non-collaboration became a principle rather than a strategy. SACOS refused to acknowledge government reforms, negotiate with white sports officials, or even enter political alliances with other resistance groups; members who dissented faced expulsion and isolation.⁴²

During the late 1980s and early 1990s, with the release of political prisoners and the unbanning of the former proscribed liberation organisations like the ANC, in the new conditions of liberalisation the ANC began engaging the apartheid regime about a constitutional democracy in South Africa. In the early days of the transition, negotiations were termed by a government-supporting newspaper as 'a different kind of war' and by the ANC as 'a new terrain of struggle'.

Certainly, the negotiation process of the early 1990s was an arena of contestation. However, if there were notions of either the essential maintenance of state power by a white minority or the simple transfer of power to an ANC-led alliance, it became increasingly clear that negotiations were less about those outcomes as much as a negotiated political settlement underwritten by a series of agreements, pacts and accords covering a variety of social spheres. Once negotiation became the major instrument of politics, the way was open for its operation over a wide and diverse area of concerns. Indeed, a feature of the transition was the extent to which, alongside the negotiating structure around political and constitutional issues, negotiating forums came into existence, often under pressure from civil society formations, around various other issues.

Given the balance of power and the trajectory of negotiations around political and constitutional issues, negotiating forums were likely to be about the incremental reform and reconstruction of structures, institutions, policies and practices rather than about the immediate, rapid, sweeping and total displacement of those in existence. In this context, 'a group of SACOS members formed a rival anti-apartheid sports organisation. It eventually brokered a new sports order in South Africa. SACOS, however, refused to negotiate and effectively denied itself the means of struggle.' In sum, despite SACOS's immense contribution to the struggle for non-racial sport 'its doctrinaire philosophy of non-collaboration politically paralysed [it]. In the end, a refusal to distinguish between opportunistic participation in apartheid sporting institutions, and participation to advance the struggle, caused a split within SACOS and eventually forced it to disband.'[43]

In Bergman's view, after 1994 non-racial tennis gravitated away from its old clubs and locales such as Elsies River, Athlone, Bosmont and the Jeevan Kara Centre in Durban to clubs in the former white areas and places with better facilities – like Westridge Park in Durban, Ellis Park in Johannesburg and similar places.[44] The top black players became members of well-equipped clubs in the formerly white areas. Non-racial tennis in its old strongholds suffered, there were fewer opportunities for prospective tennis players from impoverished backgrounds, and long-existing and once-thriving clubs like Progressive became a shadow of themselves or ceased to exist.

Bergman agrees that to date no black tennis player has risen to any great heights nationally or internationally, but notes that it is much the same with white players. The last major successes were Byron Bertram, who won Junior Wimbledon in 1969 and 1970 and Ilana Kloss who won Junior Wimbledon in 1972. The absence of a major tournament in South Africa like the SA Open of the early 1970s – buttressed by Sugar Open tournaments from which people could gain entry – is a big drawback.

As with other institutions in post-1994 South Africa, sport and its organisations and leaders have not been immune from problems of dubious leadership, corruption and mismanagement. Already in 1996, President Nelson Mandela established the Pickard Commission to 'enquire into the financial affairs and administration of the South African Football Association and the National Soccer League and other related matters'.⁴⁵ Alegi notes that 'the Pickard Commission report was . . . one of the earliest examples in the democratic era to probe new challenges for South African sport not directly linked to the apartheid past'. The report provides one example of corruption, bribery, sexism and homophobia undermining sport in the new era of political liberalisation and economic globalisation.⁴⁶

Bergman says that he engaged with a Tennis South Africa (TSA) head about recognition for non-racial tennis players of the past and restitution, but that 'nothing came of it'.⁴⁷ This has been the case in most sports after 1994. Where there has been some recognition, it has been superficial and partial. As for meaningful and substantive restitution that effectively changes conditions in tennis and makes the sport more socially diverse and inclusive, there has been none. Substantive transformation in tennis 'would ensure that communities have easy access to well-maintained tennis facilities and a good standard of coaching at school, local and provincial level'. This would need to be part of 'a well-resourced national development strategy for tennis' that prioritises those who were historically marginalised, including women and girls.⁴⁸

A key issue that arises from the 1971 tour is the question of institutional change: what brought about the advent of non-racial tennis and sport in South Africa? Judging by the fawning today by sport journalists over the likes of Gary Player, Ali Bacher and their ilk, one could gain the impression that they were in the vanguard of realising non-racialism in South African sport.

The evidence tells a different story. Player was an unequivocal apologist for apartheid and the likes of Bacher promoted multinational sport, which was fully congruent and aligned with the bantustan and separate development policy of the apartheid regime. They actively collaborated with the regime in other words and deviously used state funds to entice black sportspersons away from non-racial sport and thereby undermined non-racial sport organisations. The Bachers of sport disingenuously dressed up their reprehensible shenanigans as a concern for black sport development. Others, like SALTU's Alf Chalmers, personified the crude *baaskap* mentality and arrogance of racist white sport administrators. The latter were the frontline bureaucrats who implemented apartheid sport based on the racist policy frameworks that the apartheid-era whites-only sports leadership promoted. Both kinds of sports administrator went to great and sometimes despicable lengths to stave off the international isolation of white sports teams.

These apartheid-era sports administrators found willing collaborators in their racist endeavours in international sports officials like Basil Reay. Often imbued with a colonial mentality, international sports administrators like Reay chose not to uphold human rights in sport and colluded with racism, trampling on the dignity of black sportspersons. It was the sacrifice, courage and tenacity of non-racial sportspersons and their organisations, linked with the mass-based anti-apartheid democratic movement and the international sports boycott campaigns, that finally defeated state sanctioned, institutionalised racism in sport. These anti-racist struggles locally and globally paved the way ultimately for the emergence and victory of non-racial sport just prior to and after 1994.

More than omission is at stake. If legitimacy or legitimating relies on the act of forgetting, it also, simultaneously, depends upon the act of remembering.[49] As noted, it must be of great concern how few black sportspersons who were custodians of non-racial sport – who played, organised, administered, promoted and sacrificed to advance it, often at great costs to themselves and their families – have been appropriately recognised for their pivotal roles and contributions.

Ariel Dorfman introduces an interesting thought when he writes:

> It is members of the new government, often the very people who led the resistance against the dictatorship, who are all-too-often the ones who preach a selective amnesia, asking their citizens to focus on the future and not on what happened yesterday. Investigating the horror, they say, dragging up old crimes, putting former officials on trial, only diverts attention from the most urgent task at hand, the primary goals of national reconciliation.[50]

In so doing, they fail 'to realize that this mythic coming together of a fractured nation could not possibly be attained by ignoring the pain of the past'; they also do 'not realize that the cost of allowing the former ruler and his followers utter impunity [leads] to the erosion of the rule of law and the mortgaging of our ethical future'.[51]

Recognising the injustices of our past entails, on the one hand, knowledge and understanding of the horror and brutality of apartheid in all its myriad and diverse forms: systemic, structural, economic, social, political, psychological, collective and individual. On the other hand, it requires the persistent and assiduous unveiling of little-known pernicious features of our colonial and apartheid past and drawing these to the attention of new generations and the wider public. Dorfman insists that 'a fragile democracy is strengthened by expressing for all to see the deep dramas and sorrows and hopes that underlie its existence and that it is not by hiding the damage we have inflicted on ourselves that we will avoid its repetition'.[52]

The preamble to the South African Constitution proclaims: 'We, the people of South Africa, recognise the injustices of our past, honour those who suffered for justice and freedom in our land.'[53] It is the constitutional imperative to acknowledge 'the injustices of the past' that animates this book on the 1971 non-racial tennis tour. In illuminating the circumstances in which that tour occurred, the outstanding and talented young black tennis players who undertook the tour and the dynamics associated with it, the book simultaneously honours those who stood firm on the principle and practice of non-racial sport, despite the impediments and personal hardships this caused them. Colonialism and apartheid perpetrated great injustices against black sportspersons and denied them the facilities, opportunities and human dignity to realise their talents. To realise social justice in South Africa means determinedly cultivating a prophetic memory.[54]

This prophetic memory entails remembrance of our brutal and traumatic past and the great sacrifices that were made to achieve democracy; critique of the growing amnesia about the injustices of the past, which threatens to undermine the achievement of constitutional ideals; the consciousness that in the light of our history, South Africa needs to be boldly and fundamentally transformed in the interests of all its people so that all may lead decent, secure, rich and rewarding lives; the imagination to conceive of creative new, just and humane ways of being and doing things; and, above all, the desire to reconstruct, remake, transform and develop our country.

This book will hopefully contribute to cultivating such prophetic memory.

Part Two

12

The Dhiraj Squad

The 1971 Dhiraj Squad, so termed by the veteran tennis administrator Ebrahim Osman, was unique in that it was the first official overseas tour organised and supported by the avowedly non-racial SnALTU. In that sense, it was historic.

It was certainly the longest tour at that time undertaken by black South African tennis players, lasting over four months.

The six young tennis players who constituted the Dhiraj Squad were, however, not the first black South Africans to tour and compete in the UK and Europe. They were preceded by the legendary David Samaai, who, sponsored by his Paarl community, competed in the French Open and Wimbledon tournaments in the late 1940s and early 1950s.

The Dhiraj Squad with the green tour van bought at an auction for £20.
Left to right: Hira Dhiraj, Hoosen Bobat, a Dutch colleague, Jasmat Dhiraj, Charmaine Williams and Oscar Woodman.

Later, the Dhiraj brothers undertook tours in 1968 and 1969, with funding raised from individual supporters and non-racial sports clubs. Oscar Woodman and Alwyn Solomon participated in the so-called 1969 Sunshine Tour, which was supported by the non-racial Western Province tennis union. Only the two youngest players, Hoosen Bobat and Cavan Bergman, had not travelled overseas and played tennis internationally.

The 1971 Dhiraj Squad tour was meant to be the first of further and regular official SnALTU organised international tours. They were intended to provide promising young black tennis players with opportunities to develop their craft, become familiar with different playing surfaces and conditions, compete with the best in world, and in the process inspire new generations of non-racial tennis players.

The badge for the SnALTU in 1971.

The Dhiraj Squad at the Surrey Hard Court Championships, Guildford.
Front row sitting, left to right: Hoosen Bobat, Alwyn Solomon and Hira Dhiraj.
Back row, left to right: Cavan Bergman and Jasmat Dhiraj.
Standing: Charmaine Williams and Darroll Carolissen.

Future tours, it must be hoped, would have become more equitable, diverse and inclusive in their composition, providing opportunities, too, for women, African South Africans and promising juniors.

Unfortunately, there were no more international tours, even though non-racial tennis continued to thrive during the 1970s and 1980s.

The Dhiraj Squad at Hurlingham with Anne Coleman of Australia (*Leader*, 28 May 1971).

The 1971 Dhiraj Squad. Left to right: Cavan Bergman, the youngest touring player and high school student; Hoosen Bobat, first-year student at the University of Durban-Westville; Alwyn Solomon, first-year student at the University of the Western Cape; Hira Dhiraj Soma, squad member; Oscar Woodman, squad member; and Jasmat Dhiraj Soma, squad captain.

13

Jasmat (Dhiraj) Soma

Jasmat (Dhiraj) Soma was born in 1941 and grew up in the Asiatic Bazaar area of Pretoria, also known as Marabastad. He was aged 30 at the time of the tour and was employed by the education division of the Department of Indian Affairs as a history and physical education schoolteacher at the Pretoria Indian High School in Marabastad.[1]

In 1960, Jasmat enrolled at the University of the Witwatersrand. Unable to get used to travelling from Pretoria to Wits, in 1961 he registered at the Transvaal College of Education (TCE) in Fordsburg and graduated in 1963 with a Teacher's Diploma.[2] A fellow student at TCE was Ahmed Timol, who later 'worked in the underground structures of the ANC and SACP [South African Communist Party]', was arrested in 1971, and was murdered in political detention at the age of 29 when his 'his body was thrown from a window of the 10th floor of John Vorster Square Police station'.[3]

Jasmat Dhiraj, 1973.

Like other areas such as District Six in Cape Town, Sophiatown in Johannesburg and Cato Manor in Durban, Marabastad was a racially and culturally diverse area. Black people had lived in Marabastad since 1890.[4] A key landmark was the Hindu Mariamman Temple, associated with the Pretoria Tamil League, which was built in the early 1900s and was the oldest temple in Pretoria.[5] In the early 1900s, members of the Pretoria Tamil League resisted colonial state restrictions on Indians in the old Transvaal. As part of the satyagraha movement, the chairperson of the Pretoria Tamil League, V.S. Pillay, 'suffered two terms of imprisonment totalling nine months with hard labour in 1909'. In 1913, Pillay's partner 'was a member of the second batch of Transvaal women who went to Natal to persuade the workers to strike' in opposition to a tax that was 'imposed on workers who completed indenture and their wives and children to force them to sign another contract or return to India' and which 'caused enormous suffering'.[6] For crossing the then Transvaal-Natal border, she served a three-month sentence with hard labour in prison in Pietermaritzburg.[7]

As part of racial engineering and segregationist policies, cities and towns were reserved for white occupation and black residents were herded into racially defined townships some distance away. In 1945, the African residents of Marabastad were forcibly removed to Atteridgeville. Later, under the 1950 Group Areas Act, from 1963 onwards coloured people were relocated to Eersterus and from 1968 onwards Indians to Laudium.

At the time of the tennis tour in 1971, Jasmat continued to reside in Marabastad with his partner Deanna Starkey and children Natasha (aged five) and Shaline (aged five months). Jasmat was an all-round athlete who 'had no interest in tennis in his early years and only played football in the dusty streets of Marabastad'. He also took part in athletics and cricket and represented Transvaal in both sports. At 'the age of 14, an uncle of his, Mr. D.D. Patel, bought him a tennis racket and taught him the game'. A short four years later, in 1960, at the age of eighteen he won the South African Indian Lawn Tennis Association's biennial national championships men's singles in Durban 'with a decisive four-set victory' over Parbhoo Roopnarain and also the men's doubles and the mixed doubles.[8]

Described as possessing 'a wonderful temperament, physical fitness, and a large variety of fluent strokes', he retained his national singles

AGE VERSUS YOUTH

THE LEADER, JUNE 11, 1971

Can the vast experience and courtcraft of veteran Parbhoo Roopnarain tame the aggression and bold stroke play of young Ismail Asmal? This is the question that has to be answered in the 5-set final of the Challenge Series of the Southern Natal Lawn Tennis Union.

Roopnarain had to battle for his 6-4, 6-3 victory over Girish Raniga to win section two and challenge Asmal for the crown.

The match should provide a stirring tussle between age and youth. Asmal is bang on form, but Roopnarain cannot be underestimated, and the Royal junior will need to produce perhaps the best display of his career to win the coveted challenge series title.

Roopnarain's stamina for a 5 setter is highly suspect and he will to tame Asmal early in the match. Should the match last the full 5 sest, it is unlikely that Roopnarain can remain in command in the latter stages, and Asmal's superior fitness and all round play could carry him to victory. It should be the match of the season.

Fixtures — Sunday 13/6/71 — A Division — Challenge Series. Singles Final — Best of 5 sets — R. Roopnarain v. I. Asmal.
A Division — Shah Jehan League: Isipingo Beach 1 v. Northdale 2; Northdale 1 v. Avoca; Tech 1 v. Isipingo Beach 2; Crescent v. Tech
The remaining doubles matches in the A Division Challenge series will also be played on Sunday.

Hira Dhiraj, a member of brother Jasmat's tennis squad has gained invaluable experience from playing against some top-notch exponents of the game in the UK.

Jasmat Dhiraj
(*Leader*, 11 June 1971).

and mixed doubles titles in 1962. In the early and mid-1960s he won numerous Southern Transvaal, Western Transvaal and Natal tennis tournament titles. In 1963, Jasmat played and lost to the non-racial tennis legend David Samaai in the South African Open men's singles final, organised under the auspices of the newly formed SnALTU. He and Samaai were selected to play in the United States in the President Eisenhower Invitation Tournament. They would have been the first to represent SnALTU, but the lack of funding meant that the tour could not proceed.[9]

The tour squad took its name after the national champion Jasmat, who was known in tennis circles as Jasmat Dhiraj. Jasmat explains the matter of the name:

> My registered official name is Jasmat Soma. My tennis name is Jasmat Dhiraj. Gujerati tradition is that you take on your father's first name as your surname. My father's name was Dhiraj Soma. I became Jasmat Dhiraj. When I entered my first tennis tournament, my coach D.D. Patel entered me as Jasmat Dhiraj, which remained throughout my tennis career.[10]

Jasmat's nickname was 'sapa', which he says 'became "saps" and strangely more people call me Saps. It originated via an aunty who joked and called me "sappo" – stupid – which became "saps"'.[11]

In 1966, in the lead-up to the Southern Transvaal championships at the Newlands Stadium tennis courts in Johannesburg, a headline asked 'Can Dhiraj Beat Abrahams'?[12] The answer was 'yes'. After an absence of three years, Jasmat defeated the reigning champion Herman Abrahams 4-6, 6-3, 6-3, 6-3. In winning the 1966 singles title, Jasmat used 'his long reach and height to advantage'. Unlike Abrahams, he did not exert 'energy chasing balls that were nigh impossible' but 'saved his energy'.[13] He was like 'a darting cat' and it was 'his speed, service and directness on court' and 'immaculate scoring shots' that 'won him the coveted trophy'.[14]

He had previously won the singles title at the age of nineteen in 1961 and retained it in 1962.[15] He also won the doubles title with Herman Abrahams when they beat Leslie Metherell and Barney la Pere 9-7, 6-2, 6-2. Later, in 1966/early 1967 at the SnALTU open championships at the Braelyn courts in East London, he defeated Ronnie Samaai in the quarter-finals 4-6, 6-3, 6-4, 8-6, but then lost to Arnie Poole in a hard-fought, two-and-a-half-hour semi-final 10-12, 3-6, 8-6, 3-6. The final was won by David Samaai.[16]

In 1967, Jasmat won the Natal Open singles, defeating Conrad Johnson of the Western Cape 3-6, 6-4, 6-1, 6-1.[17] Building on that victory, his major triumph was to win for the first time the Southern Africa singles title in front of a crowd of 1 000 at the Green Point Track tennis courts in Cape Town. He defeated Herman Abrahams, who had to overcome Ronnie Samaai and Arnie Poole to reach the final, 6-2, 4-6, 6-4, 6-4. En route to the final, Jasmat beat Trevor Lawrence of Western Province 6-2, 6-4, 6-2 in the quarter-finals and fellow Transvaaler Leslie Metherell 6-1, 6-2, 6-2 in the semi-finals. It was reported that he 'played magnificently to win the singles title'. He suffered cramp in the arm in the final set but was assisted by his opponent Abrahams in a great show of 'sportsmanship'. For good measure, Jasmat and partner Abrahams triumphed in the doubles; the 'formidable Dhiraj-Abrahams combination' beat David and Ronnie Samaai 6-2, 4-6, 6-1, 5-7, 8-6.[18]

The year 1968 was a good one for Jasmat. He defeated fellow schoolteacher Abrahams in a 'gruelling five set marathon singles final' 2-6, 6-3, 3-6, 6-3, 6-4 to win the title at the Transvaal Open at the Phefeni tennis courts in Orlando West, Soweto.[19] Then, at the Bellville tennis courts in Cape Town he defeated Arnie Poole 6-2, 6-4 to become the Western Province singles champion. Partnering Gerald Samaai, he also won the doubles tournament, defeating brothers David Samaai and Ronnie Samaai 6-3, 6-3.

The late sports reporter Farook Khan wrote about plans and fundraising by the Transvaal tennis unions for South African singles and doubles champion Jasmat and his doubles champion partner Abrahams to play in competitions in the UK, including Wimbledon. The intention was to try to send black players annually to compete in overseas tournaments as a way to improve the standard of tennis.[20] A UN report observed that non-racial tennis players took part in European tournaments in 1968 and 1969: 'In 1968, Jasmat Dhiraj and Herman Abrahams won the North of England Men's Doubles Championship and in 1969 Dhiraj won the South of England Singles Championship. Dhiraj and Ms. Paddy Orchards also won the Mixed Doubles Championship in that year.'[21]

Regarding the 1968 tour, Jasmat's friend and Pretoria sports administrator Basil Bhanabhai, who was working with his brother Vernon who resided in London, stated that 'we have applied for entry forms and an itinerary of the various English tournaments'. He had been in touch with the secretary of the British Lawn Tennis Association, Basil Reay, and other European tennis associations to appeal for support

Jasmat Dhiraj (right) and doubles partner Herman Abrahams (*Post*, 27 November 1966).

for Jasmat and Abrahams. A UK newspaper had expressed interest in providing sponsorship, but Bhanabhai said they were not taking chances and collecting funds locally. Herman Abrahams was quoted as saying that 'some years ago I was hopeful that I would make a trip overseas with David Samaai but I did not go and as the years passed I gave up all hope of playing overseas'.[22]

Jasmat and Abrahams played exhibition matches in various places, including Roodepoort, Marikana, Potchefstroom, Rustenburg and Johannesburg to mobilise funds for their overseas tour. The first match in Roodepoort raised R500 through the effort of a Dr Hassim. One of the exhibition matches could not proceed because Abraham's partner, Thelma, was injured in a motor accident. The organiser accused Jasmat of lying about Thelma's accident, but said he was still open to providing a donation to Jasmat alone. Jasmat turned down the donation, but eventually the organiser believed him and contributed funding. Eventually funds were raised for air tickets and some subsistence, with support also from the Pretoria and District Football Association and the Northern Transvaal Cricket Union. The pair toured between April and July 1968, with part of their itinerary being arranged by Dunlop, the tennis racket and ball manufacturer, in London.

For their first competition, the North of England tournament, they travelled to St Annes-on-Sea near Blackpool on the north-west coast of England. They made a great beginning, losing in the singles semi-finals and winning the doubles competition, in the process reaping prizes of £4 vouchers. Returning by train to London, they sought out the Hurlingham Club near the River Thames in Putney, the venue of their next tournament. In Putney, Abrahams stopped Jasmat and said: 'Did you hear that – someone shouted Saps.' Jasmat replied, 'Don't be silly, nobody knows my name Saps in London.'[23] But someone did: Ramjoo Khoja, a fellow tennis player from the Northern Transvaal had recognised him. He took the pair in his truck to his apartment, across the Thames from the tournament venue. He left the keys with them, returned to cook them dinner and said that they could stay with him between tournaments. The free hospitality was a welcome boon!

Jasmat was satisfied with his and Abrahams' performances on the 1968 tour – they reached the quarter-finals or semi-finals in all their tournaments. They gained knowledge and experience and made good contacts, one of whom advised them to use his name to try to secure sponsorship from a 'Fred Perry outlet in the centre of London, near Trafalgar Square. They gave us free clothing – we also got free Dunlop rackets.' He observes that 'at tournaments we realised that there were regular tennis players who played the tennis circuit each year'. They included squads from England, Australia (Geoff Masters), India (the Amritraj brothers) and Pakistan (Iqbal, Meer and Rahim) seeking to qualify for Wimbledon. Jasmat was impressed by the seriousness with which the Australian players practised.[24]

He played his first match on grass at the Surrey Grass Court Championships in Surbiton, south-west London. Grass courts require regular practice and he lost to the Pakistani, Iqbal. Jasmat and Abrahams did well enough to enter the qualifying rounds of the Wimbledon Tennis Championships held at Roehampton but, unfortunately, they lost in the first round. He and Abrahams did get free tickets for Wimbledon, which they enjoyed and it was a short journey from Khoja's apartment in Putney. Given the parlous state of their finances, they were 'lucky to have met Rajoo and indebted to him' and those who provided them welcome hospitality during their tournaments. They were able to visit key tourist sites in London but Jasmat realised that tours had to be 'properly organised, practice facilities arranged, and money for travelling and meals [was] important'.[25]

On his return from the UK, in late 1968, Jasmat won the Western Province Tennis Championships by beating Arnie Poole in straight sets, 6-2, 6-4, at the Bellville South courts. The *Cape Herald* reported that 'the powerful driving and smashing of Dhiraj was a rarity and when Arnie's passing shots and overhead lobs effectively coped with Dhiraj's advances to the net, the latter was content to fight out the baseline duel into which the game eventually developed'. He also won the doubles final with Gerald Samaai, beating David and Ronnie Samaai 6-2, 6-4.[26]

There was more success at the 1968–1969 national championships. Sport journalist Harold Pongolo wrote that 'the magnificent, dynamic Jasmat Dhiraj provided once again that he's the king of our tennis courts when he blasted his doubles partner and also a teacher, Herman Abrahams, in three straight sets to retain the 1968/69 national singles title 6-1, 6-2, 6-3.' Pongolo added that 'he played really powerful and brilliant tennis throughout the 53 minutes the three-set clash lasted'. He 'conceded only 18 games out of 70 in the six matches from the first round to the final'. In the doubles, Jasmat and Abrahams easily beat Trevor and Quinton Lawrence 6-3, 6-1, 6-3.[27]

In 1968, Jasmat was one of six sportspersons selected by *Post* sportswriters as a potential 'Sportsman of the Year' sponsored by Smirnoff Vodka and chosen by *Post* readers. Fellow candidates were golfer Papwa Sewgolum, Mackeed Mofokeng, the boxing welterweight champion, athletics star Joseph Leserwane, David Isaacs, a bodybuilder, and Anthony Morodi the bantamweight boxer.[28]

In 1969, Jasmat again toured the UK. He won the South of England singles title and the mixed doubles. Unfortunately, he failed to make it to the qualifying rounds of Wimbledon.[29] He successfully defended his Southern African Open singles title and won it for the third time in succession in 1969-1970 in Port Elizabeth when he beat Arnie Poole 6-0, 6-3, 7-5. His 'strong serves and powerful backhand drives were too much for the gallant Poole'. He also won the doubles title three times in a row, this time partnering his brother Hira as his usual partner Abrahams was on holiday. The pair defeated brothers Trevor and Quinton Lawrence 6-2, 6-3, 6-2.[30]

In December 1969, he applied for the first time to play in the white-controlled and traditionally white-only SALTU South African Open Tennis Championships. He was probably the first black player to apply and his application 'was aimed at getting a definite clarification'. As he noted, 'If I am not allowed to enter, I want to know why.' Jasmat anticipated a possible basis for excluding him: that he was 'not a member of a body affiliated to the white organisation'; in that case, he wished 'to know why he was allowed to play in tournaments sanctioned by the international body'. The president of SALTU Alf Chalmers' response was that Jasmat's entry was 'unacceptable because only members of bodies recognised by the I.L.T.F. were eligible' – precisely the lame and illogical reasoning that Jasmat anticipated.[31] It, of course, did not answer why Jasmat and other SnALTU players were able play in international tournaments.

Jasmat was hugely successful during the 1970-1971 season tournaments in the Cape. At the R450 (the R450 denoting the total prize money) Lansdowne Tennis Club Tournament in late 1970, 'Jasmat Dhiraj walked off with the major prizes and R200. He won R150 for his 6-2, 6-3 win over former S.A. champion David Samaai and R50 as his share in the men's doubles match.'³² Jasmat and Herman Abrahams beat David Samaai and Ronnie Samaai 6-3, 7-5.

The *Leader* wrote that 'national champion Jesmet [sic] Dhiraj became undisputed king of South African tennis when he beat David Samaai'.³³ The *Post* commented that 'they never come back is an old boxing proverb. It proved equally true of tennis when the spectre of David Samaai was laid to rest by Jasmat Dhiraj at Lansdowne.' Dhiraj was, however, generous in victory, observing of the 43-year-old champion who had reigned supreme for over two decades that 'I am sure Samaai would have beaten me in his heyday. Samaai is one of the greatest players South Africa has produced and I don't mean among [blacks] only.'³⁴

> It is important to recall David Samaai, an educator described as 'humble, gracious, caring and of course passionate about the game of tennis' and as a genuinely 'true gentleman'.³⁵ Samaai was 'a talented music teacher for 45 years, a dedicated school principal for 25 years, choir leader for 50 years, church organist for 60 years, an exceptional tennis player and non-racial tennis champion for 21 years and the first South African black tennis player to play at Wimbledon'.³⁶
>
> He was born in 1927. Recognising his talent, in 1949 the Paarl community sponsored him to tour overseas. He played at Wimbledon in 1949, 1951 and 1954 and in the French Championships in 1951.³⁷ Samaai promoted tennis by conducting tennis coaching countrywide, and also served as a tennis administrator.
>
> His biography was published in 2020.³⁸ Beyond illuminating the life of Samaai, the book is 'an artefact to recall the inequities of the past'. It notes that Samaai's life was intertwined with that of a community 'that once lived' in a 'beautiful settlement called Old Garden' on the 'banks of the picturesque Berg River in Paarl'. The Group Areas Act removed the community to Paarl East, where 'they had to rebuild their lives. They built a new high school, new primary schools, a new church, a new mosque, new sports facilities and new tennis courts: one in David's own back yard.'

They 'managed to overcome apartheid' because of 'inspirational leaders like David Samaai, who refused to lie down submissively'.[39] Samaai passed away in 2019 at the age of 92.

David Samaai.

The 1970 Western Province Open Championships in Stellenbosch were very much a Dhiraj family affair. Jasmat won all three titles. He 'walked off with the men's singles title when he crushed a game younger brother, Hiralel [sic] 6-3, 6-1 in the final'. In the men's doubles final, he and his long-standing partner, the 'evergreen' Abrahams, defeated Winston Petersen and Gerald Samaai 6-4, 6-2. In the mixed doubles, Jasmat and Brenda Petersen beat Cavan Bergman and Lynette Thomas 6-1, 3-6, 6-1.[40]

The *Cape Herald* heaped praise on Jasmat. It commented that while

> these wins were expected ... the manner in which they were achieved, however, left an impression of invincibility about the tall, dark-haired champion. His booming serves, crushing topspin drives, which at times flattened the ball on the surface of the court, and the lightning-like moves to the net for the volley, left a trail of easy wins behind him. He dropped only sixteen games in five matches to win the title.[41]

Described as the 'unsmiling champion', in a great compliment Jasmat was said to have 'no equal as a tennis player in the country' and that

Jasmat Dhiraj (Leader, 25 December 1970).

his 'class, determination, dedication and all-round ability' was likened to that of 'David Samaai at his best'.[42]

There was more to come. A week later, in early 1971 he achieved the incredible national treble. Under the headline 'Jasmet [sic] Dhiraj the invincible', the *Cape Herald* wrote: 'What else can he be called after his so successful visit to Cape Town.' Jasmat retained his Southern African Open title in Stellenbosch, winning for the fourth time in a row. It was suggested that 'it will be some time before he will be dethroned'. He combined with Hermie Abrahams to win the doubles tournament 8-6, 6-2, 4-6, 7-5 in a thrilling final against David Samaai and Ronnie Samaai. For good measure he also won the mixed doubles with Brenda Petersen 6-4, 6-3, defeating Winston Petersen and Yvette Petersen.[43]

The *Cape Herald* recalled that seven years previously 'at Green Point, it was the 35-year-old maestro David Samaai who, with panther-like speed and uncanny anticipation beat the young, tall, lithe 22-year-old Pretoria schoolmaster, Dhiraj, in their only and last S.A. clash'.[44]

A *Post* article in 1971 observed that one of the myths that 'White sports unions have used for years to keep Black players off their fields' was '"We'd love to have them. But they're not really good enough"'. Ironically, it was a white South African player, Cliff Drysdale, who 'began to hit [this myth] out of court'. In early 1971, Jasmat played Drysdale,

Jasmat Dhiraj (*Cape Herald*, 9 January 1971).

who at the time was one of the top seeds in world tennis, in a privately arranged match. Although 'Drysdale won the best of three sets match 6-4 and 7-5', it was a commendable performance by Jasmat, given the inequalities in facilities, coaching and opportunities faced by black tennis players. Drysdale's view was that Jasmat 'was very good', 'a great player: a really nice guy too'. He added that 'it was a crying shame that [Jasmat] wasn't allowed to compete' in the South African Open in 1971; and that he 'should be a member of the South African Davis Cup team'. Sam Ramsamy, a leading non-racial sport administrator commented that in the prejudiced view of white officials, Dhiraj, as a black South African 'was never considered "good enough"'.[45]

Pushing the boundaries of what was permitted under apartheid, Jasmat applied from London for membership of the predominantly white South African Tennis Players Association (SATPA) formed in 1970 'to represent the interests of the country's top-class tournament players'.[46] He appeared to put much hope in SATPA as 'a great breakthrough in the relationships between Black and White sportsmen' and assumed that through it 'the plight and setbacks of the Non-White player will come to the fore'; and that it could also help 'bring about complete equality in tennis'.[47] His application was 'provisionally approved – pending verification that his membership [was] not prohibited by Government legislation'. Alan Schwarz, the chair of SATPA, indicated that at its 1971 meeting 'it was unanimously carried by a quorum of 42 members' that should Jasmat apply for membership he would 'be welcome as a member' as SATPA's 'constitution contains no racial qualification for admission', only 'ability as a tennis player'.[48]

There was talk of a '"mass demonstration" by leading players at Ellis Park' in support of multiracial sport – including Cliff Drysdale, Frew McMillan and Ray Moore – the last saying that 'I would have been a willing party to a demonstration'.[49] However, SATPA stated that 'we have grave

Jasmat Dhiraj at Johannesburg airport with his wife, Deanna Starkey, and daughters, Natasha (5) and Shaline (18 months) (*Post*, 18 April 1971).

doubts as to whether such a move would be legal and we are accordingly taking counsel's opinion on that point'. It also clarified that if Jasmat's membership was 'prohibited by Statute we will have no alternative but to reject your application'.[50] In essence, SATPA's stance was ambiguous and far from principled. It was a variation of the statement 'We'd love to have them. But they're not really good enough', becoming in essence 'We'd love to have them. But only if the [racist apartheid] state sanctions it.'

For all its supposedly progressive stance on membership, SATPA and its white player members were, ultimately, not prepared to take a principled and bold stand on non-racialism in tennis and kowtowed to the apartheid state. In doing so, they, like many other institutions and individuals during the apartheid period, sorely confused what was legal with what was moral, ethical and just. In any event, 'membership of SATPA would not [have made Jasmat] eligible' for the South African Open Tennis Championships under the auspices of the white SALTU.[51] SATPA did not have any impact on advancing non-racial tennis in South Africa.

As was noted, because of a delay in the renewal of his passport Jasmat did not travel with the other members of the squad on 10 April and left five days later. On his departure, he told *Post* newspaper that 'he resigned from the teaching profession because the Indian Education Department, unlike the White one, has no regulation permitting unpaid leave'. He said that he planned 'taking up part-time teaching overseas if I'm not tied down to a series of engagements during the campaign' and hoped to 'approach English tennis coach Tony Mottram' in that regard as 'he is well known there and might be of some help to keep me going'.[52]

Jasmat's flight to London was not smooth. Fog in Brussels meant that the plane could not land and was diverted to Luxembourg and then returned to Brussels. This meant a delay in the onward flight to London. In London, Jasmat discovered a large bag of clothing was missing, presumably not loaded in Brussels onto the plane to London.

Jasmat understandably had modest success on the 1971 tour, playing in senior tournaments against leading and regularly touring international players. In mid-May, he expressed disappointment with his form; he was 'struggling to find his touch' and 'nothing [seemed] to be going right for him'.[53]

Tournament results[54]

UK tournament 2: Rothmans Sutton Hard Court Championships, south London, 26 April–1 May 1971
Beat UK player Owen Hanson 6-1, 6-1 in the first round. In the second round, lost to top South African and Junior Wimbledon champion Byron Bertram.

UK tournament 3: Rothmans Surrey Hard Court Championships, Guildford, 3–8 May 1971
Lost in the second round to Australian Adi Kourim 2-6, 4-6.

UK tournament 4: Bio-strath London Hard Court Championships, Hurlingham, 10–15 May 1971
Lost to the Chilean number two Patricio Cornejo 2-6, 5-7. (Cornejo holds the record for playing, in the 1973 Davis Cup American Zone final, 'the longest Davis Cup rubber in terms of games', when he and Jaime Fillol lost 'to Stan Smith/Erik van Dillen from the US team 9-7, 39-37, 6-8, 1-6, 3-6 ... The second set is the world record for the most games in a Davis Cup set.')[55] Jasmat and Hira lost in the doubles to Hank Irvine and Andrew Pattison 2-6, 4-6.

UK tournament 5: Bio-Strath Droitwich Spa Tournament, Worcestershire, 17–22 May 1971
Defeated top Australian player Paul Kronk 5-7, 9-8, 6-3. Lost to the Pakistan number three seed, Saeed Meer, 9-8, 6-8, 2-6.[56]

UK tournament 6: Rothmans Surrey Grass Court Championships, Surbiton, 24–29 May 1971
Lost to Derek Schroeder, number 3 ranked among whites in South Africa, 5-7, 6-4, 4-6.

UK tournament 7: Rothmans Chichester Tennis Tournament, West Sussex, 31 May–5 June 1971
Results unavailable.

> UK tournament 9: Bio-Strath Wolverhampton Tournament, West Midlands, 7–12 June 1971
> Beat a local player, A. Pinson, 6-0, 6-0 in the first round. Fell to Rhodesian Andrew Pattison, 6-1 6-2 in the second round.
>
> UK tournament 10: Rothmans South of England Open Championships, Eastbourne, 14–19 June 1971
> Won the singles, doubles and mixed doubles titles. Officially, he and his partner, Orchard (sister of P. Orchard), shared the mixed doubles trophy with Bobat and P. Orchard.

Jasmat was by far the most prominent as well as most outspoken member of 1971 tour. In a newspaper article, he took issue with the international tennis bodies for their support of the racist white tennis union and its competitions 'where politics dominate sport', and 'from which 13 million Black South Africans are excluded for racial or political reasons'.[57]

He said that those participating in competitions in South Africa had to understand that by doing so they were supporting racism. Their participation in racist sport insulted and degraded black players by denying them their rights as sportspersons and humans. By staying silent in the face of racism, they also degraded themselves and turned their backs on the 'fight for sports justice'. He made an impassioned plea for international bodies and players to support black players and their 'human dignity and . . . rights' as tennis players and as people.[58]

A teacher colleague in Pretoria warned Jasmat that the security police had visited the school and that the headmaster was told that he would be in trouble if he returned to South Africa. In the light of those circumstances, Jasmat contemplated exile in the UK. Under the headline, 'Dhiraj Shock', the *Leader* dramatically reported that 'tennis ace Jasmat Dhiraj may soon become another of South Africa's Basil D'Oliveiras' by settling in the UK. It noted that Jasmat had applied to attend a university in London and hoped 'to further his studies'.[59]

M.N. Pather commented that 'Jasmat's choice to stay over for a longer period is within reason' given conditions experienced by black tennis

Jasmat Dhiraj with Arthur Ashe at Wimbledon
(*Leader*, 16 July 1971).

Jasmat Dhiraj at Wimbledon
(*Leader*, 16 July 1971).

players in South Africa. He pointed to the example of Hoosen Bobat: 'He gave up his studies and is virtually playing tennis 7 days a week. Though he is anxious to complete his degree, at the back of his mind he has this call for competitive tennis – and that you don't get here.'[60]

Immediate challenges for Jasmat in the UK were accommodation and funds for subsistence. The Bhanabhai family came to the rescue and SANROC provided a modest stipend. With no immediate job prospects and income in South Africa, and therefore plans for his family to join him in London, Jasmat's wife Deanna and children Natasha and Shaline had to relocate to Fordsburg to live with her family. Speaking about 'my uncle Jasmat, and dad, Hiralal', Hira's son Viren Soma says that after the 1971 tour Jasmat

Jasmat Dhiraj in London, with St Paul's Cathedral in the background, c.2018.

had to stay in England where he had some friends. Then my dad joined him. They were both involved with the ANC and SANROC . . . which helped them settle in the UK. Both groups ensured that South Africa was kept out of international sport [and the Olympics] until apartheid was ended. Sport is so big in South Africa that exclusion from international sport really hurt.[61]

In 1973, Jasmat qualified as the first officially recognised black professional tennis coach in England. He has lived in the UK since 1971, working for many years as a teacher. Today he is retired and resides in Brockenhurst, Hampshire, with his wife Pauline Brown. Former wife Deanna and his daughters also reside in the UK.

In 2018, Jasmat received the Andrew Mlangeni Green Jacket award of the Department of Sport and Recreation, which recognises 'unsung heroes of sport from the Apartheid era' and 'especially players and administrators who were never afforded the opportunity to represent their country'.[62]

14

Hiralal (Dhiraj) Soma

Hiralal (Hira) Dhiraj was born in 1945 in Marabastad, Pretoria. He attended the local primary school and in 1965 completed matric at the Pretoria Indian High School. He spent a year attending the TCE, but left after he failed the first year. He immediately found a job as an assistant librarian but changed jobs from time to time in search of a better salary. Earning his own income made him 'feel free and independent' and he could support his 'sport and other interests'.[1]

He was 'always passionate about sport' and 'strived to be as good as I could'. Soccer was 'always [his] first love, then came tennis'. He was 'a talented footballer during his school days while his brother Jasmat Dhiraj chose tennis'. Jasmat 'persuaded his younger brother Hira to play tennis so that he would have someone to practise with'. He confesses that he 'enjoyed the social side of tennis and was guilty of not taking the playing side more seriously'. This, however, 'all changed in Durban, when I upset the top seed Arnie Poole and lost to Hoosen Bobat in the Natal Open'. Over time, he grew to love 'both tennis and soccer'.[2]

Hira won the South African junior title in Johannesburg in 1962 at the Wits University tennis courts. He represented Transvaal on numerous occasions and won numerous singles and doubles provincial titles. At the time of the 1971 tour, he was 25, single and lived in Laudium with his parents. He was a despatch clerk with the company Beutron, from which he was forced to resign in order to take part in the tour.

Hira's first foray overseas was in 1969, when he, Jasmat and Nasim Bismillah toured England, courtesy of friends 'who made a collection to fund the tour'. They played in some smaller tournaments that followed Wimbledon. Although it was a short tour, he says, 'The experience stood us in good stead, as we knew what we had to concentrate on to improve.' The 'most important lesson was practice, practice and more practice' and to 'work harder'.[3]

Hira Dhiraj and Vernon Bhanabhai at Heathrow airport.

In 1970, in an all-Dhiraj affair, Hira lost 6-3, 6-1 to Jasmat in the singles final of the Western Province Open in Stellenbosch. He, however, won the mixed doubles competition, partnering Brenda Petersen.[4]

In London, Hira and brother Jasmat stayed with Vernon Bhanabhai, who had settled in the UK in the 1960s and lived at 4 Palace Road, Hornsey in north London. As was noted, the other squad members lived in a YMCA hostel, a short walk from the Bhanabhai home.

One weekend, squad members helped the Bhanabhais extend their kitchen. Carolissen was a builder by trade and Hira and Woodman were technically adept and so Bobat (see below) was put to work mixing the dagha (mix of cement, lime and water), manual work that he had never done previously – or subsequently on his return to South Africa.

Hira Dhiraj supervising young Hoosen Bobat during renovations to the Bhanabhai home, 1971.

Tournament results

UK tournament 2: Rothmans Sutton Hard Court Championships, south London, 26 April–1 May 1971
Playing a UK opponent, J. Hill, Hira lost the first set 4-6 but eventually triumphed, winning the next two sets 6-3, 6-3. The Australian Adi Kourim beat Hira 6-2, 7-5.[5]

UK tournament 3: Rothmans Surrey Hard Court Championships, Guildford, 3–8 May 1971
In the second round, Hira played fellow South African and Junior Wimbledon champion Byron Bertram and lost 2-6, 3-6. This was a slightly better performance than brother Jasmat who had lost to Bertram the week before.

UK tournament 4: Bio-Strath London Hard Court Championships, Hurlingham, 10–15 May 1971
In the first round, Hira defeated another South African Frank Briscoe, 6-4, 3-6, 6-2. In the second round he lost to the top

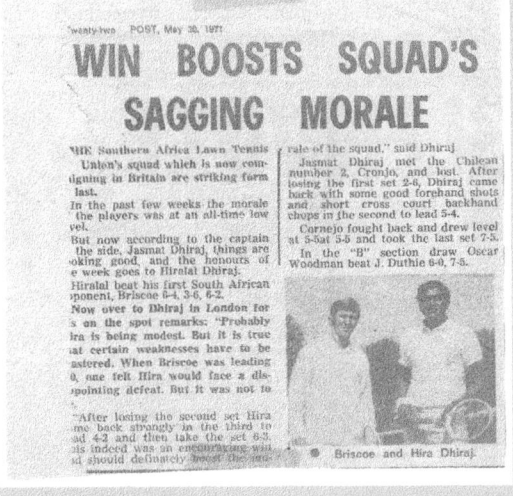

Hira Dhiraj and defeated opponent Frank Briscoe at Hurlingham (*Post*, 30 May 1971).

Rhodesian player Hank Irvine 5-7, 0-6. Being one of the first semi-professional tournaments, Hira recalled winning £25. In the doubles, Hira and Jasmat lost to Hank Irvine and Andrew Pattison 2-6, 4-6.

UK tournament 5: *Bio-Strath Droitwich Spa Tournament, Worcestershire, 17–22 May 1971*
In the second round, Hira beat J. Coe 6-2, 6-0.[6]

UK tournament 6: *Rothmans Surrey Grass Court Championships, Surbiton, 24–29 May 1971*
Hira lost to British player Philip Siviter 3-6, 2-6.

UK tournament 7: *Rothmans Chichester Tennis Tournament, West Sussex, 31 May–5 June 1971*
Results unavailable.

UK tournament 9: *Bio-Strath Wolverhampton Tournament, West Midlands, 7–12 June 1971*
Hira says that 'one of the best sets I ever played was against British Davis Cup player and number one seed Stanley Matthews in a grass court tournament in Wolverhampton'.[7] He won the first set 6-4 but coming under 'relentless pressure', eventually succumbed in three sets.[8]

UK tournament 10: *Rothmans South of England Open Championships, Eastbourne, 14–19 June 1971*
Won the doubles title with brother Jasmat.

Hira recalls that 'the weather was the biggest problem' and that it would sometimes rain for days and not a ball could be struck. They had to learn to adjust to different courts – clay, shale, grass and tarmac. They arrived a day or two before tournaments to get in as much practice as they could and supported each other with encouragement and advice.[9]

He remained with Jasmat in the UK for a while after Bobat and Woodman returned to South Africa in August 1971. He came back to South Africa a changed person, more 'focused on everything, [he] did, whether it was [his] work, sport and relationship with [his] girlfriend'. He had to adjust to life back in South Africa and find a new job. Contemplating his future, he concluded that it was not in South Africa and he began saving to return to the UK.[10]

In January 1972, he partnered fellow Transvaaler Chota Vawda to win the 1971-1972 Southern African Open doubles in Kimberley, defeating Oscar Woodman and Arnie Poole 6-3, 6-3, 6-3.[11] In 1969-1970, he had won the national doubles title with brother Jasmat, and had also won the mixed doubles once.

Soon afterwards, in April 1972, he turned out at the Athlone Stadium for a select Transvaal United soccer team against top-ranked Cape Town Spurs in a benefit match in aid of a disaster in Pakistan. The match was played under the auspices of the non-racial South African Soccer Federation. The Transvaal United team included Bluebells United Football Club notables such as Louis Jeevanantham, Prega Thandrin, Alan Moonsamy and Goona Padayatchi, with whom Hira 'played together several times and formed a good friendship'.[12]

Hira says that 'I was mad about football' and 'tried to give it up to concentrate on my tennis but failed', though 'tennis did take priority'. As a junior he played for a Pretoria club, All Bharats Football Club. Later he played for Delfos Football Club, for whom he played his last game the day before he departed for London. In December 1972, Hira's girlfriend Edith, also from Laudium, gave birth to their oldest son Viren. This was not part of the plans and rather than set up house, Hira and Edith continued to live with their own parents until definite arrangements could be made to leave South Africa. This was a tough situation for Edith, who was now an unmarried and working mother. 'Can you imagine the gossip in our community,' Hira commented.[13]

In the 1972-1973 national tournament in Durban, Hira was very much in contention to become singles champion, having beaten Arnie Poole, the eventual winner, in the Western Province Open. However, he 'made a painful exit', when he had to retire in his quarter-final match against Nasim Bismillah because of cramp. Poole commented: 'I felt sorry for Hira ... Always a difficult man to beat, our meeting again, so soon after he'd beaten me at Bellville, would have been a titanic struggle.'[14]

At the 1973 Natal Open, Hira lost in the singles semi-finals to the eventual winner and reigning national champion Arnie Poole 7-5, 2-6, 6-2. He combined with Poole to win the doubles final against Bobat and his cousin Ismail Asmal 6-4, 6-4, 3-6, 6-2.[15] In December 1973, Hira won the Western Province singles title by defeating Poole. He was one of the favourites to win the 1973-1974 national title in Bellville South, but lost to Woodman in the quarter-finals. He in turn was defeated by Solomon, the eventual champion, in the semi-finals.[16]

In 1974, out of the blue, Jasmat called Hira to say that there was a possible job as an assistant tennis coach with his friend Bill Osterberg, who was a lecturer but coached part-time mainly in Hertfordshire. To the surprise of his family and friends, he immediately arranged to depart and left within a week. His partner Edith 'was very understanding'. They had married secretly in 1973, as Hira's parent were not keen on Edith 'as she was not a Gujerati'. The expectation to marry a fellow Gujerati was a familiar one in the Indian community. Edith had been living with her parents with their two-year-old son Viren. Rumours circulated that Hira had 'run off to London' and had abandoned Edith and his son!'[17]

Hira arrived in London in June 1974 and after a weekend with Jasmat and his family he started to work with Osterberg as an assistant coach. He assisted Osterberg by coaching groups over the school summer holidays. He recalls that 'it was a bit scary at first as I had no experience of working with white kids' and nor did he have tennis coaching experience. When Osterberg enquired of Hira what his plans were after the summer holidays, he replied that he was seeking any clerical job where the employer would apply for a working visa for him. Hira had arrived in the UK on the pretext of playing tournaments and had been given a six-month visa. Osterberg encouraged Hira to study at the Polytechnic of North London (PNL; subsequently the University of North London) at which he worked.

Aspiring to be a Physical Education teacher, Hira applied to PNL. Things began looking up for him. He was accepted by PNL for a three-year course. He then successfully landed a job as a dispatch clerk and had to choose quickly between taking the job and raising funds to study. Turned down by two organisations that supported refugees, he was waiting to hear from a third, the International University Exchange Fund (IUEF). He telephoned the IUEF and was told that they would pay his tuition fees and provide living expenses of £125 per month.

The IUEF was the same organisation infiltrated by 'Craig Williamson: police informant, Cold War spy and apartheid assassin'.[18] Williamson was deputy director of IUEF, which supported African students through scholarships. Using this cover, he infiltrated the banned ANC until he was exposed as a spy in 1980.[19]

When Hira arrived in the UK in 1974, he contacted SANROC, which was helpful in various ways. He contributed to SANROC's efforts to isolate racist sport and represented SANROC at some meetings to build unity across race lines and to build non-racial sport. However, he says that Jasmat was more involved than he was. In 1975, Hira began higher education studies. It was not easy studying and supporting a family in a foreign country. He coached at weekends with Osterberg to supplement his IUEF stipend. He also undertook a three-part British Lawn Tennis Association coaching course over two years, qualifying in 1976.

Securing suitable accommodation was a major challenge and for a while he lived with Edith and young Viren in one room of Vernon Bhanabhai's home in Hornsey. Months of searching yielded no results. Landlords were reluctant to rent to families with young children. In desperation, they considered Edith, who was pregnant, returning to South Africa. His sponsors came to the rescue and promised they would find him a suitable apartment within two weeks; and they did, within one week! Hira says they were overjoyed with their one-bedroom apartment in Highbury among students from Africa and countries from the Global South. For commuting to PNL and tennis coaching over weekends he bought a 50cc scooter.

Hira's son, Viren Soma, notes: 'I was born in Pretoria, but my mum and I joined my dad... here in London when I was two, in 1974.' In 1975, younger son Hitesh was born. There was quite a lot of moving around: 'We were first at Crouch End, then Aberdeen Road, then Highbury New Park, then Blackstock Road and then Stoke Newington. I went to school at Highbury Quadrant and then to Highbury Grove – all my friends were in Islington.'[20]

Apart from coaching tennis, Hira continued to play tennis and won the inter-college singles competition three years in a row. He graduated from PNL as a teacher in 1979. Should he teach or coach? Jasmat, already a teacher, advised him to coach as he would be his own boss and earn better. The end of his studies, however, meant that they had to give up their apartment as it was only for students. Fortunately, the local council stepped in and found the family a three-bedroom apartment in 'Highbury, in North London, two minutes from the famous Arsenal football stadium'.[21] In 1983, they purchased their own home in Stoke Newington, North London, where they continue to live to this day.

Hira has been coaching since 1979. At first, he coached all over London and enjoyed his chosen occupation. Later, he based himself in Battersea Park, south London, where he still coaches. When he turned 45 in 1990, he began playing tournaments again, with veteran events becoming popular. He played in Italy and Spain and won a small tournament in Spain for a few years.

He began reaching the finals of the national grass court tournament played at Aorangi Park, Wimbledon, and was selected several times to represent Great Britain at the world championships. There were also considerable successes in over 50s, over 55s and over 60s tournaments. In 2000, he was ranked a fantastic 20th in the world in the over-55 division.

Hira Dhiraj with Brakpan-born fellow South African professional, Pat Cramer, 1999.

In 1992, in the Remington national father and son tournament, Hira and Hitesh had a great victory over David Lloyd and his son Scott. They came from 1-5 down in the first set and 2-5 down in the second to win 7-6, 7-6. Thereafter, in 'an epic final' they went down 7-5, 5-7, 6-2. They went on to represent Great Britain at the world championships in Austria.[22]

Hira Dhiraj and fellow 1999 Great Britain team members in the Netherlands.

Hira Dhiraj was the Bournemouth Clay Court Championships singles finalist in the 60s age group (he lost to Peter Adrigan, left). He was the doubles winner with Jasmat, 2005.

Viren Soma (right) and Hira Dhiraj with Hitesh Soma (below).

Viren (51) and Hitesh (48) live near Hira, so they get to see each other regularly. Both sons are tennis coaches at Highbury Fields, with Viren 'going straight into tennis coaching' when he left school at 18.[23] Viren and his Australian partner Melinda have two children, Joakim (14) and Martha (18), both of whom play tennis. Grandfather Hira coaches them whenever he can. After fetching them from school daily, he takes them three

Hira Dhiraj with his granddaughter, Ayala, 2020.

times a week to the tennis courts. When Viren is busy Hira also takes Joakim to tournaments. Hitesh and his English wife Charlotte have a three-year-old daughter, Ayala and a one-year-old daughter, Lilia.

Now aged 78, Hira is semi-retired and lives with Edith in Stoke Newington, north London. He coaches a few hours almost every day. He continues to play competitive tennis turning out in county matches for Middlesex and on the veterans' circuit. He says that he 'would love to have one more go at playing in the World Champs' once the Covid-19 pandemic is over. Hira was enthusiastic that this book should be produced because of the need 'to get a message' to black communities 'that we did play sport under apartheid. Even with all the obstacles presented by the [racist] government, we produced some great sportsmen and sportswomen.'[24]

Implicit in Hira's words is the important observation that, try as it did, the apartheid regime and racism were not able to entirely suppress or destroy the determination of black South Africans, men and women, to express themselves through sport, to strive to excel despite impoverished facilities, to test and improve themselves in competition against others irrespective of colour, and to dream about a future where sport would be a human right and would uphold and enhance human dignity.

15

Alwyn Solomon

Alwyn Wesley Solomon was born on 13 April 1950 in Elsies River and grew up in that suburb of Cape Town, designated for coloured South Africans.

Born into a tennis family, Alwyn's interest was nurtured by his family from a very young age. His mother, Esme Solomon, was the champion of the tennis club Progressive based in Elsies River, to which the family belonged. His brother, James, achieved Western Province colours and was a formidable doubles player.[1] Uncles and aunts saw Alwyn's potential at an early age and gave him every opportunity to grow his love for the game. Having a tennis court in his backyard, extremely rare among black families, also gave him a distinct advantage.

Solomon excelled in both sport and academic work. He was a 'former head student at Elsies River High where he matriculated in 1968' with a first-class pass.[2] He attained Western Province colours in athletics and was also an accomplished soccer player, playing for the popular St Lukes club. He was accepted at the University of the Western Cape (UWC) to study for a B. Pharm. degree. Soon after, influenced by exposure to the theories of the economist John Maynard Keynes, he switched to a B. Com. In 1970, he completed the first year and was a second-year student at the time of the 1971 tour.

Solomon became a member of the Progressive Club. In a profile on Progressive in a local newspaper, Darroll Carolissen, described as one of the key forces behind the club, commented:

> At our club we always strive to be the best. We arrange as many [coaching] clinics as possible and participate in as many tournaments as we can. Our purpose is to always have our players compete against the best. [We believe] that with that kind of competition and exposure, they must inevitably come out on top.

Alwyn Solomon.

The Progressive club motto was 'For the love of the game – sacrifice and dedication for the love of the game'. The club prided itself on cultivating outstanding junior players: when Alwyn won the 1971 Southern African Open in Kimberley, another Progressive player, fourteen-year-old Lorraine Samuels won both the under-19 and under-15 singles titles. The previous year, Progressive's Lynette Thomas won the under-19 singles championship.[3]

Carolissen observed about his nephew Alwyn Solomon that 'his lean physique belies his strength. His powerful shots have often raised eyebrows. He kicks the ball just as hard on the soccer field, where he likewise shines.'[4] In his first year at UWC in 1969, he was chosen to be part of the Sunrise Squad to tour Europe with player/manager Conrad Johnson, and fellow players Oscar Woodman, Danny Beukes and Trevor Lawrence in order to pursue the dream of a career in tennis. His selection was not surprising, as in 1968–1969 he had won the under-19 national title, defeating Nasim Bismillah 6-3, 6-1.[5] The tour encompassed England, Germany and the Netherlands – Solomon spoke of the beautiful green fields with numerous adjacent soccer pitches. The Netherlands was the one place where they could not use the team's secret weapon – 'speaking Afrikaans'!

Playing on clay courts was one thing for which the Sunrise Squad members were not prepared. They learned very soon that a serve and volley game did not work. Unaccustomed to the clay surface, there was the hilarious situation of the players finding themselves sliding past the ball. The team also learnt to curb their enthusiasm the hard way. Each tournament had two divisions, an A (professional) division and a B (aspiring professional) division. All the players entered both divisions and also singles and doubles draws. Solomon reached the last sixteen of both divisions at a German tournament, but was so exhausted that he could not cope. Next time he would be more selective.

We are fortunate to be able to draw on letters that Solomon sent home while he was on tour between June and early August 1969. They provide useful insight into aspects of the tour and his performance. On 6 June 1969, he wrote: 'Played in a small tournament in Beckenham, Kent. Won first round match to local club player and lost in 2nd round to an Australian. Learnt to fight to the end . . . the one who masters the court first wins the match. Every night has chips, eggs, etc. . . . tennis partner, Angela Carter from America, played serve and volley.' Five days later, he recounted while playing at Beckenham that in the class B singles under-21 he beat the Swedish junior champion in three sets and was to play a white South African, Brian Ansley, in the third round. 'Every match,' he wrote, 'is like a final.' He went on: 'Grass courts are just great. I never volleyed so much in my life. One is forced to play power tennis . . . one seldom sees long rallies, it's short and sweet.'

He expressed the view that the team members were possibly too inexperienced and not yet ready for the level of tennis that they were encountering on tour. He bemoaned the expensive entry fees, which were £9/10/- for the five players at every tournament but commended the great tournament organisation. At every tournament, they met people of different races and nationalities. He was thankful that 'so far, reporters have not pestered us about South Africa'. He was awaiting sponsored tennis rackets from Dunlop. Unfortunately, they could not play at Wimbledon as there were too many entries. Moreover, they would miss Junior Wimbledon under-18 and under-21 because of being scheduled to return home.

On 15 June 1969, his missive noted that he had played in Malvern and that 'here I learnt how to concentrate and fight for every point'. He felt that the standard of every first-round match he played was higher than that in South Africa. A few days later he said that they had heard that the African tennis union had affiliated to the all-white SALTU. He was concerned that non-racial players would 'have no right to play tennis' internationally and that the ILTF had 'the power to prevent us from participating in any future tournaments overseas'. No one had yet approached them on the matter of apartheid. He was of the sentiment that non-racial players from South Africa should have participated in overseas tournaments years ago because skin colour did not count. He had lost in the second round to one M. Bolton from Canada.

In late June 1969, Conrad Johnson reported that Arthur Ashe wished to meet the squad. They did meet and greeted Rod Laver, Ken Rosewall, Roy Emerson, Pancho Gonzales and Pierre Barthes. Ashe spoke at length to the squad and asked whether they could play in the United States for three weeks during late July. He indicated that he would do his best to get them there. Barthes from France also extended an invitation. John Newcombe suggested that they form a group and travel internationally for a whole year.

On 27 June 1969, Solomon wrote with the good news that Ashe had said he had raised funds for a month in the US, including hospitality, for tournaments in San Francisco, New Orleans, Chicago and New York. He had also obtained for them special seats at Wimbledon Centre Court and court number one to see his first-round match against Marty Riessen (which Ashe won 1-6, 11-9, 6-3, 7-5) and Ken Rosewall's second round match against Roger Taylor (won by Rosewall 6-1, 6-4, 8-6).[6]

Writing on 7 July 1969 from Belgium, Solomon said that everything was expensive in Brussels and that he couldn't understand the people linguistically. He had played in the A division, won his first-round match but lost in the quarter-finals to the Belgian Marc Bolle. He also played in the B division, losing in the semi-finals. He had his first experience of European slow clay courts, which he called 'red-ground sand' and said were wet five minutes before every match. Playing in a tournament at Eindhoven in the Netherlands, he wrote that he could understand Dutch. He had a walkover in the first round and won his second-round match against one Meyer. In the third round he lost to Jan Hajer, the Dutch Davis Cup player and doubles partner of the well-known Dutch player Tom Okker. Oscar Woodman also lost in the third round to an Australian.

Alwyn Solomon, Western Province sportsman of the year, 1971 (*Die Burger*).

On the 1969 tour, Solomon's talent did not go unnoticed. Coaches commented that they could not teach him much more, but he had to remain in Europe if he wanted to be a professional tennis player. Of course, financial support to live overseas, to travel, and to play tournaments was a critical issue. The 1969 tour had a great positive impact on Solomon's tennis: it taught him areas of his game to which he had to give attention; and being able to see tennis greats such as Rod Laver and Arthur Ashe in action inspired him to take his own game to new heights.

In early 1971, Solomon and Woodman were shortlisted as possible Western Province sportsmen of the year. Solomon won the award at a function at the Grassy Park Hotel, the Basil d'Oliveira trophy being presented by the South African-born England international cricketer himself.[7] D'Oliveira, who was classified Cape Coloured, was born in Signal Hill, Cape Town. Being black, Dolly, as he was nicknamed, could not thrive as a cricketer in South Africa nor represent South Africa.

He 'played county cricket for Worcestershire from 1964 to 1980, and appeared for England in 44 Test matches and four One-Day Internationals between 1966 and 1972'.[8]

The infamous D'Oliveira affair was to result in the exclusion of South Africa from test cricket from 1968 until 1990. In 1968 white South African cricket officials feared that Dolly's inclusion in the England cricket team to tour South Africa 'would lead to the cancellation of the tour, and probable exclusion of South Africa from Test cricket'. They exerted pressure on English cricket officials, who shamefully did not pick him, resulting in an outcry in the media. When a tour player was injured, Dolly was included in the squad. The South African government rejected a black player playing among whites in South Africa and the tour was cancelled leading to South Africa's isolation from world cricket.[9]

Prior to the Dhiraj Squad tour in 1971, Solomon's best tennis year was in 1968. He defeated Stephen Dietrich of Western Province 6-2, 1-6, 6-1 to win the under-19 singles title at the Southern Africa Open at the Green Point Track tennis courts in Cape Town. He reached the final of

Alwyn Solomon (second from right), with Oscar Woodman (to his left) and Jasmat Dhiraj (right), in London.

the Bellville Open, losing to Arnie Poole in three sets.[10] And he won the junior singles and doubles titles at the Bellville Open.[11]

His wins in the 1970-1971 season over Woodman in the Belville tournament and over Bobat in the Lansdowne R450 competition established him as one of the top young stars in the country. In early 1971, Carolissen enquired from SnALTU whether the possibility of a four-year scholarship for Solomon at a university in the United States that had been discussed with Arthur Ashe still stood. The response from SnALTU's M.N. Pather was in the affirmative.[12] Nothing, however, materialised.

When Solomon was chosen to be part of the Dhiraj Squad, the family rallied together and organised events to raise funds for his trip. A major funding source was Rubins Sports in Parow. Having learnt from experiences on his first 1969 tour, he was better prepared for the UK weather, braving the cold wrapped in blankets. He was more content with the less windy conditions in the UK compared to Cape Town.

Tournament results

UK tournament 1: Oxfordshire Junior Tournament, Norham Gardens, Oxford, 19–24 April 1971
Solomon was triumphant, beating fellow South African squad member Woodman 6-3, 6-2 in the singles final. En route to the final, he beat Bobat in the semi-final 6-0, 6-4.

UK tournament 2: Rothmans Sutton Hard Court Championships, south London, 26 April–1 May 1971
In a first-round loss in bitterly cold weather, Solomon was soundly beaten 6-0, 6-0 by Geoff Notman of Britain.[13]

UK tournament 3: Rothmans Surrey Hard Court Championships, Guildford, 3–8 May 1971
No results available.

> UK tournament 4: Bio-Strath London Hard Court Championships, Hurlingham, 10–15 May 1971
> No results available.

On tour, Solomon hung out mainly with fellow Progressive club member Cavan Bergman and the two did much sightseeing together. Fish and chips seems to have been the standard meal for Solomon. His son Wesley recollects that his father saved some of his pocket money to enjoy strawberries and cream at Wimbledon.[14] Fellow squad members recall that Solomon missed his girlfriend, Joy Thomas, terribly and that he wrote to her almost daily. This was the pre-cellphone and digital media era, international telephone calls were expensive, and air mail or surface mail letters were the main forms of communication. He returned home early on 21 May 1971 because he could not secure additional leave of absence from the University of the Western Cape. He expressed the desire to return to rejoin the tour, but that was dependent on his performance in his mid-year examinations and on securing sponsorship.[15]

On his return, Solomon reached the finals of seven SnALTU national championships, winning five times. He also won numerous Western

Alwyn Solomon and Jasmat Dhiraj sightseeing in London, 1971.

Alwyn Solomon (*Cape Herald*, 30 January 1971).

Province and Boland singles and doubles titles. He became known for his formidable single-handed backhand with the ability to place the ball anywhere he chose. He was a disciplined individual, whose positive qualities were manifested on court and off-court.

In 1971–1972, Solomon won his first Southern Africa title in Kimberley, defeating Andrew Jansen Abrahams in straight sets 7-5, 6-1, 7-5. Poole commented that 'Alwyn is a thinking player with a fine all-round game, and I'm glad he won the title'.[16] Reigning champion Jasmat

Alwyn Solomon and Cavan Bergman, 1971.

Dhiraj did not participate, now being in exile in the UK. Solomon teamed up with Winston Petersen to win the doubles title also.[17] The following year, he was losing finalist to Arnie Poole at the Southern African championships in Durban, but he bounced back in 1973-1974 to beat Poole in a three-and-a-half-hour five-setter in Belville South. He retained his doubles title with Winston Petersen when they defeated Poole and Woodman 6-3, 4-6, 7-6, 2-6, 6-1.[18] In 1974, Solomon was ranked number one by SnALTU.[19]

In 1974-1975, Solomon and Petersen reigned supreme again in the national doubles championships, defeating Peter Lamb and Quinten Lawrence, in the process winning the title three times in a row.[20] However, he did not have success in singles tournaments, losing three times in a month to Lamb. Lamb had the better of him in both the Boland and Western Province Opens, as well as in the national championships when he lost to the eventual winner in five sets in the semi-final.[21]

Solomon had an especially good year in 1975-1976. He won the national singles title for the third time in five consecutive tournaments and in what was his fourth appearance in the national singles final, defeated the top seed Winston Petersen in four sets by 1-6, 6-2, 6-3, 6-1 in Paarl. He retained his national doubles title for the fourth time in four years, when he and partner Petersen defeated Herman Abrahams and Cavan Bergman.[22] He also won the Western Province Open by triumphing over Petersen, avenging his loss to Petersen in the final of the earlier Boland Open.[23]

In 1976-1977, Solomon was beaten by fellow touring party member Bergman 6-1, 6-2, 6-0, a loss that was repeated the following year when he was again defeated by Bergman 6-3, 6-0, 5-7, 6-4. However, partnering Petersen again, he retained his national doubles title in 1976-1977 for the fifth time. Partnering his singles adversary Bergman for the first time, Solomon won the national doubles title again for the sixth time in 1977-1978 when they defeated Glenn Samaai and Raymond Anthony 6-3, 6-3, 6-2.[24] The pair of Solomon and Bergman retained the doubles title in 1978-1979, giving Solomon his seventh national doubles title, when they defeated Anthony and Chota Vawda. In 1979-1980, there was an eighth national doubles title with Bergman at the first TASA championships in Benoni.[25]

Alwyn Solomon, South African Open champion, receiving the trophy from the SnALTU secretary, M.N. Pather, with the treasurer, A.Y. Moola, looking on.

In 1980–1981, the successful Solomon-Bergman combination, which had won four national doubles titles in succession, separated. Solomon linked up with Patrick Carolissen but lost in the national tournament to former partner Bergman and his new partner Anthony. That would be Solomon's last appearance in a national doubles final. A last appearance in a singles final followed in the 1981–1982 season. Solomon won the Western Province singles title beating Russell Woodman,[26] but at the national TASA championships in Paarl he was the beaten finalist, losing to Raymond Anthony. The following year, in the process of retaining his title, Anthony defeated Solomon in the semi-finals.[27] After the 1981–1982 season, Solomon did not appear in a national final again. He continued to participate and remained competitive, losing to Bergman in the semi-finals in 1985–1986 and again in 1986–1987.[28]

Solomon's record during the eleven seasons between 1971–1972 and 1981–1982 was excellent. He won three national singles titles and was runner-up four times. He made the national doubles title almost his own:

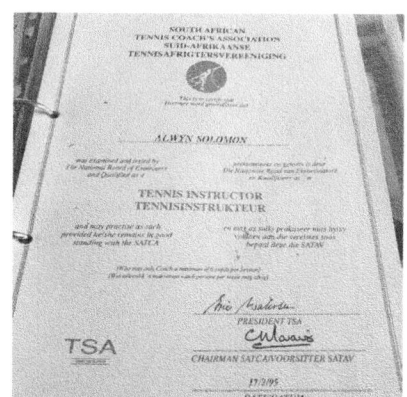

South African Tennis Coach's Association certificate awarded to Alwyn Solomon in 1995.

there were seven wins between 1972-1973 and 1979-1980, four with Winston Petersen and three more with Cavan Bergman. There was just one doubles final loss: after he and Bergman found new partners, a loss to Bergman and Anthony when he partnered Patrick Carolissen.

In 1995, Solomon was certified by the South African Tennis Coach's Association as a tennis instructor, which permitted him to coach up to six players in a single session.

In the mid-1990s, Solomon coached the under-15 Western Province team that comprised Adam Eitan, Gregg le Sueur, Peter Jon Nomdo, Raven Klaasen and Stephen Mitchell that 'earned the nickname the "dream team" after dominating the South African Interprovincials for five consecutive years from 1995'.[29]

Dream team members have competed nationally and internationally at senior levels and some have gone into coaching. Eitan, for example, was 'born into a family with a long history in tennis' and 'won many titles at provincial level'. Now with the Anthony Harris Academy in Bantry Bay, and with apartheid having 'thwarted his playing career at junior level', his dream 'is to produce an African champion'.[30]

On his return from the 1971 tour, Solomon completed his B. Com. degree and took up employment with Old Mutual in Pinelands. In 1979, he completed a B. Com. (Honours) and in 1980 an MBA at the University of Stellenbosch Business School. He left Old Mutual to take up a senior lecturer position at Peninsula Technikon and later became the head of its Marketing Department. In 1980, Alwyn married Lorna Rooy and they

Alwyn Solomon.

were blessed with three children: Wesley, born in 1981, Kim-Lee born in 1983 and Nadia-Marie born in 1986. Described as a 'role model to his family', he passed over promotions so that he could dedicate his time to be a husband and father, collect his kids from school, and coach his children and the kids from the wider community.

For Alwyn Wesley Solomon, playing tennis was a way of life. For much of his life, he played competitive tennis. His tennis ability, style and discipline were widely admired, and he continuously reinvented his approach and technique to keep abreast of new developments. Well into his 40s he could still hold his own in the first division league against top players and younger up-and-coming stars. The last trophy he racked up was in 1997, for winning the father-son doubles at the Strand Championships. Each of the Solomon children walked in his footsteps, winning provincial school colours. Daughter Nadia-Marie became one of the top junior tennis competitors in the country. She won a prestigious college tennis scholarship and makes her living coaching tennis in Texas.

Solomon passed away in February 1999 aged 49.

16

Oscar Woodman

Oscar Woodman was born at Parow, Cape Town in 1951. He grew up in Stellenbosch until the early 1960s, when the family moved to Lansdowne. After attending various primary schools, he completed his schooling at Livingstone High School in Claremont. Oscar grew up in a tennis family and played for Livingstone Tennis Club. His father, Ossie Woodman, was a very good player and partnered non-racial tennis star David Samaai to win many national doubles championships titles.[1] Oscar's siblings also played tennis and younger brother Russell became one of the top players in the 1980s.

Oscar Woodman and his father Ossie Woodman (*Cape Herald*).

Oscar Woodman retrieving a forehand.

Woodman was also talented in soccer and played for St Johns FC in league matches at the famous William Herbert Ground in Wynberg. For many years he played as goalkeeper. Later, he played for Aurora FC in Athlone as a midfielder. At the time of the 1971 tour, he worked as an architectural draftsperson at Trevor Euley Design Studio. He says that then he was 'happily unmarried' and had 'no children, that [he] knew of'; he 'still has not heard of any' from that time.[2]

Woodman previously toured Britain in 1969 as part of the Sunrise Squad, which included Conrad Johnson (manager), Trevor Lawrence, Alwyn Solomon and Danny Beukes. The tour was sanctioned by the Western Province Tennis Board but was privately sponsored through fundraising. He did not have any problems adjusting to conditions in Europe. He 'did not miss a step' as 'most of us had been there' and he does not recall 'any issues' that affected him negatively. His personal expenses on the 1971 tour were financed mainly by 'family and

Oscar Woodman (top), Charmaine Williams (middle) and Hira Dhiraj (seated) in Regent Street, London (*Leader*, 11 June 1971).

friends, and some moonlighting on my part' as he 'did not have much savings'.

Regarding how he fared in the UK tournaments, Woodman says 'not very well'. He was 'no longer a junior' and 'played senior tournaments'; he says that he got his 'arse thoroughly kicked all the time'. Despite that, he 'enjoyed every minute of it'. He was touring Europe and breathing 'rare air' and he was away from the restrictions, indignities and slights that confronted black people at every turn in apartheid South Africa. For him, 'most memorable' was the time in Katwijk aan Zee, when the squad stayed at a beach family resort and 'were heroes amongst the teenagers', who considered the Dhiraj Squad members 'super-star tennis players'.

After the tour, Woodman says that he 'went back to my mundane existence'. He 'realised that playing tennis for a living was definitely not an option at that point'. He observes that in 1969, during his first tour, we 'held our own in the junior ranks. We had good matches against juniors like John Lloyd, Vijay Amritraj' and others. Just two years later,

Tournament results

UK tournament 1: Oxfordshire Junior Tournament, Norham Gardens, Oxford, 19–24 April 1971
Woodman performed very well in his first tournament and he and Solomon played each other in the singles final. Solomon won 6-3, 6-2. En route to the final, Woodman beat the reigning champion, Chris Ronaldson in the semi-final, 5-7, 8-6, 6-1. In mid-June, he experienced tonsilitis and it was feared that he could have to be hospitalised.[3] Fortunately, he recovered.

UK tournament 2: Rothmans Sutton Hard Court Championships, south London, 26 April–1 May 1971
In a first-round defeat, Woodman lost to the Australian Geoff Perkins 6-3, 6-1.[4]

UK tournament 3: Rothmans Surrey Hard Court Championships, Guildford, 3–8 May 1971
Results unavailable.

UK tournament 4: Bio-Strath London Hard Court Championships, Hurlingham, 10–15 May 1971
Woodman beat J. Duthie 6-0, 7-5 in the singles tournament. Partnering Bobat, he reached the quarter-finals of the A-level tournament.

UK tournament 5: Bio-Strath Droitwich Spa Tournament, Worcestershire, 17–22 May 1971
As previously noted, Woodman 'provided the match of the day when he had [Paul] Kronk struggling for survival', making his opponent 'battle every inch of the way for his narrow 9-8, 5-7, 6-3 victory'. He and his partner Rana lost to Bobat and Bergman in the doubles 7-5, 6-8, 3-6.[5]

UK tournament 6: *Rothmans Surrey Grass Court Championships, Surbiton, 24-29 May 1971*
Results unavailable.

UK tournament 7: *Rothmans Chichester Tennis Tournament, West Sussex, 31 May-5 June*
Philip Siviter beat Woodman 6-4, 8-6.[6]

UK tournament 8: *Kent Championships, Beckenham Lawn Tennis Club, 7-12 June 1971*
Woodman lost to C. Russell 1-6, 4-6.

UK tournament 10: *Rothmans South of England Open Championships, Eastbourne, 14-19 June 1971*
Results unavailable.

Oscar Woodman executing a mid-court volley.

Oscar Woodman (right) and Hoosen Bobat on tour, 1971.

however, 'they were miles ahead of us. Left us in the dust'. The difference between playing and not playing regularly on the international circuit was considerable.[7]

Woodman is honest that for various reasons his 'tennis was suffering long before the tour'. He says that on both the European trips he undertook, tennis was not his 'only priority'. For him, it was also 'about new experiences', and tennis provided him the opportunity to be in other places and in new arenas and to be 'exposed to all that social interaction' that he could not experience in apartheid South Africa. The 1971 tour further 'opened [his] eyes to a complete new world, with endless opportunity' and he became 'more convinced' that he 'had to emigrate'. He became 'recommitted to getting the hell out of South Africa'.[8]

His exit from South Africa took some time and during the 1970s Woodman continued to play competitive tennis. While he was not as successful as Solomon and Bergman and won no major singles titles, he performed credibly and won numerous doubles titles. In 1971–1972, he and Arnold Poole were national doubles finalists, losing to Hira Dhiraj and Chota Vawda 6-3, 6-3, 6-3.[9] At the national championships in Durban the following year, he 'slammed' Petersen in the quarter-finals 6-4, 6-0, 6-0, only to be defeated by Solomon in the singles semi-finals.

The Woodman family: Candace, Valerie, Oscar and Lauren.

It was observed that Woodman's semi-final match with Solomon 'provided spectators with the proof of what two overseas visits had done to improve the play of the two Western Province players. In particular, it showed Woodman as an immeasurably improved player.'[10]

Woodman was also a semi-finalist in the doubles with Poole when they lost to the Samaai brothers. There was, however, success in the mixed doubles, when he and 1971 tour mate Charmaine Williams defeated Trevor Lawrence and Alfreda Abrahamse.[11]

In 1974, SnALTU ranked Woodman number three nationally.[12] In 1973-1974, he and Williams retained their national mixed doubles title 7-5, 6-4 against the sibling pair of Winston and Yvette Petersen.[13] This was the second of three national mixed doubles titles with Williams between 1972-1973 and 1974-1975 – they succumbed in 1975-1976 to victors Cavan Bergman and Sandra Petersen.[14] Woodman was losing national doubles finalist on two occasions, each time partnering Arnie Poole.

Woodman left South Africa for Canada in 1999. Between 1980 and 1984, he attended and graduated from the British Columbia Institute of Technology in Vancouver. Today, aged 72, Woodman lives in Port Moody, twenty minutes up the Burrard Inlet from Vancouver. He is 'happily married' to Valerie and has two daughters, Candace aged 42 and Lauren 40, both born in Vancouver.

17

Hoosen Bobat

Born in 1952, at the age of 18 Hoosen Mia Ahmed Bobat was the second youngest tour member and the only player selected from Natal. At the time of the 1971 tour, he lived with his parents in Reservoir Hills and was a first-year B. Com. degree student at the University College for Indians at Salisbury Island, Durban. The tour was his first overseas trip.

Bobat grew up in Mansfield Road in the Botanic Gardens area of Durban and 'developed a passion for all forms of sport from an extremely early age'. He regarded himself as 'a street sportsman, especially as all over Durban . . . the roads were marked out into tennis courts, cricket pitches and soccer grounds'. Growing up and 'living in an extended family, his early experience in sport was influenced by his dad, Ahmed Bobat, and uncle Bill Asmal'. Initially he was a 'jack of all sports', including 'cricket,

Hoosen Bobat (Graphic, 9 April 1971).   Hoosen Bobat with trophies.

Royals B, from left: Cassim Asmal, Ismail Asmal, Hoosen Bobat and Nasim Mayat, 1968 (*Leader*, 22 November 1968).

tennis, table tennis, swimming and fishing'. He 'took up tennis seriously at the age of 12'.[1]

Bobat recalls that in the 1960s there was 'a serious lack of facilities and it was difficult finding courts to play on. We had to travel great distances to play, and the only available courts were in Isipingo, where we played twice a week.' Of great help was 'playing for hours on end against the garage door'. His tennis improved through 'lots of practice, training and dedication' and 'by reading tennis books'. His 'first junior tournament [was] in 1967 at the age of 15' and he 'won both the singles and doubles' in his age category. His 'tennis hero was David Samaai from Paarl', who 'inspired [him] to work harder'.[2] Bobat played club tennis for Royals under the auspices of the non-racial Southern Natal Lawn Tennis Union (SNLTU), an affiliate of SnALTU. In 1968, Bobat's team, Royals B, triumphed 'in the league in singles, doubles, and cup competitions'.[3]

Considered 'Natal's most promising tennis youngster', in the five years prior to the tour he won provincial colours and represented Natal in the South African Senior Schools Sports Union competitions and in senior interprovincial competitions. He was holder of the Natal and Western Province junior titles, and the Southern African national junior singles champion and doubles champion (with Nasim Mayat, also from

Hoosen Bobat (above) and Nasim Mayat (below) (*Graphic*, 11 December 1970).

Hoosen Bobat (second from right) with fellow players (*Leader*, 22 November 1968).

the Mansfield Road area and later a professional soccer player with Berea).[4]

At a tennis coaching clinic in 1969, Bobat hugely impressed the legendary David Samaai with his ground strokes. Samaai commented that he had been waiting a long time for a player with a backhand like his own and extracted a promise from Bobat's father to visit his home in Paarl so that he could spend some time with the promising younger Bobat.

This duly happened in late 1969, when the Bobat family undertook a 1 700 kilometre trip to holiday in the Western Cape so that he could play in tournaments. On their first day together, Samaai educated Bobat about the qualities required to succeed in tennis. Bobat recalls that Samaai had a drawing of a tennis court on his study wall and instructed him on preparing for matches, match strategies, visualising strokes against opponents, and so forth.

At the Western Province Open, Bobat lost in the second round to Trevor Lawrence 6-2, 6-2.[5] Travelling east to Gqeberha (then Port

Hoosen Bobat at the courts at Sastri College, Durban.

Elizabeth) for the 1969-1970 Southern African Open tournament, Bobat achieved great success. He beat Oscar Woodman 6-4, 6-3 to become, at the age of seventeen, the national junior champion in the under-19 singles category. He also won the national junior under-19 doubles title, when he and partner Nasim Mayat triumphed over Cavan Bergman and K. Martin 6-2, 7-5.[6]

During 1970, 'Bobat, [Nasim] Mayat and [Ismail] Asmal led Young Royals to victory in the league competition to end the decade-long dominance of Avoca Moonlighters'.[7] Bobat represented Natal in the SnALTU Interprovincial Tournament in Durban and was a semi-finalist in the Coca Cola Winter Open in Durban, won by Jasmat Dhiraj. He was also part of the Natal squad selected to compete in the Western Province Open and the Southern African Open.[8]

In December 1970, Bobat flew to Cape Town, courtesy of the Lansdowne Tennis Club, to play against Alwyn Solomon in the new Ben Crowie Challenge Tournament, 'a sort of champion of champions affair'.[9] He lost to Solomon in a closely fought encounter 6-4, 6-4. He 'put up a brave fight', but having concentrated on his matric exams 'he was out of match practice and nowhere near his peak form.' Still, 'he gave a good account of himself all the same'.[10] At the R450 Lansdowne Tennis Club tournament in Cape Town, Bobat, the reigning national junior champion, 'was crushed 6-4, 6-0 by Alwyn Solomon'. The *Cape Herald* commented that 'the poor display' of Bobat against Solomon, bore 'out the remark of a wag that "Bobat needs more match practice and not a REST", the latter being the reason given for Bobat's withdrawal from the Bellville Tournament'.[11] The real reason for withdrawing from the Bellville Tournament was that Bobat was advised that it was connected with Conrad Johnson, who the Western Province Tennis Board and SnALTU expelled for accepting funds from the Coloured Affairs Department for the 1969 overseas Sunshine Tour.

Bobat reached the final of the under-21 Western Province Open tournament in Stellenbosch, where he met Oscar Woodman. It was reported that the 'aggression expected ... was absent' and that Bobat 'left Woodman off the hook', going down 6-4, 6-8, 1-6. In the senior doubles tournament, there was a credible semi-final loss when he and partner Hira Dhiraj went down to eventual winners Jasmat Dhiraj and Hermie Abrahams 2-6, 5-7.[12] A week later, Bobat lost again to Woodman

Discussion on the forthcoming tour, 1 March 1971. From left: M.N. Pather, SnALTU secretary; Ebrahim Osman, SNLTU secretary; Mohamed (Ginger) Mahomedy; Hoosen Bobat; and Ahmed Bobat, Hoosen's father (Moosa Badsha).

Carrying the best wishes of all tennis fans is Hoosen Bobat (centre) Natal's national junior champion who left by air for an overseas campaign recently. And there to see him off were Mr. Ebrahim Osman (right) president of the Natal Lawn Tennis Union and veteran player Parbhoo Roopnarain.

SNLTU administrator Ebrahim Osman (right) and fellow tennis player Parbhoo Roopnarain (left) seeing Hoosen Bobat off at Durban airport (*Leader*, 22 April 1971).

in the under-21 competition at the Southern African Open, going down 1-6, 9-7, 2-6.[13] There was a perception of jerrymandering associated with the age grouping for the junior competition to favour the Cape players: whereas during the previous year the junior tournament was restricted to those under nineteen, in 1970-1971 it was changed to include those who were under 21. Bobat's major success in 1970 was to reach the quarter-finals of the South African Open, where he 'lost narrowly to the eventual finalist Herman Abrahams'.[14]

Universities usually make special arrangements for students who are selected to take part in national and international sports events. Despite the honour of being selected for the 1971 tour, the largely white officials of the University College for Indians, many of whom were supporters of the apartheid regime, obstinately refused to provide Bobat leave. A first application for leave was summarily rejected. A supportive American lecturer attempted to intervene, trying to get other lecturers to facilitate Bobat's continued studies, but with no success. Bobat eventually resigned himself to withdrawing from his first-year courses in order to take part in the tour.

On 10 April 1971, family, friends, tennis players and administrators gathered at Louis Botha airport on the Durban south coast to see Bobat off to Johannesburg, accompanied by M.K. Naidoo (SnALTU president) and M.N. Pather (SnALTU secretary).

Hoosen Bobat at Durban airport with his granny, mum, dad and sisters Ameena and Razia.

Tournament results

UK tournament 1: Oxfordshire Junior Tournament, Norham Gardens, Oxford, 19–24 April 1971
At the first tournament of the tour, Bobat won his early rounds easily. He eventually fell to compatriot Alwyn Solomon in the semi-finals 6-0, 6-4. He and Bergman shared the honours in the doubles final when rain precluded play.

UK tournament 2: Rothmans Sutton Hard Court Championships, south London, 26 April–1 May 1971
Results unavailable.

UK tournament 3: Rothmans Surrey Hard Court Championships, Guildford, 3–8 May 1971
Bobat narrowly lost to the top American junior D. Crawford 8-6, 3-6, 7-9 after leading 5-2 in the final set.

UK tournament 4: Bio-Strath London Hard Court Championships, Hurlingham, 10–15 May 1971
Although 'he was expected to be beaten easily by the ranked Australian, Geoff Masters', Bobat 'put up a fighting display',

losing 7-9, 3-6 and earning 'the praise of critics'. Jasmat noted: 'Credit must be given to Bobat. The first set was oh so close!'[15]

Bobat partnered Woodman and reached the quarter-finals of the A-level doubles tournament.

UK tournament 5: Bio-Strath Droitwich Spa Tournament, Worcestershire, 17–22 May 1971
Bobat lost in the singles to the Rhodesian Sheridan Towers 6-0, 6-1. In the doubles, Bobat and Bergman beat Woodman and Rana 5-7, 8-6, 6-3.[16]

UK tournament 6: Rothmans Surrey Grass Court Championships, Surbiton, 24–29 May 1971
Results unavailable.

UK tournament 7: Rothmans Chichester Tennis Tournament, West Sussex, 31 May–5 June 1971
In the singles, Bobat beat D.J. Mercer 6-2, 6-1; but then lost to fellow South African Derek Schroeder 6-0, 6-0.[17]

UK tournament 8: Kent Championships, Beckenham Lawn Tennis Club, 7–12 June 1971
Bobat narrowly went down in the singles to R. Andrews 4-6, 6-8. In the doubles, ranked Americans Stan Smith and Erik van Dillen defeated Bobat and Bergman 6-1, 6-1.[18]

UK tournament 10: Rothmans South of England Open Championships, Eastbourne, 14–19 June 1971
Bobat and P. Orchard and Jasmat Dhiraj and P. Orchard's sister shared the doubles prize.[19]

During the tour Bobat was troubled with back injury. Fortunately, he soon 'fully recovered' and said he was 'looking forward to taking part [in] the European circuit' with the Dhiraj brothers and Woodman following the UK tournaments.[20] With respect to adjusting to conditions in Britain, Bobat notes:

> Coming from a background where we had very limited tennis court facilities and limited different playing surfaces, we were suddenly thrust into a completely new tennis world. We were now exposed to many different surfaces such as sand courts, clay, synthetic and wood floors. All these courts had varying speeds and bounce. It took us a few tournaments to adjust to varying conditions.[21]

While on tour, he wrote that 'the players are doing their best to get accustomed to playing in the cold wet weather on slow damp courts'. He observed that 'service is one of the most important aspects of play in overseas tournaments' and that the players were 'learning fast'.[22] Moreover, 'being on the international circuit and participating in all the tournaments leading up to Wimbledon' meant that 'we were now competing with the best players in the world and had to quickly adapt and raise our standard'.[23]

Hoosen Bobat waiting patiently for his opponent to turn up at the Hurlingham tournament (*Leader*, 18 June 1971).

Hoosen Bobat (right) and Oscar Woodman on tour.

Looking back, Bobat reflects:

> Personally, I had a good first ever tour especially in my age group as a junior. I had some notable performances in the men's open division against top players from around the world. Proof of my performance in the junior division was my acceptance by the All-England Tennis Club to play in Junior Wimbledon, which was based on performance and ranking among the juniors. I also had notable performances in doubles tournaments, (winning a title with Oscar Woodman) and in the mixed doubles (runner-up in one tournament).[24]

Tragically, as we have noted, Bobat was denied entry to the Junior Wimbledon championships because of the machinations of the white SALTU and the ILTF's Basil Reay. He recounts that he 'was ecstatic – it was a goose bump moment, the culmination of my years of training, sacrifice and passion for the sport'. To his knowledge, 'he was the first and only black South African to have had that honour'.[25]

Bobat elaborates that 'four weeks before Wimbledon I was invited to play, then two weeks before the tournament I got my acceptance goodies. Then one week before the tournament I received a telegram from the International Lawn Tennis Federation requesting an urgent meeting.'

He recalls that at the meeting, which he attended with Jasmat Dhiraj, 'I was informed that my entry was terminated.' It was, of course, 'an incredible shock to have the "singular honour" of playing at Wimbledon snatched away'. The 'ugly reality of apartheid reared its head in the form of the white SA Tennis Union, under Alf Chalmers, who objected to his entry'.[26]

Bobat in his own words

This is my story of what happened.

Many terms were used in the press and by others to describe the incident of my exclusion: turned down, blocked, prevented and terminated. A few weeks into the tour, all the squad members applied for entry to the Wimbledon championships. Cavan Bergman and I applied for Junior Wimbledon. The criteria for acceptance at the time were that you had to be the number one or two ranked junior in your country together with your performances in the past twelve months. Also, you had to be a member of your national body and affiliated to a club that was a member of the ILTF.

Cavan and I satisfied all the criteria and sent in our entries for Junior Wimbledon to the All-England Lawn Tennis Club, which traditionally handled entries for Wimbledon. On tour, all our correspondence was directed to our equipment sponsor, Dunlop, whose representative used to bring our mail daily to the tournaments we were playing. I recall being handed a telegram by the Dunlop rep from the All-England Lawn Tennis Club. With shaking hands, I opened the telegram and saw the words, 'Congratulations you have been accepted for Junior Wimbledon 1971.'

Wow! You can imagine my elation receiving this news. It was surreal. I remember reading the telegram over and over again. This was the culmination of years of sacrifice, training and practice with no formal coaching, no access to proper facilities and no sponsorship.

Back home, the black tennis fraternity celebrated as it would be the very first time that a black tennis player from South Africa was accepted to play at Junior Wimbledon. I recall receiving a call from our tennis president, Mr Ebrahim Osman, from Durban expressing the joy and celebration back home at this news. For me it was a dream come true to compete on the highest tennis stage in the world, Wimbledon.

About ten days before the start of Wimbledon, I received another telegram, but this time from the ILTF, requesting me to come to their head office in London with my team captain. I was not aware of the reason for the meeting. Fifty-one years later, I still vividly recall that day. I was accompanied by my captain Jasmat Dhiraj. At the ILTF office the receptionist told us that we were to meet Basil Reay, who at that time was the secretary of the ILTF.

When we entered Reay's office we were shocked to see Alf 'Baas' Chalmers there in a corner of the room. Chalmers was the head of the white SALTU in South Africa. I remember thinking 'what the heck is "Baas" Chalmers doing here!' He had flown all the way from South Africa for this meeting. I remember, Jasmat being incensed at the presence of Chalmers. He asked Reay 'What is "Baas" Chalmers doing here?' Reay got straight to the point and told us that the all-white SALTU had objected to my entry for Wimbledon.

SALTU alleged that I was not the number one junior in South Africa and that Byron Bertram was the number one. Jasmat asked how SALTU could claim that Bertram was number one if he was not allowed to play against black players for racial reasons. Chalmers ignored that truth and said that I was not affiliated to the ILTF-recognised national body in South Africa, which was the all-white SALTU. Jasmat told Reay that as blacks we were not allowed to belong to SALTU.

Reay said that we did not belong to any ILTF-recognised club. Jasmat told him that was not true. On arriving in the UK, we had become members of an ILTF-recognised club, the Coolhurst Tennis Club, and had already played in several tournaments that were under the auspices of the ILTF. Jasmat emphasised that I satisfied all the criteria for Junior Wimbledon.

There was much heated back-and-forth discussion, but it was clear that Reay had already made up his mind. He wanted me out of the Wimbledon draw to appease 'Baas' Chalmers.

Reay's final words at the conclusion of the meeting kept ringing in my ears: 'Tomorrow I will instruct the All-England Club to remove your entry from the main draw of Junior Wimbledon.'

And just like that, it was all over! No 'Love all!' Game set and match. Apartheid abetted by its international collaborators won in straight sets without even the toss of the coin! I really couldn't understand the impact of it all at that time. I was only eighteen years old. I remember thinking, 'who are all these people in suits who can decide your fate by the stroke of a pen?'

I had many questions about the decision by Reay and the ILTF. Did the ILTF have a meeting? Were there any minutes of the meeting? Or did Reay make the decision on his own? Had 'Baas' Chalmers flown all the way from South Africa just to remove this young black kid from playing in Junior Wimbledon?

A very interesting incident occurred eighteen months prior in Durban, South Africa. Basil Reay was in South Africa as a guest of SALTU. Together with 'Baas' Chalmers he went around the country, trying to woo black tennis administrators and players to join SALTU as honorary whites. They had very limited success. This is what we referred to as window dressing to show the world that blacks and whites play together in South Africa. At that time, apartheid South Africa was starting to feel the pressure from the international community about racism in sport.

In late 1969, Reay and Chalmers had a meeting in Durban with our non-racial tennis officials, M.N. Pather and Ebrahim Osman. They brought a document for us to sign in which we agreed to join the white SALTU as honorary whites and play in a few selected tournaments. Ebrahim Osman writes in his autobiography that 'after 10 minutes we showed Basil Reay and Chalmers the door.' For months after, there was much poking of fun that the two left with their tails between their legs.

> Join the dots! This was the same Reay and Chalmers who six months later got their own back at being shown the door and embarrassed. I, an eighteen-year-old black kid on the cusp of the dream of playing Junior Wimbledon was their victim.

Bobat, instead, proceeded to play tournaments on the European continent, winning two trophies in the Netherlands as a losing finalist in singles and doubles tournaments. On tour, the Dhiraj Squad members ran into Claude Lister, who was white 'South Africa's long-serving captain. Lister led the white team in 1974', when it won the Davis Cup – 'the only nation ever to win without playing a final'. This happened after 'India refused to play South Africa because of apartheid, a decision commended by millions who considered that the South Africans should not have been allowed back into the Davis Cup, having been expelled a few years before'.[27] Lister indicated to the team members that he would facilitate their entries at some tournaments in the Netherlands. Later, they would discover that it was quite the opposite: Lister engineered their exclusion.[28] Their entries for the junior Dutch Open were referred to Lister. He indicated to the squad juniors that the tournament entries were full, but they later discovered that was not true when they were asked by Dutch officials why they did not turn up.[29]

In 1977, when South Africa was placed in the Davis Cup American zone since many countries in that region either openly collaborated with the apartheid government or refused to take a principled stand on racism in sport, Lister partnered Byron Bertram who had defeated Jasmat Dhiraj on the 1971 tour. The pair lost to Bob Lutz and Stan Smith, but not before the match 'was interrupted in the third set . . . when two black demonstrators went on court and spilled oil that took 45 minutes to clean. The police wrestled them to the ground and handcuffed them.'[30] Smith (with Van Dillen) had defeated Bobat and Bergman in 1971 in a doubles match at the Beckenham Championships.

For Bobat there were many memorable moments related to the 1971 tour. To begin with, it was 'getting a phone call from Ebrahim Osman, to tell me I have been selected for the tour, followed shortly by a call from M.N. Pather'. Another great 'highlight was receiving a telegram from the All-England Club confirming that I was accepted to play in Junior Wimbledon in July 1971. This was a dream come true.'[31] Other special moments were 'meeting Arthur Ashe and other tennis idols such as Ken Rosewall, Rod Laver, Roy Emerson and Stan Smith' and 'playing a doubles match in the men's open division with my partner Cavan Bergman against one of the world's top doubles pairs at the time, Stan Smith and Erik van Dillen'. In addition, there was the opportunity to have 'a ten-minute on court practice with Billie Jean King.'[32]

Bobat cherished meeting SANROC stalwarts Chris de Broglio and especially Dennis Brutus while on tour, with the latter leaving a lasting impression on him. He also met Peter Hain, who headed up 'many of the disruptions in South Africa's white touring sports teams'. Hain considered that 'the banning of South African sports tours was integral to the dismantling of apartheid' and was 'arrested and detained for his role in the disruptions'.[33] Hain recalls that 'we would run onto the pitch in the middle of cricket matches and always end up in handcuffs'. At 'other times we would inject solidifying agent into the locks and hinges of the hotel doors so that the players couldn't get out of their rooms. We helped to ensure that white South Africa never toured.'[34]

Another memorable moment for Bobat was, unfortunately, also one of the 'worst moments in [his] life', hearing Basil Reay of ILTF utter the words to [him], 'Tomorrow I will instruct the All-England Club to terminate your entry from Junior Wimbledon.'[35] But the tour was 'an exhilarating experience'. According to him, the white South African tennis players like Ray Moore, Derek Schroeder and Terry Ryan that they met were helpful; and that Moore was 'particularly friendly' and a 'great guy'.[36]

In Bobat's view, his tennis greatly improved during the four-month Dhiraj Squad tour. He says that 'my tennis game went to a whole new level by the end of the tour. I soaked up the experience of playing on different surfaces and meeting and playing against the best players in the world at the time. I learnt about the importance of not only stroke play or shot making but the equally important mental and physical aspects of the game.' He feels that 'it would've been ideal for us to have gone for at least two or three more tours to fully break in on the international circuit. I believe we all had the potential to go much further'.[37] However, as noted, he bemoaned the lack of competition locally, the dearth of tougher competition and the lower standard of tennis relative to overseas.

For Bobat, captain Jasmat Dhiraj was an outstanding leader from whom he gained much as he also did from 'meeting Dennis Brutus, and being on the tour'. He says that Jasmat was 'a truly amazing, strongly principled person'.[38] He considers Jasmat not returning to South Africa a major setback for South African tennis. The adverse meeting with Basil Reay was also an important life lesson. The Durban weekly, the *Leader* dubbed 1971 'Bobat's year'. It observed that by 'campaigning in England and the Continent from April to August' he had 'blazed a trail for an exciting adventure for our up-and-coming tennisites'.[39]

The tour gave a fillip to the SNLTU, which expressed great hopes for 'more international competition', more overseas tours, 'regular organised coaching at all levels, the building of a proper tennis stadium and a national championship in Durban'.[40] On tour, the University of Minnesota tennis coach approached Bobat to consider joining the Minnesota Golden Gophers, as the University's sports team was known, on a sports scholarship. Bobat was keen to take up the opportunity, but his father preferred him to remain in Durban and complete his university studies.

While this book was in its final draft, Bobat's 95-year-old father reminded him that somewhere in their business office, notwithstanding many moves over the years, there should hopefully be a journal of letters that he wrote to him during the 1971 tour. Indeed, there was and we are fortunate to be able to draw on ten letters that date between 14 April 1971 (four days after Bobat left on tour) and 9 August 1971.[41] The letters communicate news about the family, and about developments in local tennis such as the results of club matches and the performances and progress of Bobat's cousin. But they also ask questions about happenings on the tour, request information on squad plans, provide counsel on various matters, and express mild exasperation at the lack of letters from Bobat while on tour.

In the first letter, Mr Bobat observes that his son would be in a new and different world and he encourages him to 'treat this all with level headedness', to 'enrich' himself, and to 'come back with your horizon broadened'. He counsels, 'Practice at every opportunity, look for players from other parts of the world and talk to them about your tennis, get them on to court for practice, and learn all you can about tennis.' Not least, Bobat should 'analyse and learn to sum up the strong points and weaknesses of [his] tennis, teammates and leading players'. And he had to 'keep in trim by exercising regularly and by eating only good wholesome food'. Mr Bobat remarks that 'the squad has been so much in the news that all eyes will be on you all and we just pray and hope that you all acquit yourselves meritoriously'.

In a second letter on 1 May 1971, Mr Bobat says he has been reading about the cold weather in England and urges Hoosen to, if necessary, buy warm clothing and to keep warm. He reports that a local sports dealer, Mr Kirby, who specialised in tennis equipment was 'anxious to hear about your progress with Dunlop rackets and Fred Perry clothing'. He enquires whether squad members were 'aiming to play at Wimbledon' and 'if so, what is the procedure'. He enclosed some articles so that Bobat was 'aware of the vicious campaign in the local papers to prove that we are not fit enough for top level competition' – 'whose fault?' he asked.

A letter of 29 May 1971 expresses relief at Hoosen's recovery from his 'cold and back trouble'. He urges his son to keep warm and eat 'nourishing foods'. He advises that if his back gives further trouble Hoosen should 'arrange a thorough check-up at a hospital'. In a strong affirmation of support, Mr Bobat says that 'we are all satisfied that the squad is doing better than expected and some of your performances have really excited the whole of non-white South Africans' and that 'we are confidently looking forward to some upsets'. He conveys disappointment at a black South African not defeating a white South African: 'If Jasmat could only have beaten . . . Derek Schroeder . . . then we could really have gone to town.' He asks Hoosen to thank Jasmat for sending information on tournament matches to *Post* reporter Farook Khan. Khan had kindly telephoned and shared letters with Bobat senior. Mr Bobat urges, 'I do hope that you keep the full results of all the players at each tournament that you and other members of the squad participate in so that we can study the details when you get back home.'

He requests more information on the idea of the squad playing on the Continent, the tournaments that would be played, talk of pooling of funds from different unions and the costs that would be involved. He indicates that M.N. Pather and Ebrahim Osman were 'sympathetic but would like to have more definite details'. Mr Bobat resigns himself that 'it does appear that your studies will suffer considerably this year'. He was enquiring about withdrawal from university, the matter of fees and arrangements in that regard.

A fourth letter on 4 June 1971 drills Hoosen on numerous matters to do with tennis:

> In what department of your game have you improved most? What about your service and smashing? Do you exercise regularly - any special exercises? Any particular forms of practice on the court - do you get sufficient practice? Of the squad who has made the most progress? Will Dunlop and Fred Perry be issuing you with further rackets and clothing? Do you think any members of the squad can make the grade in top tennis? Does one have to wear special shoes when playing on grass tennis courts?

There is also a practical matter: 'Should we continue to post letters to Dunlop Sports Co.?'

Mr Bobat says he 'read in Wednesday's *Star* newspaper that you lost 6-0, 6-0 to Schroeder'. In a show of encouragement, he says, 'I hope you did not suffer from a complex. I have always maintained that physical aches and pains and mental stress are part and parcel of the game.' His keenness for his son to improve his tennis and learn is evident when he informs Hoosen that South African Abe Segal was playing in the same tournament as him, that Segal was 'the top coach for service faults in particular' and that he hoped that Hoosen could 'get him to the courts for valuable coaching and advice'.

He enquires, 'How do you fare against Jasmat in practice - have you been able to close the gap a little?' And he advises Hoosen that 'one of the things missing from your game was your reluctance to jump into the air when smashing. I wonder if you have rectified this glaring omission.' He encourages Hoosen to use his video camera at Wimbledon to film '[John] Newcombe's great serve from as many angles as possible' and enquires about 'best tennis magazines' to which to subscribe. Exploring possibilities for more competition for black players, he requests Hoosen to enquire of 'the Rhodesian players the dates when important Rhodesian tournaments take place and where'.

A letter on 23 June 1971 implores Hoosen to send required information on the impending trip to the Continent so that SnALTU could mobilise the necessary finances. And had he contacted Mr Paruk from South Africa to collect R200 that was sent for him? A letter on 28 June 1971 addresses the matter of money again and informs Hoosen that he can collect another R250 from Mr Suleman Paruk in London. In response to Hoosen's concern about buying gifts for family and friends, his father responds that it 'should be your least concern. You are there to learn, gain experience, to observe and to widen your horizons – not on a shopping expedition.'

Eleven weeks into the tour there is an evident ambivalence about the lengthening of the tour. Mr Bobat says that 'you full well must realise that in spite of opposition and concern I am allowing your trip to be extended'. He counsels Hoosen that 'you must always conduct yourself in a way that does the family proud. It is because I have full confidence in you that I have allowed this trip of yours. I expect you to leave for South Africa by the middle of September and not later.' Perhaps as a response to Hoosen not providing requested information, Mr Bobat remarks that 'your itinerary for your continental trip will also clarify my further directions in this matter'.

On 1 July 1971, in a seventh letter Mr Bobat says that he will send Hoosen's steel racket with a Mr Bobby Maharajh from Durban. His anxiety about the tour to the Continent is manifest when he says, 'Please do look after yourself on the Continent – what I read regularly gives me grey hairs! No one is an angel – but there are certain limits which must not be exceeded.' Another letter a day later on 2 July 1971 confirms that a racket would be brought over by Mr Maharajh. It also asks whether Hoosen is over his back trouble completely and if he needs any clothing sent over.

On 7 August 1971, Mr Bobat writes to a relative in London. He requests him to pass on a money draft from M.K. Naidoo, the SnALTU president, as a gift to the squad. He says that he estimated that the squad would return to England from the Continent by mid-August. He observes that 'the squad seems to be in an embarrassing position financially on the Continent and their van is giving them endless trouble. The tour has gone sour now.' The relative is told to tell Hoosen that 'he must return home as soon as possible'. And he must express family concern about Hoosen's overgrown hair – he had to cut his hair so that he was presentable when he returned home. A final tenth letter on 9 August 1971 shortly before Hoosen returned home commented that 'it appears that in spite of your squad's woes you seem to be enjoying yourself immensely in Holland'.

On 25 November 1971, Mr Bobat wrote to Hira Dhiraj requesting the return of floating trophies that he and Jasmat won at the 1970 SNLTU tournament. He comments that 'Hoosen cannot stop talking about the trip and the warm companionship he found with the members of the team'. On his return in mid-August 1971, Bobat was unable to return to university immediately, 'as they had denied me leave for the tour'. He, therefore, 'wasted six months of my studies as they had told me to withdraw from campus and re-register in 1972'. He 'tried to keep fit' and maintain his level of tennis at that which he had reached on tour.[42]

In coming years, he continued to play competitive tennis. In the 1971–1972 national championships in Kimberley, Bobat lost in the quarter-finals to Hermie Abrahams.[43] In 1972, he was ranked number five in South Africa. In the 1972 SNLTU Coca Cola Winter Open Championship, playing with 'superb coolness and judgement', he 'out-stroked, out-thought and out-manouvered Ismail Asmal in the men's singles final' winning 6-2, 6-4, 6-4.[44] Partnering Asmal in the men's doubles final, they came up against the formidable Boland brothers David and Frank Samaai and lost 3-6, 4-6, 7-5, 2-6.

In the 1972 Western Province Open won by Hira Dhiraj, he was beaten by the losing finalist, Woodman, 6-2, 7-9, 6-4.[45] In the 1973 Natal Open, when defending his title, there was a convincing victory over Hira Dhiraj in the semi-final but he succumbed to Poole in the final 1-6, 7-5, 6-2, 6-3. Poole and Dhiraj beat Bobat and Asmal in the doubles final 6-4, 6-4, 3-6, 6-2.

A 'shoulder injury while bowling in a cricket match slowed [him] down', there were no honours at the 1973–1974 national championships after retiring with a foot injury, and by 1974 his national ranking had dropped to tenth.[46] The 'disappointment' of not being able to take up a tennis scholarship in the US killed his 'competitive edge'.[47] As he observed: 'Here I was, one minute on top of the world ... and the next I was offered a scholarship to the US and couldn't go.'

By 1973, the correspondence with US universities came to an end and at the age of 21 'the competitive chapter in [his] tennis career

Hoosen Bobat, University of Durban-Westville graduation, 1978 (African News Agency).

ended, and the passion dropped a couple of notches'. Thereafter, he confined himself to playing tennis socially, took up golf, and coached juniors at the Jeevan Kara Tennis complex in Springfield.[48]

Bobat graduated with a B. Com. degree from the University of Durban-Westville in 1978 and acquired further professional qualifications

Hoosen Bobat with juniors at the Jeevan Kara Centre, Springfield (*Independent on Saturday*, 26 November 2006).

Hoosen Bobat in his 1970s green provincial blazer at Bobat Wealth Solutions in Morningside, Durban.

as a financial planner. In 1980, he joined the family business, Bobats Insurance Brokers CC and helped it grow into a highly successful company. Located in Morningside, Durban and now called Bobats Wealth Solutions, it celebrates its 93rd anniversary in 2023.

In 1980, he married Zulekha Moosa with whom he had two boys Siraaj and Zaheer. A widower since 2006, he has two grandsons, the oldest of whom, Hamza, aged ten, is a regular on the tennis court and shows great promise. He continues playing tennis to maintain fitness. A keen fly fisherperson, he is involved in various environmental and social welfare causes.

18

Cavan Bergman

Cavan George Bergman was the youngest member of the Dhiraj Squad, turning seventeen while on tour. He was born on 24 April 1954 in Athlone, Cape Town, and attended Alicedale Primary School in Athlone and later Athlone High School. Bergman's father was a hotel manager and in 1964 took up a new post at the Reo Hotel in Elsies River, when Cavan was ten years old. The whole family relocated there. Cavan, however, continued to commute daily to the English-medium schools in Athlone, a one-hour journey.

He took up tennis at the age of ten, when he came across the tennis court used by the Progressive Tennis Club in Elsies River that was associated with the Carolissen and Solomon families. There was only one other clay court, owned by the Samuels family. Basil Carolissen invited him to attend coaching, which he did under the supervision of David Isaacs. Bergman recalls that in those days Alwyn Solomon was the outstanding junior. The likes of him and Lynette Thomas (later Clarke, after her marriage to sport administrator Colin Clarke) had to join a long queue of youngsters to play the top juniors. You could only remain on court if you won, but most times he was 'annihilated' by the likes of Solomon, who was four years older. Club policy motivated him strongly, making him realise that he had to become serious and practise if he wanted game time. Progressives produced many junior and senior champions – Alwyn Solomon, Lynette Thomas, Lorraine Samuels, Charmaine Carolissen, Patrick Carolissen, Roxanne Thomas, Alwyn Solomon's daughter Nadia Solomon, and Bergman himself.

Just prior to the 1971 tour, the Bergman family moved to Bosmont, Johannesburg, when Cavan's father became the manager of the Bosmont Hotel. From 1962 onwards, coloured South Africans from the inner-city areas of Johannesburg were forcibly relocated under the Group Areas Act to Bosmont.[1] Bergman enrolled at St Barnabas College, an independent

Std. VI Class.
Cavan Bergman (front row, third from left) at St Barnabas College.

school established in 1962 in Bosmont, which later became the first school to be open to all students irrespective of race.[2] The agreement with St Barnabas was that he could go on tour if he became a boarding student on his return so that he could catch up on the months of schooling that he would lose; and if he took his schoolbooks with him. He recalls opening his biology textbook on the aeroplane when they departed Jan Smuts airport; thereafter the textbooks were ignored!

A St Barnabas graduate, who 'grew up in a "poor, beautiful and solemn village" in Hammanskraal', is Trudi Makhaya, a Wits graduate, Oxford University Rhodes Scholar and economic adviser to president Cyril Ramaphosa.[3] She comments that the college's success was due to being

> an institution that believed in us. Michael Corke [the long-serving headmaster] made sure that we understood that we were taken seriously, and that made us take ourselves seriously. He used to tell a story about the days in which he was raising funds for the school and he shared his plans with the businessmen of the

day. Some were quick to tell him that the facilities he envisaged were too good for black children from poor backgrounds. The beautiful building which stands in Bosmont today is testament to the fact that he believed that we had talent worth nurturing. This is the work of someone who was beyond lamenting the fact that his learners were not from the 'right side of the tracks'.[4]

Corke himself adds that 'the college's recipe for success was to treat' the students 'as individuals and to insist that they think for themselves'. The school supported students to 'protest apartheid but at the same time made sure they were given a quality education'. It allowed students 'to argue while subjecting them to a firm study regime'. Instead of being focused entirely on the matric exams, it tried 'to provide a programme to unlock other latent talents they might have'.[5]

Bergman was surprised at his inclusion in the Dhiraj Squad because he was still very young, but his selection was deserved and is testimony to the SnALTU's commitment to cultivate and support promising juniors. In 1967-1968 he had won both the under-16 and under-14 championships at the Southern African Open held at the Green Point Track tennis courts in Cape Town, when he beat Thomas Nunes of

Cavan Bergman (Leader, 18 June 1971).

Southern Rhodesia 6-4, 6-4 and Y. Galdien of Western Province 3-6, 6-4, 6-4.[6] The following year at the national championships at the Wits University courts, Bergman beat Girish Raniga of Natal 6-4, 6-4 in the under-15 singles finals. He was losing finalist to Raniga and Asmal in the doubles under-15 finals.[7]

Immediately prior to the 1971 tour, at the 1970-1971 national junior championships in Cape Town, he was beaten in the semi-finals by Bobat 6-3, 3-6, 6-3.[8] After winning junior titles he received sponsorship from tennis goods manufacturers Dunlop and, later, from Wilson. Now, he receives sponsorship from Babolat, the brand of racket used by Rafael Nadal.

In his view, the tour was overlaid with some minor politics. For one, the designation Dhiraj Squad gave a certain status to Jasmat, though he acknowledges that Jasmat was the natural leader and spokesperson of the squad. For another, the precise status of Carolissen – whether he was the official or the volunteer manager on the tour – was not clear. The Progressive Tennis Club and Woodman's club did not always see eye to eye.

Tournament results

UK tournament 1: Oxfordshire Junior Tournament, Norham Gardens, Oxford, 19–24 April 1971
Bergman beat P. Saunders 6-3, 6-3 in the first round and then defeated R. Battersby 6-2, 6-1 in the second round. In the quarter-finals he lost to the reigning champion, Chris Ronaldson, 5-7, 8-6, 6-1. Bobat and Bergman shared the honours in the doubles final when rain prevented play. Bergman and a British partner, Lyn Maxwell, shared the mixed doubles prize when rain also washed out their final.[9]

UK tournament 2: Rothmans Sutton Hard Court Championships, south London, 26 April–1 May 1971
Bergman lost to J.P. Malvin 6-8, 2-6.[10]

UK tournament 3: *Rothmans Surrey Hard Court Championships,*
Guildford, 3–8 May 1971
Results unavailable.

UK tournament 4: *Bio-Strath London Hard Court Championships,*
Hurlingham, 10–15 May 1971
Results unavailable.

UK tournament 5: *Bio-Strath Droitwich Spa Tournament, Worcestershire,*
17–22 May 1971
Bergman was defeated by Mandelstrom 6-0, 6-1. Bergman and Bobat had 'a good doubles win over Woodman and Rana', winning 5-7, 8-6, 6-3.[11]

UK tournament 6: *Rothmans Surrey Grass Court Championships,*
Surbiton, 24–29 May 1971
Results unavailable.

UK tournament 7: *Rothmans Chichester Tennis Tournament, West*
Sussex, 31 May–5 June 1971
Bergman beat A.J. Cottis 6-3, 6-8, 6-3.[12]

UK tournament 8: *Kent Championships, Beckenham Lawn Tennis*
Club, 7–12 June 1971
Bergman lost to the number one seed, United States player Erik van Dillen 6-1, 6-1.[13] In the doubles tournament, Bobat and Bergman were defeated by top Americans Stan Smith and Erik van Dillen 6-1, 6-1.[14]

UK tournament 10: *Rothmans South of England Open Championships,*
Eastbourne, 14–19 June 1971
Results unavailable.

Hoosen Bobat (front), Cavan Bergman (middle) and Alwyn Solomon on tour, 1971.

The youngest squaddies on the 1971 tour: Hoosen Bobat, 18 (left) and Cavan Bergman, 17 (right).

Bergman returned to South Africa at the close of the squad's UK schedule, while the rest of the group moved on to the European continent. He is of the view that, notwithstanding challenges, the 1971 tour impacted him strongly and 'was positive'. He recognised that in 1971 'I was not a good tennis player'. The tour was the catalyst that drove him to play tennis better than he was doing. He had previously been coached to play with one grip (continental) for all his strokes, which meant he possessed only a sliced backhand. On the tour, he came to understand the importance of varying his grip and it made him an accomplished all-round and especially serve-and-volley player.

He recalls meeting on the tour SANROC officials like Dennis Brutus, which made him become more politically aware. For Bergman, one memorable moment of the 1971 tour was when he either beat the UK's John Lloyd or strongly extended him. Another special occasion was holding his serve when he and Bobat played and lost 6-1, 6-1 to the top US doubles pair of Stan Smith and Erik van Dillen. Then, there was the visit to Wimbledon and especially to the Centre Court, where he watched Bob Hewitt, an Australian who became a South African citizen through marriage.

Hewitt won all the Grand Slam (Australian Open, French Open, Wimbledon and US Open) doubles and mixed doubles titles, and in 1992 'was inducted into the International Tennis Hall of Fame'. Bergman alleges that Hewitt held the view that 'blacks don't have the acumen to be good tennis players'. In 2015, Hewitt was found guilty of 'rape and sexual assault of minors [girls he was coaching in the 1980s and 1990s] . . . sentenced to an effective six years in jail, and was subsequently permanently expelled from the International Tennis Hall of Fame'.[15]

Bergman says that being a secondary school student he was the *laaitie* (youngster) of the tour. Because of 'his junior status, he had to look after the equipment in the Ford Thames van whose door would not lock'. He 'accepted it as part of status and of life'.[16]

On his return, in early 1972 Bergman won the Southern African under-19 title in Kimberley, beating Claude Moonieyan of Border 1-6, 6-4, 6-2. He teamed up with Natal's Ismail Asmal to win the under-19 doubles tournament 2-6, 6-4, 6-1, defeating brothers Claude and Gavin Moonieyan. Unlike Bobat, who David Samaai invited to spend time with

From left: Oscar Woodman, Hoosen Bobat, a representative of sponsor Bio-Strath, Hira Dhiraj and Cavan Bergman (*Post*, 11 July 1971).

him for coaching, Bergman was overlooked, perhaps because Samaai did not see in him a future senior champion – a forgivable error of judgement. That only made him more determined to succeed. Samaai opened the door to him only when he was already the senior SnALTU champion. Much later Samaai invited Bergman to coach his grandson; he accepted, seeing this as acknowledgement of his coaching abilities and as the extension of an olive branch.

Like Bobat, who felt that the age eligibility for junior championships was adjusted to favour Western Cape players, Bergman's perception was that draws for tournaments were stacked against him. He says that in almost every tournament he was drawn to meet Girish Raniga of Natal, as it was known that he struggled against Raniga and left handers like Japie Klaasen. He shared that observation with a prominent Western Cape tournament referee, thanking him for giving him tough draws and for bringing out the best on him.

A turning point in his life was when as the junior champion he played Hira Dhiraj in the quarter-finals at the Top 16 tournament in Vryburg in the early 1970s. He lost in three sets, but it confirmed to him that he could become the senior champion in the years to come. In Bosmont, meeting Herman Abrahams, a fellow resident who mentored him, was also important. He met Charlton Eagle, a young tennis talent whom he encouraged. Eagle emigrated to Australia in 1976, went on to play Boris Becker at the 1988 Stella Artois Championships at Queen's, and as a coach worked with 'with Martina Navratilova, Mary Pierce, Pam Shriver, Zina Garrison' and others.[17]

Completing his schooling at St Barnabas in the mid-1970s, Bergman did not consider going to college or university. He had dreams of becoming a professional tennis player. But his hopes were set back when his partner Janice Fortuin, sister of the soccer player Leroy Fortuin, fell pregnant and he had to earn a living. Through the St Barnabas headmaster he got a job at the Carlton Centre in Johannesburg's central business area. Later, he worked for the Chamber of Mines. He ran to tennis practice every day – before and after work.

At some point, he approached Alwyn Solomon to play doubles with him but was rebuffed. He then partnered Raymond Anthony who was from Vryburg, had lived and been coached in Paarl by the Samaais, and later settled in Johannesburg. Sometime later, Solomon approached Bergman to become his doubles partner and, though mindful of the earlier rejection, he accepted.

Despite beginning to defeat Solomon, Darroll Carolissen maintained that his nephew Solomon was the better player. Bergman's response was that the results had to speak. In his view, although Alwyn was very good 'he was mentally and psychologically fragile', a weakness that he exploited. Once, before a tournament, Solomon asked him how his game was. He replied emphatically that he was on top of his game. He was, but he said it forcefully to unnerve Alwyn psychologically! Carolissen took issue with him for expressing his condition with such gusto; Bergman's response was that having been asked, he had responded honestly. For him, such repartee was part of the game.

Bergman maintains that while some of his contemporaries may have been technically better players, mental strength combined with physical fitness is critical. 'It's all about the legs. If the legs can't get you to do the wide balls you're in trouble.' As a measure of the seriousness with which he took his tennis, he says: 'I was the fittest player on the circuit. No one was fitter than me. If the opponent didn't win the first set, he was in trouble.'

He did 200 metres and 400 metres speed training with marathon runner Mark Plaatjes, who won the Port Elizabeth marathon in 1985 and then sought political asylum in the US in 1988 because he 'didn't want [his] daughter to grow up in a country where she felt inferior'. Plaatjes

Cavan Bergman (Independent Media/African News Agency).

subsequently won the Los Angeles marathon in 1991 and, representing the US, 'was the marathon champion at the 1993 World Championships in Athletics in Stuttgart'.[18]

Bergman learned early on that he had to be analytical, strategic and tactical. Having been taught only the continental grip by Isaacs at the Progressive Club, he came to understand by trial and error that it was good only for serve and volley. He spent considerable time analysing his opponents and putting together a game plan – much as David Samaai had educated Bobat in 1969. He was also of the philosophy that 'attack is the best form of defence'. Bergman's approach paid handsome dividends.

In 1972, still only eighteen, he partnered Hira Dhiraj to win the first of his senior titles, the doubles at the Western Province Open against Trevor and Quentin Lawrence.[19] The following year, though, was lean. He lost to Hira in four sets in the Transvaal Open championships at the Newlands courts and had no success in the Cape tournaments or the national championships.[20]

In 1974, he was ranked seventh by SnALTU and vindicated his status as losing finalist in the 1974-1975 Southern African championships in Port Elizabeth to the fifteen-year-old teenage prodigy Peter Lamb, who became the youngest-ever national singles title holder and added that to his Western Province title.[21] It was a remarkable five setter: Bergman won the first two sets 5-7, 3-6, only for Lamb to fight back and win the next two sets 6-2, 6-3. In the final set, Lamb led 5-0 but Bergman levelled at 5-all, only to be vanquished 8-6. In mid-1974, he had also suffered a loss at Lamb's hands in the Coca Cola Natal Open in Durban.[22]

In 1975-1976, he was again a losing finalist when Solomon and Petersen beat him and fellow-Transvaaler Herman Abrahams in the Western Province Open doubles final. There was success, however, in the mixed doubles at the national championships: Bergman and the promising Eastern Cape player Sandra Petersen ended the Woodman and Williams run of three consecutive national mixed doubles titles.[23]

The national title that eluded him for many years was finally made his in 1976-1977 at the age of 22. At the De Beers Country Club in Kimberley, he ended the Western Cape domination of the national title when he thrashed Solomon, who was appearing in his fifth singles final since the 1971 tour and was three-time champion, 6-1, 6-2, 6-0.[24] This was to be the beginning of the Bergman domination of the national singles title. He retained his title the following two years in Pretoria and Cape Town respectively, in 1977-1978 defeating Solomon again 6-3, 6-0, 5-7, 6-4 and the next year beating an up-and-coming Raymond Anthony 7-6, 7-5, 6-3.

Solomon had approached him to become his doubles partner and in 1977-1978 the pair won the national title, Bergman's first, when they defeated Glenn Samaai and Raymond Anthony 6-3, 6-3, 6-2.[25] This was to be the first of his remarkable trebles, after he also won the mixed doubles with the rising star Charmaine Carolissen. There was a repeat of the treble of the national singles, doubles and mixed doubles titles in 1978-1979. It was noted that 'Cavan Bergman has established himself as the best tennis player in South Africa, completing the triple in the second successive year' in a context of limited playing opportunities and strong opposition in Transvaal.[26] Bergman was described as 'fit and immovable', and it was reported that 'Cavan Bergman's unrelenting pressure and determination to win again came to the fore ... Bergman depends a lot on his service to win games for him ... but his unyielding determination is even more powerful and it is this which eventually gave him the title again.'[27]

In so far as provincial titles are concerned, in 1978 Bergman won the Western Province title, the first of three that he would win in succession. The following year he retained this title, defeating Oscar Woodman's younger brother, Russell, 7-6, 6-3. It was observed that 'Cavan Bergman isn't as good as he was a year ago. He's even better than that.' He won with 'tireless effort' and 'at times near perfection' and was likened to a 'tennis machine'. Bergman again defeated Woodman in 1980 6-0, 7-5. In 1980, too, he reached the Boland Open final, but rain washed out his match against Petersen.[28]

During the late 1970s and early 1980s there were numerous other provincial singles, doubles and mixed doubles titles. Bergman won the Natal Open singles title three years in a row and five times until 1987, when Hussein Mahomedy defeated him. There were many mixed doubles victories with Charmaine Carolissen and doubles triumphs with either Alwyn Solomon or Raymond Anthony after 1978.[29] At the Western Province Open, there were a handful of trebles in the late 1970s and early 1980s.

The early 1980s were, however, barren years in so far as the prized national singles title was concerned. In 1979-1980 Bergman was denied a fourth straight national singles title when he lost in the first TASA Open in Benoni to Winston Petersen; the only match he lost in four years! As with Lamb five years previously, he won the first two sets only to lose in five sets.[30] However, he won the doubles title with Solomon and the mixed doubles title with Charmaine Carolissen.[31] There was defeat again in 1980-1981 in Port Elizabeth, when Natal's Hassan Mahomedy beat Bergman, the first player from Natal to win a national title in decades under the SnALTU and TASA. Consolation came in the form of the doubles title being retained with a new partner Raymond Anthony and the mixed doubles title with Charmaine Carolissen.[32]

In 1981-1982 Bergman did not feature in the national singles final for the first time in six consecutive years, when there was a semi-final defeat to doubles partner Raymond Anthony who won his first national title. Again, Bergman had to settle for national doubles victories, retaining the doubles with Anthony and the mixed doubles with Charmaine Carolissen.[33] There was disappointment also in 1982-1983. Anthony retained his national singles title by defeating Bergman in the final, despite the latter playing great tennis. Anthony, however, reportedly 'suddenly turned on the power'.[34] Bergman, though, once more successfully defended his doubles title with Anthony and the mixed doubles title with Carolissen.

Four years of disappointment eventually ended in Gqeberha (Port Elizabeth) in 1983-1984 when Bergman denied Raymond Anthony a third consecutive national singles title by defeating him in five sets.[35] It was also the third of his national trebles, as he won the doubles with Anthony and the mixed doubles with Carolissen. Anthony blamed the infamous Gqeberha wind, saying that 'the wind had me beaten. I could not control my play enough to beat Cavan'. The 'Port Elizabeth gale certainly wreaked havoc... as it howled across the court, making it unpleasant for spectators and even worse for the players'. There was an especially poignant dimension to Bergman's victory. Six months previously he 'was told he would never play tennis again. But he did not listen, transferred his account from his doctor to the gym instead and last week he proved medical science wrong when he won the [1983] singles title at the Tennis Association of South Africa McIver National Championships.'[36] Bergman commented that 'I don't do road work as that is bad for my knees. But I do a lot of work in the gym.' He recounted:

> I was devastated when I had operations on both knees, and the doctor made it clear to me that my knees would never be the same again. I am more happy about winning it after being told firstly that I will never play tennis again and secondly that I have proved wrong the critics who labelled me as being all washed up.[37]

Bergman's victory meant that the national men's singles trophy went to a Transvaal player for the sixth time in eight years, once to a Natal player and just once to a player from the Western Cape, the traditional hothouse of tennis stars. Over the next four years, between 1984-1985 and 1987-1988, Bergman appeared in every national singles final, winning twice – against Anthony and Marcelo Winlock – and then losing twice to Hussein Mahomedy. In 1986-1987, nineteen-year-old Mahomedy, building on his Western Province singles victory, defeated Bergman in an 'epic battle which lasted 210 minutes and went to the full five sets', the final set being won 12-10.[38]

The following year he again lost to an unstoppable Mahomedy, who won the grand slam of the Natal, Boland, Western Province and South African open titles in a single season. He was, however, no pushover: he only succumbed in Bloemfontein after a four-hour, five-set battle.[39] During this four-year period, Bergman won the doubles title every year with partner Anthony. The mixed doubles was won twice with Charmaine Carolissen with one defeat in the final while partnering Vera du Plessis in 1987-1988.

Overall, Bergman had remarkable success in the national Southern Africa Open and was undoubtedly the outstanding player of his era, which also featured other greats like Alwyn Solomon, Raymond Anthony, Winston Petersen and Hussein Mahomedy. None, however, enjoyed such consistent and sustained success as he did. The closest in success was Solomon, who between the early 1970s and early 1980s won three national singles titles and was runner-up four times; and won seven national doubles titles (three with Bergman) with just one loss.

During the sixteen-year period between his first appearance in a national final in 1974-1975 and 1989-1990 Bergman appeared in thirteen singles finals, winning six times, twice in three consecutive years 1976-1977 and 1978-1979 and 1983-1984 and 1985-1986, and losing seven times.[40] There were fourteen doubles finals appearances, with twelve victories, eleven in consecutive years between 1977-1978 and 1987-1988, with just two losses. Eight titles were won with Raymond Anthony, three with Alwyn Solomon and one with Hussein Mahomedy. There were also eleven mixed doubles finals, with at least nine triumphs, the trophy being shared once because of inclement weather, and one loss. Charmaine Carolissen was his partner in eight triumphs and Sandra Petersen once. There were also a remarkable five trebles, three in consecutive years, when he won the national singles, doubles and mixed doubles titles, the matches all being played on a single day.

In the mid-1970s, Owen Williams, a former South African tennis player, entrepreneurial tournament director and prominent tennis official connected with the racist white union and committed to keeping South African tennis within international competition approached Bergman. Williams indicated that Gary Player wished to sponsor Bergman to the tune of R100 000 and that facilities and coaching would be available for him at Ellis Park. Of course, Bergman would have to give up playing non-racial tennis under SnALTU and move over to a club linked to the African union that was affiliated to SALTU as a subordinate member. It struck Bergman that were he tempted to pursue Williams' overture, one of his problems would be getting from Bosmont, a coloured township, to Ellis Park, a white township, as the two areas were not well-connected by public transport. This practical matter further brought home to him the iniquities of apartheid and heightened his political awareness.

In 1979, he bravely resigned from the Chamber of Mines, cashed in his benefits and at his own expense travelled to Virginia to attend a United States Professional Tennis Registry coaching course. He also attended the US Open at Flushing Meadows. At that time, he was the only qualified

Cavan Bergman
(Independent Media/
African News Agency).

tennis coach in the newly established TASA. He initiated coaching within TASA and in 1987 'tennis coaching entered a new dimension when TASA held its first training course for coaches . . . under the direction of three of its most experienced coaches', including Bergman. Some '36 trainee coaches attended the first course' with plans to run courses annually.[41]

In 1984, Bergman was TASA Sportsperson of the year. The 1984 SACOS Sportsperson of the Year function brochure observed:

Cavan has been one of our most consistent champions for more than a decade. During that period he has won titles at provincial and national levels. He is the 1984 triple national champion. Despite the lack of regular top-class competition throughout the season he has maintained a consistently high standard of play by assiduously applying himself to improve his game and correct any shortcomings. None of the top players in our code at present has been able to maintain such a high standard for so long.[42]

It was noted that when there were moves in the Southern Transvaal, to which Bergman belonged, to join the racist sport establishment 'despite threats and victimisation he was one of the leaders who sought to keep Southern Transvaal within the non-racial ranks. He fought hard, though unsuccessfully, to serve the non-racial cause. He never wavered and today he is still the respected member of TASA and the non-racial fraternity that he has always been.' There was recognition that Bergman 'at his own expense, qualified as a tennis coach in the United States. Because of a lack of finance he could not be employed as a full-time coach. Yet, he remained true and loyal to the non-racial fraternity.'[43]

Around 1990, through the efforts of SANROC, he and David Samaai spent time in the UK to enhance their coaching expertise. Duncan Crowie, the well-known Cape soccer star and later coach, travelled with him to the UK to attend training in soccer coaching. Bergman undertook the Lawn Tennis Association's course at different levels of coaching. In London, they were invited to a meal at the home of Sam Ramsamy, who emphasised the need to coach and develop tennis in African townships. Although willing to do so, he met with strong opposition from the TASA leadership and was prohibited from doing so because many clubs in African townships continued to associate with the white SALTU. He did,

Cavan Bergman's Sport Science certificate was awarded in 2000.

Cavan Bergman receiving one of his many trophies (Independent Media/African News Agency).

however, find ways of connecting with clubs in Soweto, Meadowlands, Pimville, Atteridgeville and elsewhere.

In 1993, at the age of 39 he began to play over-35 tennis tournaments – a rather late start because of the tennis set-up under apartheid. He was hugely successful, achieving number one ranking in South Africa under a unified national tennis body after just a few tournaments. He represented South Africa in the world veteran championships in Barcelona, held a year after the city hosted the 1992 Olympics, and also played in Turkey.

Unification brought with it numerous challenges at the personal and social levels, such as the racism and condescending behaviour of some white players, coaches and administrators who assumed that they alone possessed knowledge, expertise and experience on tennis matters and demonstrated little or no or respect for people like Bergman. He had to confront various indignities and constantly prove himself and his knowledge, expertise and abilities in the face of white arrogance, notions of superiority and disrespect. It was, of course, infuriating and trying.

He recalls a white woman who ran tournaments. Ronnie van t'Hof his doubles partner and a former chair of seniors tennis advised her to seed Bergman otherwise it would be both unfair on him and others. Her attitude was to question whether Bergman could really play tennis and she refused to seed him. On one occasion he was watching the world doubles championships at midnight on a Friday at the Standard Bank arena at Wanderers when an official sauntered over to him and informed Bergman that he had entered him in a qualifying event for the South African Open the next day and that he was scheduled to play at 9 am. He was taken aback at being informed at such a late hour, but went along and played against someone who is today a prominent TSA official. His opponent quipped to his family that the match would not take long. It did not; Bergman beat him easily. In one tournament, unseeded, he played a well-known white player in the final. His opponent threw in the towel, commenting that he was thankful that he did not previously have to play against non-racial TASA players. When officials from the old SALTU ranks heard about his victory, he was more readily accommodated at the table. Of course, he had to prove himself; they assumed that their expertise was self-evident and they did not have to.

The transition to democracy in the early 1990s exposed Bergman to the coaching set-up for white South Africans. He discovered that many white coaches had limited coaching knowledge and used a cobbled-together manual. It also brought new opportunities for Bergman and he became involved at the higher echelons of the tennis establishment. He attended the coaching courses of the International Tennis Federation (ITF) that were held in Pretoria for the Africa region and acquired various coaching certificates. He is a licenced professional coach acknowledged as having his qualifications 'achieved in accordance with syllabus and conditions approved by the ITF'.[44]

Bergman was a key representative of South Africa in tennis coaching. In 2006, he was sent to Australia to attend a tennis coaching conference in Melbourne. He used the opportunity to attend the Australian Open, when first seed Roger Federer defeated unseeded Marcos Baghdatis, the first Cypriot to participate in a Grand Slam final, 5-7, 7-5, 6-0, 6-2.[45] He travelled to Thailand and various other places for coaching conferences. In Bangkok, he participated in a competition on feeding balls as a test of adeptness in coaching and won it (this activity involves throwing balls accurately and consistently to players being coached in a manner that allows them to execute a particular tennis stroke, such as a topspin backhand or a flat forehand). Belgian players like Kim Clijsters and Justine Henin were coming to the fore and he attended a training course in Belgium through an exchange programme between South Africa and Belgium.

He travelled around the country to share information with coaches on developments in world coaching. He was sometimes treated rather disdainfully by white coaches. Their attitude was who are you? He found himself having to emphasise that they did not need to change their coaching approach if they did not wish to; it was entirely up to them whether they wished to hold fast to old and outmoded coaching methods or wanted to learn about and embrace new developments in coaching internationally.

He became a national selector and a national coach and travelled abroad with top juniors for a decade after unification, from the early 1990s to the early 2000s. As part of qualification for the Roland Garros junior championships, many countries sent their top juniors to play in Italian junior championships and on the European junior tour. South Africa sent three of its top boys and girls in the under-14 and under-16 categories. Bergman accompanied them to various places, including Turin, Milan and Vienna. Once the juniors were settled in for the night, the coaches converged at a pub, shared information and sought to learn from each other. On the junior tour, he rubbed shoulders with eventual Grand Slam winners like Kim Clijsters. He coached Jessica Steck[46] from Bloemfontein, who used to defeat Amélie Mauresmo – later junior French Open and Wimbledon women's singles winner, 1996 junior world champion and 2006 Grand Slam senior titles winner – in tournaments.[47]

In around 2000, Bergman became president of the South African Tennis Coaching Association. He thinks this was passed on to him because someone knew that TSA was seeking to bring the association under its auspices. He saw it as a welcome opportunity to change the approach to coaching. With his executive, he introduced the ITF approach to coaching, which is still used today. There were no funds for research and development activities locally and he considered that there 'was no need to reinvent the wheel' as the ITF approach made good sense. The ITF provided a range of coaching services, which were introduced in 2000 and are still used today. The TSA website notes that its Coaches Education Training Programme is 'based on the ... ITF ... courses syllabi and tutor contact hours'.[48]

In 1995, through the efforts of the former UWC academic Denver Hendricks, who was a senior official in the Department of Sport and Recreation during the tenure of minister Steve Tshwete, Bergman became the assistant Davis Cup coach of the South African team. Some may view this as window dressing, but it was a great opportunity for Bergman to further develop his expertise and experience.

Bergman recalls an occasion when Kevin Curren requested him to conduct a scheduled television interview. To his shock, a white team member brushed past him and undertook the interview. He complained to the TSA head that he found that conduct egregious – it was, indeed, an especially callous display of arrogance associated with whiteness. Placing his hand on Bergman's shoulder, the head remarked 'My boy, you don't have to worry about it.' A furious Bergman retorted, 'Who is your "boy"?' The head's response was, 'That's the way we talk. You are over-reacting!' This incident exemplifies the appalling arrogance and insensitivity that black South Africans have at times confronted post-1994. Bergman's view on transformation in tennis was noted earlier: he agrees that there has been limited transformation, recognition for non-racial tennis players and restitution.[49]

Whiteness is both an individual and institutional problem. Sara Ahmed argues that to 'talk about whiteness as an institutional problem', to 'describe institutions as being white' is 'to point to how institutional spaces are shaped by the proximity of some bodies and not others'. In such spaces, 'white bodies become somatic norms ... Whiteness is invisible and unmarked ... the absent center against which others appear as points of deviation'; a 'habit insofar as it tends to go unnoticed'. But, of course, it 'is only invisible to those who inhabit it or those who get so used to its inhabitance that they learn not to see it'.[50] A deeply embedded culture of whiteness in South Africa is yet to yield to substantive respect for and affirmation of difference, valuing of others and the creation of inclusive cultures. It is also a major impediment to fundamental change.

Having begun coaching in 1979, Bergman continues to coach at the Bryanston Country Club in Johannesburg. He and Janice divorced some years ago and today he lives in Four Ways with his daughter Carmen Roxane Bergman Ally. His son, Jokaim Bergman, born in 1990, is a baseball catcher who began playing at the age of five. In 2016, he was part of the South African Baseball Union team that participated at the World Baseball Classic Qualifying Tournament in Australia.[51]

Notes

Notes to Introduction

1. University of the Witwatersrand Historical Papers Research Archive, AG3403 – Non-Racial Sport History Project, Transvaal, 1930s–, http://www.historicalpapers.wits.ac.za/?inventory/U/collections&c=AG3403/R/; Non-Racial Sport History Project Gauteng, 'Let the History be Told', 11 March 2021, https://www.facebook.com/1660909827469680/photos/a.1660915960802400/3071675693059746/?type=1&theater.
2. Peter Alegi, 'Beyond Master Narratives: Local Sources and Global Perspectives on Sport, Apartheid, and Liberation', *International Journal of the History of Sport* 37(7), 2020: 560, 562, 566.
3. Hein Marais, *South Africa Pushed to the Limit: The Political Economy of Change* (Cape Town: UCT Press, 2011), pp. 5–6.
4. Trevor Manuel, 'Trevor Manuel's Open Letter to Jimmy Manyi', *Independent Online*, 2 March 2011, https://www.iol.co.za/news/politics/trevor-manuels-open-letter-to-jimmy-manyi-1034606.
5. Albie Sachs, 'Foreword' in Elaine Kennedy-Dubourdieu, *Race and Inequality: World Perspectives on Affirmative Action* (Farnham: Ashgate, 2006), pp. ix, x.
6. Neville Alexander, 'Affirmative Action and the Perpetuation of Racial Identities in Post-Apartheid South Africa', *Transformation* 63, 2007, pp. 92–108.
7. Sachs, 'Foreword', p. xi.
8. The points made in this paragraph, and the following quotation from Caroline Knowles, explain why the word 'race', objectionable though it might be especially in view of its apartheid connotations, is not given in quotation marks throughout this book. Their frequency would be irritating for the reader.
9. Caroline Knowles, *Race and Social Analysis* (London: Sage, 2003), pp. 29–30, emphasis in original, cited by Ashwin Desai, *Wentworth: The Beautiful Game and the Making of Place* (Pietermaritzburg: University of KwaZulu-Natal Press, 2019), p. 4.

Notes to Chapter 1: Fifty-Two Years Ago

1. My thanks to Samiena Amien for mentioning this fact to me.
2. Margalit Fox, 'Katherine Johnson Dies at 101: Mathematician Broke Barriers at NASA', *New York Times*, 24 February 2020, https://www.nytimes.com/2020/02/24/science/katherine-johnson-dead.html.
3. Tyina Steptoe, '"What's Going On" at 50 – Marvin Gaye's Motown Classic is as Relevant Today as it was in 1971', *The Conversation*, 18 May 2021.
4. Leigh Carriage, 'John Lennon's Imagine at 50: A Deceptively Simple Ballad, a Lasting Emblem of Hope', *The Conversation*, 8 September 2021.
5. 'Jim Morrison', https://en.wikipedia.org/wiki/Jim_Morrison#:~:text=He%20died%20unexpectedly%20in%20Paris,they%20split%20up%20in%201973.
6. Julian Coman, 'John Rawls: Can Liberalism's Great Philosopher Come to the West's Rescue Again?', *Guardian*, 20 December 2020, https://www.theguardian.com/inequality/2020/dec/20/john-rawls-can-liberalisms-great-philosopher-come-to-the-wests-rescue-again.
7. 'White South Africans', https://en.wikipedia.org/wiki/White_South_Africans; Saleem Badat, *Black Student Politics, Higher Education and Apartheid: From SASO to SANSCO, 1968–1990* (Pretoria: HSRC, 1999), pp. 59–60; Saleem Badat, 'SASO and Black Consciousness, and the Shift to Congress Politics' in *Students Must Rise: Youth Struggle in South Africa Before and Beyond Soweto '76*, edited by Anne Heffernan and Noor Nieftagodien (Johannesburg: Wits University Press, 2016), p. 98; Saleem Badat, *The Forgotten People: Political Banishment under Apartheid* (Johannesburg: Jacana Media, 2012), p. 159.
8. United Nations Centre Against Apartheid, *Racial Discrimination in South African Sport: Notes and Documents* (New York: UN Centre Against Apartheid, 1980), pp. 29–30.
9. University of the Witwatersrand Historical Papers Research Archive, AG3403 – Non-Racial Sports History Project, Transvaal, 1930s–; Douglas Booth, *The Race Game: Sport and Politics in South Africa* (London: Frank Cass, 1998).
10. Douglas Booth, 'The South African Council on Sport and the Political Antinomies of the Sports Boycott', *Journal of Southern African Studies* 23(1), 1997: 51, 56; Alegi, 'Beyond Master Narratives': 567.
11. Philani Nongogo, 'The Struggles to Deracialise South African Sport: A Historical Overview' (D.Phil. thesis, University of Pretoria, 2015); Selvan Naidoo, 'Gary Player Receives Presidential Award from Trump Despite his Apartheid Role', 1860 Heritage Centre, 7 January 2021, https://www.facebook.com/1860heritagecentre/posts/1792934877547194?__tn__=K-R.

Notes to Chapter 2: Sport and Social Justice

1. Mandela on enacting the Promotion of National Unity and Reconciliation Act, 19 July 1995, cited in George Bizos, *No One to Blame? In Pursuit of Justice in South Africa* (Cape Town: David Philip Publishers, 1998), p. 1.
2. 'Archbishop Oscar Romero', https://onlineministries.creighton.edu/CollaborativeMinistry/Martyrs/Romero/index.html.
3. Jody Kollapen, 'NEPAD's Human Rights Challenge', *Connecting* February-April 2003, p. 26.
4. Murray Leibbrandt, 'The Human Tragedy of South Africa's Inequality', *New Frame*, 22 May 2021, https://www.newframe.com/the-human-tragedy-of-south-africas-inequality/.
5. Leibbrandt, 'The Human Tragedy of South Africa's Inequality'.
6. Leibbrandt, 'The Human Tragedy of South Africa's Inequality'.
7. Imraan Valodia, 'The Link between Inequality and Power', *New Frame*, 18 May 2021, https://www.newframe.com/the-link-between-inequality-and-power/.
8. 'A New Economy Means Undoing the Old One', *New Frame*, 17 May 2021, https://www.newframe.com/a-new-economy-means-undoing-the-old-one/.
9. Leibbrandt, 'The Human Tragedy of South Africa's Inequality'.
10. Leibbrandt, 'The Human Tragedy of South Africa's Inequality'.
11. Valodia, 'The Link between Inequality and Power'.
12. Valodia, 'The Link between Inequality and Power', quoting Darrick Hamilton, 'Neoliberalism and Race', *Democracy* 53, 2019, https://democracyjournal.org/magazine/53/neoliberalism-and-race/.
13. Linda Chisholm, 'Introduction' in *Changing Class: Education and Social Change in Post-Apartheid South Africa*, edited by Linda Chisholm (Pretoria: HSRC Press, 2004), p. 12.
14. 'The Freedom Charter', https://www.sahistory.org.za/archive/freedom-charter-original-document-scan; University of the Witwatersrand Historical Papers Research Archive, http://www.historicalpapers.wits.ac.za/inventories/inv_pdfo/AD1137/AD1137-Ea6-1-001-jpeg.pdf.
15. Ashwin Desai and Dhevarsha Ramjettan, 'Sport for All? Exploring the Boundaries of Sport and Citizenship in "Liberated" South Africa' in *Racial Redress and Citizenship in South Africa*, edited by Adam Habib and Kristina Bentley (Cape Town: HSRC Press, 2008); Farieda Khan, 'Anyone for Tennis? Conversations with Black Women Involved in Tennis During the Apartheid Era', *Agenda* 85, 2010: 81; Christopher Mwirigi, 'Transformation and Affirmative Action in South African Sport' (LLM thesis, University of Pretoria, 2010).
16. William Faulkner, *Requiem for a Nun* (New York: Random House, 1951), https://en.wikipedia.org/wiki/Requiem_for_a_Nun.

17. Milan Kundera, *The Book of Laughter and Forgetting*, cited in Neville Alexander, *An Ordinary Country: Issues in the Transition from Apartheid to Democracy in South Africa* (Pietermaritzburg: University of Natal Press, 2002), p. 114.
18. Primo Levi, *If This Is a Man*, cited in Alexander, *An Ordinary Country*, p. 13.
19. Cited in Terry Bell with Dumisa Ntsebeza, *Unfinished Business: South Africa, Apartheid and Truth* (Cape Town: RedWorks, 2001), p. 288.
20. Charmaine Li, 'Confronting History: James Baldwin', *Kinfolk*, https://www.kinfolk.com/confronting-history-james-baldwin/.
21. Eduardo Galeano, *The Book of Embraces* (London: W.W. Norton, 1992), p. 123, http://en.wikipedia.org/wiki/Eduardo_Galeano.
22. Alexander, *An Ordinary Country*, pp. 117–18.

Notes to Chapter 3: Reclaiming the Narrative on Tennis History

1. André Odendaal, 'Reflections on Writing a Post-Colonial History of a Colonial Game' in *Exploring Decolonising Themes in SA Sport History: Issues and Challenges*, edited by Francois J. Cleophas (Stellenbosch: Sun Press, 2018), p. 1.
2. Odendaal, 'Reflections on Writing a Post-Colonial History, p. 1.
3. Odendaal, 'Reflections on Writing a Post-Colonial History, p. 1.
4. Odendaal, 'Reflections on Writing a Post-Colonial History, pp. 1–2.
5. Odendaal, 'Reflections on Writing a Post-Colonial History, p. 3.
6. KZN Tennis Association, 'History of KZN Tennis', https://www.filepicker.io/api/file/80SLoFsUS9iyZ9PbDBv6.
7. KZN Tennis Association, 'Aceing Apartheid Tennis: A Tale of Dedication, Resilience and Big-Hearted Spirit', https://www.filepicker.io/api/file/4s3c K8RoSoy6V0zaWcRJ.
8. I am thankful to Goolam Vahed for this point.
9. KZN Tennis Association, 'History of KZN Tennis'.
10. Odendaal, 'Reflections on Writing a Post-Colonial History', p. 4.
11. André Odendaal, 'Sport and Liberation: The Unfinished Business of the Past' in *Sport and Liberation in South Africa: Reflections and Suggestions*, edited by Cornelius Thomas (Alice: University of Fort Hare Press, 2006), p. 28.
12. Khan, 'Anyone for Tennis?': 78.
13. Peter Alegi, 'Black Sport Matters: A History of Sporting Subalterns' Quest for Social Justice in Africa', Keynote address, Sports Africa Conference, University of the Free State, Bloemfontein, April 2017, p. 5, citing Brian Willan, '"One of the Most Gentlemanly Players that Ever Donned a Jersey":

The English Rugby Career of Richard Msimang (1907–1912)', *Quarterly Bulletin of the National Library of South Africa* 66(3), 2012: 15.
14. Khan, 'Anyone for Tennis?': 80.
15. Odendaal, 'Sport and Liberation', p. 29.
16. Goolam Vahed, 'Control of African Leisure Time in Durban in the 1930s', *Journal of Natal and Zulu History* 18, 1998: 67, 72.
17. 'Albert Lutuli: The Facts', https://www.nobelprize.org/prizes/peace/1960/lutuli/facts/; Peter Alegi, 'Sport, Race, and Liberation Before Apartheid: A Preliminary Study of Albert Luthuli, 1920s–1950s', http://www.sahistory.org.za/archive/sport-race-and-liberation-apartheid-dr-peter-alegi.
18. Alegi, 'Black Sport Matters'.
19. Alegi, 'Sport, Race, and Liberation Before Apartheid'.
20. Vahed, 'Control of African Leisure Time': 111, 112, 117.
21. Quoted in Vahed, 'Control of African Leisure Time': 82.
22. Quoted in Vahed, 'Control of African Leisure Time': 117.
23. Vahed, 'Control of African Leisure Time': 85, 111, 117–18.
24. Quoted in Vahed, 'Control of African Leisure Time': 118.
25. Vahed, 'Control of African Leisure Time': 118.
26. Vahed, 'Control of African Leisure Time': 121.
27. Vahed, 'Control of African Leisure Time': 121.
28. Odendaal, 'Reflections on Writing a Post-Colonial History', pp. 4–5.
29. Odendaal, 'Reflections on Writing a Post-Colonial History', p. 6.
30. Odendaal, 'Reflections on Writing a Post-Colonial History', p. 6.
31. Alegi, 'Beyond Master Narratives': 560.
32. Alegi, 'Beyond Master Narratives': 560.
33. Odendaal, 'Sport and Liberation', pp. 12–13, 35.
34. Alegi, 'Beyond Master Narratives': 571.
35. Alegi, 'Beyond Master Narratives': 560.
36. Alegi, 'Beyond Master Narratives': 560, citing Albert Fu and Martin Murray, 'Sentimentalizing Racial Reconciliation in the "New South Africa": Cinematic Representation of the 1995 Rugby World Cup', *Black Camera* 9(1), 2017: 22–46.
37. Alegi, 'Beyond Master Narratives': 560–1, citing Jacob Dlamini, *Native Nostalgia* (Johannesburg: Jacana Media, 2009), p. 156.
38. Odendaal, 'Sport and Liberation', pp. 12–13, 34.
39. Odendaal, 'Sport and Liberation', pp. 13, 15.
40. Philip Abrams, *Historical Sociology* (New York: Cornell University Press, 1982), pp. 3, 8.
41. Francis F. Piven and Richard A. Cloward, *Poor People's Movements: Why they Succeed, How they Fail* (New York: Vintage Books, 1979), p. xiii.

42. Lesley le Grange, 'Decolonising Sport: Some Thoughts' in *Exploring Decolonising Themes in SA Sport History: Issues and Challenges*, edited by Francois J. Cleophas (Stellenbosch: Sun Press, 2018), p. 16. My thanks to Peter Alegi for pointing out some exceptions: Benedict Carton and Robert Morrell, 'Zulu Masculinities, Warrior Culture and Stick Fighting: Reassessing Male Violence and Virtue in South Africa', *Journal of Southern African Studies* 38(1), 2012: 31–53; and Peter Alegi, *Laduma!: Soccer, Politics, and Society in South Africa* (Pietermaritzburg: University of KwaZulu-Natal Press, 2004), chapter 1.
43. Le Grange, 'Decolonising Sport', p. 17.
44. Arnab Sen, 'Independence Day Special: Golden Moments of Indian Sports', *Hindustan Times*, 14 August 2018, https://www.hindustantimes.com/other-sports/independence-day-special-golden-moments-of-indian-sports-part-one/story-Z3qxvsRCsY1AzomSZ0iQ0L.html.
45. Le Grange, 'Decolonising Sport', p. 17.
46. Le Grange, 'Decolonising Sport', p. 17.
47. Le Grange, 'Decolonising Sport', pp. 18–19.
48. Ashwin Desai, *The Race to Transform: Sport in Post-Apartheid South Africa* (Pretoria: HSRC Press, 2010). For a KwaZulu-Natal study of a contemporary grassroots initiative that emerges out of this historical context and social concerns, see Peter Alegi and Liz Timbs, 'The Izichwe Football Club: Youth, Sport and Masculinity in Pietermaritzburg, South Africa', *Journal of Southern African Studies* 45(5), 2019: 963–80.

Notes to Chapter 4: From Colonialism to Apartheid in Sport
1. Michael Burawoy, *The Politics of Production: Factory Regimes under Capitalism and Socialism* (London: Verso, 1985), p. 253.
2. Harold Wolpe, *Race, Class and the Apartheid State* (London: UNESCO/ James Currey, 1988), p. 23.
3. Wolpe, *Race, Class and the Apartheid State*, p. 9.
4. Abrams, *Historical Sociology*, p. xv.
5. United Nations Centre Against Apartheid, *Racial Discrimination in South African Sport*, p. 3.
6. Deborah Posel, 'What's in a Name? Racial Categorisations under Apartheid and their Afterlife', *Transformation* 47, 2001: 52.
7. Posel, 'What's in a Name?': 54.
8. Keith Breckenridge, 'The Book of Life: The South African Population Register and the Invention of Racial Descent, 1950–1980', *Kronos* 40(1), 2014: 225, 226.

9. Douglas Booth, 'Playing the Game? Desegregating South African Sport' (Development Studies Unit, Centre for Applied Social Sciences, Natal University, Durban, 1988; Working Paper 18), pp. 1-2.
10. Biographies of Sewgolum include Barry Cohen, *Let Me Play* (Cape Town: New Voices Publishing, 2020); Maxine Case, *Papwa: Golf's Lost Legend* (Johannesburg: Kwela, 2015); and Christopher Nicholson, *Papwa Sewgolum: From Pariah to Legend* (Johannesburg: Wits University Press, 2005). Videos that feature Sewgolum include Cohen's 'Let me Play: The Sewshanker "Papwa" Sewgolum Story', https://www.youtube.com/watch?v=cpBrfb2h90g; 'Discussion: Remembering the Life of SA's Golfer Sewsunker "Papwa" Sewgolum', https://www.youtube.com/watch?v=eZnw6SiemYs; and 'Papwa: Golf's Untold Story', https://www.youtube.com/watch?v=IZcxlrShtJg.
11. 'Sewsunker "Papwa" Sewgolum', https://www.sahistory.org.za/people/sewsunker-papwa-sewgolum.
12. John Barton, 'Golf in the Days of Black & White', *Golf Digest*, 2 October 2007, https://www.golfdigest.com/story/papwa.
13. Naidoo, 'Gary Player Receives Presidential Award from Trump'.
14. Naidoo, 'Gary Player Receives Presidential Award from Trump'.
15. Naidoo, 'Gary Player Receives Presidential Award from Trump'.
16. Selvan Naidoo, 'A Talent Apartheid Tragically Denied: Honouring Papwa's Memory', *Mercury*, 17 April 2018, https://www.iol.co.za/mercury/a-talent-apartheid-tragically-denied-honouring-papwas-memory-14489208.
17. Naidoo, 'A Talent Apartheid Tragically Denied'.
18. Barton, 'Golf in the Days of Black & White'.
19. Naidoo, 'Gary Player Receives Presidential Award from Trump', citing Gary Player, *Grand Slam Golf* (London: Cassell, 1966). See also Peter Hain and André Odendaal, *Pitch Battles: Sport, Racism and Resistance* (London: Rowman & Littlefield, 2021) for information on other aspects of Player's role in supporting apartheid sport in the 1970s.
20. Peter Alegi points out that there was no law prohibiting integrated sport – except boxing and wrestling – and that is why the National Party government released its first sports policy statement in June 1956, the so-called Dönges Declaration (personal communication, 11 May 2021).
21. Muriel Horrell, *Laws Affecting Race Relations in South Africa, 1948-1976* (Johannesburg: South African Institute of Race Relations, 1978).
22. Booth, 'The South African Council on Sport': 55.
23. United Nations Centre Against Apartheid, *Racial Discrimination in South African Sport*, p. 11.
24. United Nations Centre Against Apartheid, *Racial Discrimination in South African Sport*, p. 11.

25. South Africa, *House of Assembly Debates* 11 April 1967, col. 3960; Booth, *The Race Game*, p. 3.
26. Booth, *The Race Game*, p. 3.
27. South Africa, *House of Assembly Debates* 11 April 1967, cols 3960, 3961.
28. 'So. Africa Defends Policy of Apartheid', *New York Times*, 2 June 1970, https://www.nytimes.com/1970/06/02/archives/so-africa-defends-policy-of-apartheid.html.
29. John Roberts, 'Tennis: Firebrands, Flour Bombs and Frew', *Independent*, 21 September 1999, https://www.independent.co.uk/sport/tennis-firebrands-flour-bombs-and-frew-1121083.html. Alegi notes that 'in 1965 there had been similar tennis protests in the UK' (personal communication, 2021).
30. Robin Kelley, 'The Role of the International Sports Boycott in the Liberation of South Africa', *Ufahamu* 13(2-3), 1984: 29.
31. South Africa, *House of Assembly Debates* 22 April 1971, cols 5050-1.
32. South Africa, *House of Assembly Debates* 25 May 1973, col. 7559.
33. Koornhof quoting Vorster, cited in Booth, *The Race Game*, p. 4; South Africa, *House of Assembly Debates* 25 May 1973, col. 7559.
34. South Africa, *House of Assembly Debates* 25 May 1973, cols 7783-4; Juan Klee, 'Multinational Sport Participation Replaces Apartheid Sport in South Africa, 1967-1978: The Role of BJ Vorster and PGJ Koornhof', *New Contree* 64, 2012: 166.
35. *Survey of Race Relations* 1972: 416.
36. *Survey of Race Relations* 1972: 416; Booth, *The Race Game*, p. 101, cited in Ashwin Desai, *Wentworth: The Beautiful Game and the Making of Place* (Pietermaritzburg: University of KwaZulu-Natal Press, 2019), p. 21.
37. Booth, *The Race Game*, p. 4; South Africa, *House of Assembly Debates* 25 May 1973, col. 7563.
38. Roger Southall, *South Africa's Transkei: The Political Economy of an 'Independent Bantustan'* (New York: Monthly Review Press, 1983), p. 46.
39. Gustav Venter, 'Experimental Tactics on an Uneven Playing Field: Multinational Football and the Apartheid Project during the 1970s', *International Journal of the History of Sport* 36(1), 2019: 85.
40. Gustav Venter, 'White's Gambit in the Middle Game: Chess, Apartheid, and South Africa's Sporting Isolation in the 1970s', *International Journal of the History of Sport* 37(7), 2020: 2-3.
41. Venter, 'Experimental Tactics on an Uneven Playing Field': 84.
42. Venter, 'Experimental Tactics on an Uneven Playing Field': 84.
43. Booth, 'The South African Council on Sport': 55-6.
44. Booth, 'The South African Council on Sport': 55, 56.

45. Venter, 'White's Gambit in the Middle Game': 2.
46. Venter, 'White's Gambit in the Middle Game': 2.
47. Booth, 'The South African Council on Sport': 56, citing Committee of Non-Racial Organisations, 'Secretarial Report', pp. 37–8.
48. Alegi, 'Beyond Master Narratives': 567.
49. International Olympic Committee, *Olympic Rules and Regulations* (Lausanne: IOC, 1971), p. 11.
50. Booth, 'The South African Council on Sport': 53, citing Rudolf Opperman and Lappe Laubscher, *Africa's First Olympians: The Story of the Olympic Movement in South Africa 1907–1987* (Johannesburg: South African National Olympic Committee, 1987), p. 56.
51. Booth, 'The South African Council on Sport': 53.
52. Booth notes that 'like most federations athletics had a weighted voting system which, in this case, gave 37 white nations 244 votes and 99 non-white nations just 195' (Booth, 'The South African Council on Sport': 53).

Notes to Chapter 5: Tennis under Apartheid

1. 'The Sporting Sixties – Tennis', *Post*, 29 December 1969.
2. United Nations Centre Against Apartheid, *Racial Discrimination in South African Sport*, p. 26.
3. Ebrahim Osman, *I Think I Have a Story to be Told: The Life of My Days* (Durban, 2014), p. 190.
4. 'The Sporting Sixties – Tennis'.
5. Osman, *I Think I Have a Story to be Told*, p. 190.
6. B. Walley, 'Tennis Shows How to Solve Problem', *Sunday Times*, 18 April 1971.
7. 'The Tennis Link-Up', *Post*, April 1971.
8. 'The Tennis Link-Up'.
9. 'The Tennis Link-Up'.
10. Alegi, *Laduma!*.
11. Alegi, personal communication, 2021.
12. United Nations Centre Against Apartheid, *Racial Discrimination in South African Sport*, p. 27; Osman, *I Think I Have a Story to be Told*, p. 193.
13. South African Council on Sport, 'Sportsperson of the Year Award, West End, Port Elizabeth, 24 November 1984', p. 3 (Historical Papers Research Archive, University of the Witwatersrand, Johannesburg).
14. South African Council on Sport, 'Sportsperson of the Year Award', p. 3.
15. 'Dhiraj Accuses Non-Whites Who Played in Federation Cup: A Stab in the Back', *Post*, 7 May 1972.
16. 'Peter Lamb (tennis)', https://en.wikipedia.org/wiki/Peter_Lamb_(tennis).

17. Osman, *I Think I Have a Story to be Told*, p. 169.
18. Osman, *I Think I Have a Story to be Told*, p. 177.
19. The Fakir, 'An Open Letter to Our Two Most Famous Tennis Ladies', *Leader*, 14 April 1972.
20. The Fakir, 'An Open Letter'.
21. The Fakir, 'An Open Letter'.
22. Alegi, personal communication, 2021; see Christopher Merrett, *Sport, Space and Segregation: Politics and Society in Pietermaritzburg* (Pietermaritzburg: University of KwaZulu-Natal Press, 2009).
23. The Fakir, 'An Open Letter'.
24. The Fakir, 'An Open Letter'.

Notes to Chapter 6: International Collusion with Apartheid Sport

1. Nongogo, 'The Struggles to Deracialise South African Sport', p. 286.
2. Alegi, personal communication, 2021.
3. Matt Bersell, 'Sports, Race, and Politics: The Olympic Boycott of Apartheid Sport', *Western Illinois Historical Review* 8, 2017: 1.
4. Alegi, 'Black Sport Matters': p. 8.
5. United Nations Centre Against Apartheid, *Racial Discrimination in South African Sport*, p. 4.
6. United Nations Centre Against Apartheid, *Racial Discrimination in South African Sport*, p. 71.
7. See https://www.itftennis.com/en/about-us/organisation/faqs/?type=governance.
8. Alegi, personal communication, 2021.
9. 'SALTU Under Pressure from Whites – But We Won't Join, Pather Tells Reay', *Post*, 26 April 1969; 'The Sporting Sixties – Tennis'.
10. Osman, *I Think I Have a Story to be Told*, p. 218.
11. 'Overseas Tour Chance for Top Players', *Post*, 4 January 1970.
12. 'Tennis Association Spurns Affiliation Scheme', *Rand Daily Mail*, 28 April 1971.
13. Neville Grimmet, 'Geni: Manikum Nadarajan Pather', https://www.geni.com/people/Manikum-Nadarajan-Pather/6000000004246182727.
14. Krishnan Coopoosamy Pather, 'Geni: Manikum Nadarajan Pather', https://www.geni.com/people/Manikum-Nadarajan-Pather/6000000004246182727.
15. Enuga Sreenivasulu Reddy, 'A Tribute to Sam Ramsamy and Others Who Fought Apartheid Sport', https://www.sahistory.org.za/archive/tribute-sam-ramsamy-and-others-who-fought-apartheid-sport-es-reddy.

16. United Nations Centre Against Apartheid, *Racial Discrimination in South African Sport*, p. 35.
17. 'Play Ball Says P.M.: But Administrator Sees Obstacles Ahead', *Leader*, 2 April 1971.
18. 'Play Ball Says P.M.'.
19. Ashwin Desai, *Reverse Sweep: A Story of South African Cricket since Apartheid* (Johannesburg: Jacana Media, 2017), p. 16.
20. Desai, *Reverse Sweep*, p. 16.
21. Stephen Moss, cited in Desai, *Reverse Sweep*, p. 17.
22. United Nations Centre Against Apartheid, *Racial Discrimination in South African Sport*, p. 28.
23. My thanks to Peter Alegi for information on CCIRS.
24. Alegi, personal communication, 2021.
25. Chris de Broglio, 'The SANROC Story', https://onlinelaw.co.za/docs/The_SANROC_story.pdf.
26. Klee, 'Multinational Sport Participation Replaces Apartheid Sport': 160.
27. Klee, 'Multinational Sport Participation Replaces Apartheid Sport': 160, citing Richard Thompson, *Retreat from Apartheid: New Zealand's Sporting Contacts with South Africa* (London: Oxford University Press 1975), p. 6; Rob Nixon, 'Apartheid on the Run: The South African Sports Boycott', *Transition* 58, 1992: 70.
28. Alegi, personal communication, 2021.
29. Bersell, 'Sports, Race and Policy': 19.
30. Bersell, 'Sports, Race and Policy': 19, citing Richard E. Lapchick, *The Politics of Race and International Sport: The Case of South Africa* (Westport, CT: Greenwood Press, 1975).
31. Mary Corrigall, 'International Boycott of Apartheid Sport: With Special Reference to the Campaigns in Britain by the Anti-Apartheid Movement', Paper prepared for the United Nations Unit on Apartheid in 1971, https://www.sahistory.org.za/archive/international-boycott-apartheid-sport-mary-corrigall.
32. Nixon, 'Apartheid on the Run': 78.
33. Corrigall, 'International Boycott of Apartheid Sport'.
34. Corrigall, 'International Boycott of Apartheid Sport'.
35. 'Dennis Brutus', https://www.sahistory.org.za/people/dennis-brutus; Alegi, 'Beyond Master Narratives': 562.
36. Alegi, 'Black Sport Matters': p. 17, footnote 22.
37. Nixon, 'Apartheid on the Run': 77.
38. Trevor Bisseker, 'We Will Beat Czech Threat – Chalmers', *Rand Daily Mail*, 23 June 1971.

39. 'Those Whites-Only Signs are Getting Pretty Rusty: Punches that Hit Racial Sports in the Guts', *Post*, 11 July 1971.
40. 'Sporting Boycott of South Africa During the Apartheid Era', https://en.wikipedia.org/wiki/Sporting_boycott_of_South_Africa_during_the_apartheid_era.
41. 'Secret Trials: 4 "Guinea Pigs"', *Post*, 23 January 1972.
42. Farook Khan, 'Federation Cup Trials a "Farce"', *Post*, 16 January 1972.
43. Bisseker, 'We Will Beat Czech Threat'.
44. 'Those Whites-Only Signs'.
45. 'SALTU's Ruling is Silly Says Pather', *Graphic*, 12 March 1971.
46. 'Those Whites-Only Signs'.
47. 'SALTU's Ruling is Silly Says Pather'.
48. 'How the Daughter of an Ancient Race Made it out of the Australian Outback by Hitting a Tennis Ball Sweetly and Hard', *New York Times*, 29 August 1971, https://www.nytimes.com/1971/08/29/archives/how-the-daughter-of-an-ancient-race-made-it-out-of-the-australian.html; Eric Allen Hall, *Arthur Ashe: Tennis and Justice in the Civil Rights Era* (Baltimore: Johns Hopkins University Press, 2014), p. 145.
49. 'How the Daughter of an Ancient Race'.
50. 'Honorary Whites', https://en.wikipedia.org/wiki/Honorary_whites#:~:text=Honorary%20whites%20is%20a%20term,been%20treated%20as%20non%2Dwhites.
51. Soheir Morsy, 'Beyond the Honorary "White" Classification of Egyptians: Societal Identity in Historical Context' in *Race*, edited by Steven Gregory and Roger Sanjek (New Brunswick, NJ: Rutgers, 1996), pp. 175–98, quoted in Yoon Jung Park, 'White, Honorary White, or Non-White: Apartheid Era Constructions of Chinese', *Afro-Hispanic Review* 27(1), 2008: 123.
52. Jung Park, 'White, Honorary White, or Non-White': 128.
53. Eric J. Morgan, 'Black and White at Center Court: Arthur Ashe and the Confrontation of Apartheid in South Africa', *Diplomatic History* 36(5), 2012: 817.
54. Morgan, 'Black and White at Center Court': 818, 819, 835.
55. Hall, *Arthur Ashe*, pp. 143, 144.
56. Rob Skinner, 'The Moral Foundations of British Anti-Apartheid Activism, 1946–1960', *Journal of Southern African Studies* 35(2), 2009: 401.
57. Morgan, 'Black and White at Center Court': 824, citing the United Nations Centre Against Apartheid, 'Response of Artists and Entertainers to Apartheid: A Brief Review', August 1988; United Nations Notes and Documents, folder: Topical—Cultural Activities and Cultural Boycott, 1983–1992, box 30, Pan Africanist Congress of Azania United Nations

Records, National Heritage and Cultural Studies Centre, University of Fort Hare, Alice.
58. Skinner, 'The Moral Foundations of British Anti-Apartheid Activism': 411.
59. Skinner, 'The Moral Foundations of British Anti-Apartheid Activism': 413.
60. Morgan, 'Black and White at Center Court': 818.
61. Ellen Mark, 'Review of Arthur Ashe and Frank DeFord, *Arthur Ashe: Portrait in Motion*', *Africa Today* 25(1), 1978: 70, https://www.jstor.org/stable/4185753?seq=1#metadata_info_tab_contents.
62. 'SALTU's Ruling is Silly Says Pather'.
63. 'Davis Cup: Dhiraj Gets SA Banned', *Post*, 23 April 1972, 'Dhiraj Accuses Non-Whites Who Played in Federation Cup'.
64. B. Wilson, 'Davis Cup: We'll be Back in 1973 – Chalmers', *Sunday Express*, 16 April 1972.
65. 'The Sporting Sixties – Tennis'.
66. 'Dhiraj Accuses Non-Whites who Played in Federation Cup'.
67. Raymond Arsenault, *Arthur Ashe: A Life* (New York: Simon & Schuster, 2018), p. 298.
68. 'Sporting Boycott of South Africa During the Apartheid Era', https://en.wikipedia.org/wiki/Sporting_boycott_of_South_Africa_during_the_apartheid_era.
69. 'Mixed Trials to Select Davis Cup Team', *Sunday Express*, 16 January 1972.
70. 'Mixed Trials to Select Davis Cup Team'.
71. International Olympic Committee, *Olympic Charter* (Lausanne: IOC, 2020), pp. 11, 12.

Notes to Chapter 7: The Historic 1971 Tour

1. United Nations Centre Against Apartheid, *Racial Discrimination in South African Sport*, p. 28.
2. Hoosen Bobat (HB) interview.
3. Booth, 'The South African Council on Sport': 54, citing the Committee of Non-Racial Organisations, 'Secretarial Report', p. 8.
4. Farook Khan, 'Hopes for Mixed Sport Fade: Gloom Sets in as SB Quiz Pather on Talks', *Post*, 17 January 1971.
5. 'Tennis Men also Slam SB Probe of Pather', *Graphic*, 8 February 1971.
6. 'Overseas Tour Chance for Top Players'.
7. Farook Khan, 'Jasmat for U.S – and World's Richest Tourney', *Post*, 18 January 1970.
8. Ebrahim Osman, 'It's Been a Great Year for Juniors', *Leader*, 25 December 1970.

9. 'Non-White Tennis May Soon Break onto World Scene', *Graphic*, 26 February 1971; 'Tennis Union has Big Plans', *Leader*, 5 February 1971.
10. My thanks to Peter Alegi for raising this matter (personal communication, 2021).
11. Inflation Tool, https://www.inflationtool.com/south-african-rand/1971-to-present-value; 'Tennis Union Has Big Plans'.
12. HB interview.
13. Osman. *I Think I Have a Story to be Told*, pp. 184, 185; 'Wimbledon Here we Come!', *Leader*, 9 April 1971; 'Natal's Bobat to Campaign Overseas', *Graphic*, 8 January 1971.
14. 'Tennis Association Spurns Affiliation Scheme'.
15. Julian Coman, 'Interview – Michael Sandel: The "Populist Backlash Has Been a Revolt Against the Tyranny of Merit"', *Observer*, 6 September 2020, https://www.theguardian.com/books/2020/sep/06/michael-sandel-the-populist-backlash-has-been-a-revolt-against-the-tyranny-of-merit.
16. Alegi, personal communication, 2021.
17. Sandel, quoted in Coman, 'Interview'.
18. South African Students Organisation, 'SASO Policy Manifesto'.
19. Steve Biko, *I Write What I Like*, edited by Aelred Stubbs (London: Heinemann, 1987), p. 149.
20. 'SASO Policy Manifesto'.
21. Pandelani Nefolovhodwe, quoted in an interview in Julie Frederikse, *The Unbreakable Thread: Non-Racialism in South Africa* (Johannesburg: Ravan Press, 1990), p. 108.
22. Alegi, personal communication, 2021.
23. *Leader*, 4 June 1971.
24. 'Champs Jasmat and Brenda Grab Crown' (Parvati Soma clippings).
25. Jasmat Dhiraj Soma (JDS), interview.
26. 'The Captain Went Later', *Cape Herald*, 24 April 1971; 'Good Luck Jasmat', *Post*, 18 April 1971; *Rand Daily Mail*, 16 April 1971.
27. 'Springbok colours', https://en.wikipedia.org/wiki/Springbok_colours; David Black and John Nauright, *Rugby and the South African Nation* (Manchester: Manchester University Press, 1998); Bruce Murray and Christopher Merrett, *Caught Behind: Race and Politics in Springbok Cricket* (Pietermaritzburg: University of KwaZulu-Natal Press, 2004).
28. Alegi, personal communication, 2021.
29. Alberto Melucci, *Nomads of the Present: Social Movements and Individual Needs in Contemporary Society* (Philadelphia: Temple University Press, 1989), p. 76.
30. 'Dhiraj Squad All Set for U.K. Tennis', *Leader*, 2 April 1971.
31. Oscar Woodman (OW) and Hira Dhiraj Soma (HDS) interviews.

32. HB interview.
33. HB interview.
34. Lorna Solomon (LS) interview.
35. Farook Khan, 'Dhiraj Squad Starts Well', *Post*, 2 May 1971.
36. 'What's a "Fast Court" or a "Slow Court"?', https://tt.tennis-warehouse.com/index.php?threads/whats-a-fast-court-or-a-slow-court.244766/#:~:text=What%20makes%20a%20court%20surface,the%20court%20and%20the%20ball.&text=If%20the%20court%20is%20a,the%20ball%20and%20the%20court.
37. 'What's a "Fast Court" or a "Slow Court"?'
38. 'What Are Tennis Courts Made of? (The 11 Surfaces)', https://mytennishq.com/the-different-types-of-tennis-court-surfaces-explained/.
39. 'What Are Tennis Courts Made of?'
40. JDS interview.
41. HDS interview.
42. HB interview.
43. JDS interview.
44. HDS interview.
45. HB interview.
46. HB interview.
47. HB interview.
48. HB interview.
49. Cavan Bergman (CB) interview.
50. CB interview.

Notes to Chapter 8: UK Tournaments

1. Bergman beat R. Battersby 6-1, 6-4 rather than the score indicated in the article that follows (*Reading Evening Post*, 22 April 1971).
2. 'Juniors Good Start in Britain', *Leader*, 30 April 1971.
3. 'Juniors Good Start in Britain'.
4. 'Miss Goolagong Takes Tennis Final in England', *New York Times*, 2 May 1971, https://www.nytimes.com/1971/05/02/archives/miss-goolagong-takes-tennis-final-in-england.html?smid=em-share.
5. 'Evonne Goolagong Cawley Career Statistics', https://en.wikipedia.org/wiki/Evonne_Goolagong_Cawley_career_statistics.
6. '"Think Pro", Says Dhiraj', *Cape Herald*, 8 May 1971.
7. *Rand Daily Mail*, 28 April 1971.
8. Justin Dowling, 'Dhiraj Meets Bertram in the Next Round', *Star*, 28 April 1971; 'Easy Win for Byron Bertram', *Rand Daily Mail*, 28 April 1971.

9. *Times*, 29 April 1971.
10. Dowling, 'Dhiraj Meets Bertram in the Next Round'; Justin Dowling, 'First Test for Dhiraj', *Pretoria News*, 28 April 1971.
11. Dowling, 'Dhiraj Meets Bertram in the Next Round'; Dowling, 'First Test for Dhiraj'; 'Easy Win for Byron Bertram'.
12. 'Tennis Tourers Growing Up Fast', *Graphic*, 7 May 1971.
13. 'Dhiraj Speaks His Mind', *Post*, 16 May 1971.
14. 'Opposition is What We're After', *Cape Herald*, 15 May 1971.
15. 'Dhiraj Speaks his Mind'.
16. HB interview.
17. Derek Hook, *Fanon and the Psychoanalysis of Racism* (London: LSE Research Online, 2004), p. 114, http://eprints.lse.ac.uk/2567/1/Fanonandthepscyho.pdf.
18. Hook, *Fanon and the Psychoanalysis of Racism*, pp. 116, 117.
19. Cited by Hook, *Fanon and the Psychoanalysis of Racism*, p. 119.
20. 'SASO Policy Manifesto'.
21. Baruch Hirson, *Year of Fire, Year of Ash: The Soweto Revolt: Roots of a Revolution?* (London: Zed Press, 1979), p. 296.
22. Biko, *I Write What I Like*, p. 15.
23. 'Dhiraj Speaks his Mind'.
24. 'Dhiraj Hits White Press for Bias', *Graphic*, 28 May 1971; 'Dhiraj Slams White Press', *Leader*, 28 May 1971.
25. 'Dhiraj Slams White Press'.
26. '"Don't play" Jasmat Tells Whites: Dhiraj Calls for "Genuine Action"', *Cape Herald*, 3 July 1971.
27. 'Bertram Again', *Rand Daily Mail*, 4 May 1971; 'Bob Maud Keeps His Cool', *Star*, 4 May 1971.
28. 'Solomon Draws First Blood', *Leader*, 7 May 1971.
29. 'Tennis Tourers Growing up Fast'.
30. 'Solomon Draws First Blood'.
31. 'Win Boosts Squad's Sagging Morale', *Post*, 30 May 1971.
32. 'Win Boosts Squad's Sagging Morale'.
33. 'Bobat Put up Brave Display', *Graphic*, 21 May 1971.
34. CB interview; 'Geoff Masters', https://en.wikipedia.org/wiki/Geoff_Masters.
35. 'Alwyn Solomon's Back Home Again', *Cape Herald*, 22 May 1971.
36. 'Solomon Rocks the Boat', *Post*, 30 May 1971.
37. 'Dhiraj Outlasts Top Aussie', *Graphic*, 4 June 1971.
38. Christopher Clarey, 'How Are Ties Broken in Tennis? That Depends', *New York Times*, 12 January 2019, https://www.nytimes.com/2019/01/12/sports/tennis/how-are-ties-broken-in-tennis-that-depends.html.

39. 'Dhiraj Outlasts Top Aussie'. The victory over Kronk is also recorded as 5-7, 8-6, 6-3 (*Birmingham Daily Post*, 19 May 1971).
40. 'Paul Kronk', https://peoplepill.com/people/paul-kronk/.
41. *Birmingham Daily Post*, 20 May 1971; JDS interview.
42. *Birmingham Daily Post*, 19 May 1971; 'Dhiraj Outlasts Top Aussie'.
43. *Birmingham Daily Post*, 26 May 1971.
44. 'SNLTU Men May Return Home Early', *Cape Herald*, 5 June 1971; 'Kevin Briscoe Through', *Rand Daily Mail*, 25 May 1971; *Birmingham Daily Post*, 25 May 1971; *Daily Mirror*, 25 May 1971.
45. *Reading Evening Post*, 3 June 1971.
46. *Times*, 1 June 1971, 2 June 1971.
47. 'Bobat Turned Down', *Cape Herald*, 19 June 1971.
48. 'Dhiraj's Squad Fails to Qualify for Wimbledon Test', *Graphic*, 25 June 1971; 'Hard Luck Chaps', *Leader*, 18 June 1971.
49. 'Stan Smith', https://en.wikipedia.org/wiki/Stan_Smith.
50. T. Cox, 'W'ton Tennis Tournament Scare: Matthews Falters Then Wins', *Express and Star*, 8 June 1971; 'Bobat Turned Down'.
51. HDS interview.
52. 'Hard Luck Chaps'.
53. Within South Africa there has been talk at different times about Nasim Bismillah, who toured with the Dhiraj brothers in 1969, playing at Junior Wimbledon. This is most unlikely and there is no evidence to this effect.
54. Osman, *I Think I Have a Story to be Told*, p. 185.
55. 'Those Whites-Only Signs'.
56. HB interview.
57. 'Those Whites-Only Signs'.
58. 'Give Us a Chance Implores Dhiraj', *Leader*, 16 July 1971.
59. 'Give Us a Chance Implores Dhiraj'.
60. 'Dhiraj and the SALTU', *Leader*, 26 February 1971.
61. 'Give Us a Chance Implores Dhiraj'.

Notes to Chapter 9: The Rest of the Tour

1. JDS interview.
2. Nirode Bramdaw email, 14 June 2021.
3. '1971 Wimbledon Championships – Men's Singles', https://en.wikipedia.org/wiki/1971_Wimbledon_Championships_%E2%80%93_Men%27s_Singles.
4. HDS interview.
5. 'Tennis Squad are Touring in Sweden', *Post*, 25 July 1971. The headline is incorrect.

6. HDS interview.
7. HDS interview.
8. L. Kramer, 'London Bridge Sold to an American 45 years Ago Today', *Londonist*, https://londonist.com/2013/04/londonbridge.
9. HDS interview.
10. JDS interview. Alegi recalls both Chileans from the 1976 Davis Cup final between Chile and Italy. He was a young boy in Rome and there was controversy surrounding the Italians' decision to play in Chile under the brutal dictator Augusto Pinochet. The USSR had refused to do so in the semi-final and lost in a walkover. Owing to his progressive politics, Italian Adriano Panatta, the 1976 French Open winner, had to be convinced to go to Santiago but did travel and won both his singles matches and the doubles as Italy took its first and only Davis Cup title. The Alegi family still possesses, in its apartment in Rome, the long-playing vinyl record of the radio broadcast highlights from that epic moment in Italian sports history.
11. '1974 Davis Cup', https://en.wikipedia.org/wiki/1974_Davis_Cup.
12. JDS interview.

Notes to Chapter 10: Lighter Moments and Tour Lessons

1. HB interview; CB interview.
2. HDS interview.
3. 'Fred Perry', https://en.wikipedia.org/wiki/Fred_Perry.
4. HDS interview.
5. 'John Lloyd (tennis)', https://en.wikipedia.org/wiki/John_Lloyd_(tennis).
6. CB interview.
7. JDS interview.
8. HB interview.
9. 'SNLTU Men May Return Home Early'.
10. 'SNLTU Men May Return Home Early'.
11. 'Alwyn Solomon's Back Home Again'.
12. JDS interview.
13. 'Alwyn Solomon's Back Home Again'.
14. John Rawls, 'The Best of All Games', *Boston Review*, 1 March 2008, http://bostonreview.net/rawls-the-best-of-all-games.
15. '"Think Pro", Says Dhiraj'; 'Think Pro: Dhiraj Tells Juniors', *Star*, 4 May 1971.
16. 'Give Us a Chance Here Says Bobat', *Graphic*, 28 August 1971.
17. *Leader*, 4 June 1971.
18. '"Think Pro", Says Dhiraj'; 'Think Pro: Dhiraj Tells Juniors'.

19. 'Opposition is What We're After'.
20. 'Praise from Top Coach for Squad', *Post*, 25 July 1971.
21. 'Give Us a Chance Here Says Bobat'.
22. 'Give Us a Chance Here Says Bobat'.
23. 'Bobat on Tennis Tour', *Leader*, 20 August 1971.
24. 'UK Tennis Tour "Good Deal of Wasted Effort"', *Cape Herald*, 10 July 1971.
25. 'Obituary: Tony Mottram, Tennis Player Appointed GB National Coach in 1970s', *Scotsman*, 25 October 2016, https://www.scotsman.com/news/obituary-tony-mottram-tennis-player-appointed-gb-national-coach-1970s-1464130.
26. 'Angela Buxton', https://en.wikipedia.org/wiki/Angela_Buxton.

Notes to Chapter 11: Conclusion

1. HB interview.
2. HB interview.
3. CB interview.
4. 'Experiment a Smashing Success: Champagne Tennis at Championship . . . Overseas Tour Squad Show Class', *Post*, 16 January 1972.
5. 'Charmaine's Champ – But oh so Sad', *Cape Herald*, 1 January 1972.
6. 'Dedicated Arnie, Plucky Yvette Win SA Titles', *Cape Herald*, 23 December 1972.
7. 'Solomon is Tennis Champ', *Cape Herald*, 12 January 1974.
8. 'Dhiraj is Following His Brother', *Cape Herald*, 30 December 1972.
9. 'Dedicated Arnie, Plucky Yvette Win SA Titles'; 'Salute Arnie and Yvette – They're the Greatest', *Leader*, 12 January 1973; 'Solomon is Tennis Champ'.
10. 'Dedicated Arnie, Plucky Yvette Win SA Titles'.
11. 'Solomon is Tennis Champ'.
12. 'Experiment a Smashing Success'.
13. 'Charmaine's Champ'.
14. 'Brilliant Charmaine', *Cape Herald*, 8 January 1972.
15. 'Brilliant Charmaine'.
16. 'Brilliant Charmaine'.
17. Farook Khan, 'Dhiraj Gives Warning on Overseas Tour Squad', *Post*, 19 January 1972.
18. 'Experiment a Smashing Success'.
19. Barry Hopwood, 'TASA Players Deserve Pat on the Back', *Cape Herald*, 16 January 1982.
20. 'TASA Can be Proud', *Cape Herald*, 15 January 1983.

21. 'TASA Can be Proud'; Barry Hopwood, 'No Sponsorship but TASA can . . .', *Cape Herald*, 10 January 1981.
22. Hopwood, 'No Sponsorship'.
23. 'TASA Can be Proud'; Hopwood, 'TASA Players Deserve Pat on the Back'.
24. HDS interview.
25. OW interview.
26. HB interview.
27. 'Curren SA's New Davis Cup Captain', 5 November 2001, https://www.news24.com/News24/Curren-SAs-new-Davis-Cup-captain-20011115.
28. Posel, 'What's in a Name?': 69.
29. Eric Hobsbawm, 'Old Marxist Still Sorting Global Fact from Fiction', *Times Higher Education Supplement*, 12 July 2002: 18–19.
30. Colin Bundy, cited in Alexander, *An Ordinary Country*, p. 133.
31. Alegi, 'Beyond Master Narratives': 569.
32. Ashwin Desai and Ahmed Veriava, 'Creepy Crawlies, Portapools, and the Dam(n) of Swimming Transformation' in *The Race to Transform: Sport in Post-Apartheid South Africa*, edited by Ashwin Desai (Pretoria, HSRC Press, 2010), pp. 51–2.
33. Dale T. McKinley, 'Transformation from Above: The Upside-Down State of Contemporary South African Soccer' in *The Race to Transform: Sport in Post-Apartheid South Africa*, edited by Ashwin Desai (Pretoria, HSRC Press, 2010), p. 84, cited in Alegi and Timbs, 'The Izichwe Football Club': 965.
34. Alegi and Timbs, 'The Izichwe Football Club': 964.
35. Osman, *I Think I Have a Story to be Told*, p. 249.
36. Khan, 'Anyone for Tennis?': 81.
37. Osman, *I Think I Have a Story to be Told*, p. 249.
38. Robbie Naidoo, personal communication, 20 June 2021.
39. Khan, 'Anyone for Tennis?': 81.
40. CB interview.
41. Tennis South Africa, 'The Future of Tennis: A Presentation to the Portfolio Committee of Sports and Recreation, August 2012', https://static.pmg.org.za/docs/120807tennis.pdf; 'Demographics of South Africa', https://en.wikipedia.org/wiki/Demographics_of_South_Africa.
42. Booth, 'The South African Council on Sport': 51.
43. Booth, 'The South African Council on Sport': 51.
44. CB interview.
45. Pickard Commission, 'Report', https://www.playthegame.org/fileadmin/documents/Pickard_Commission_Report.pdf.
46. Alegi, 'Beyond Master Narratives': 569.
47. CB interview.
48. Khan. 'Anyone for Tennis?': 82.

49. L. Gordon, 'Race and Higher Education', Roundtable, Rhodes University, 12 July 2011.
50. Ariel Dorfman, *Exorcising Terror: The Incredible Unending Trial of General Augusto Pinochet* (New York: Seven Stories Press, 2002), p. 198. Dorfman had to flee into exile after the 1973 US-supported military coup in Chile toppled the democratically elected government of Salvador Allende and installed the brutal dictator Pinochet.
51. Dorfman, *Exorcising Terror*.
52. S. Marais, 'The Precision of Violence/the Approximation of Language: Ariel Dorfman's *Death and the Maiden*', unpublished mimeo, 2010.
53. 'Constitution of the Republic of South Africa, 1996', https://www.gov.za/documents/constitution-republic-south-africa-1996.
54. Harvey J. Kaye, *Why Do Ruling Classes Fear History and Other Questions* (New York: St Martin's Press, 1996).

Notes to Chapter 13: Jasmat (Dhiraj) Soma

1. 'Good Luck Jasmat'.
2. JDS interview.
3. Ismail Vadi, 'Speech Delivered at the Transvaal College of Education Reunion, 2018', https://www.kathradafoundation.org/2018/08/14/speech-delivered-at-the-transvaal-college-of-education-re-union/.
4. K. Chinappa, 'The History of the Asiatic Bazaar in Pretoria, 1885–1914' (Honours thesis, University of Durban-Westville, 1984), p. 29.
5. Johan Swart, 'The Story of a Remarkable Hindu Temple in Pretoria's Inner City', *The Conversation*, 22 March 2020.
6. Enuga Sreenivasulu Reddy, 'Gandhi, Tamils and the Satyagraha in South Africa', https://www.sahistory.org.za/archive/gandhi-tamils-and-satyagraha-south-africa-es-reddy.
7. 'List of Satyagraha Members', https://www.sahistory.org.za/sites/default/files/archive-files/list_of_satyagraha_members.pdf.
8. Joe Latakgomo, 'Athletics, Cricket, Football All Come Easy to Jasmat: A Star from Pretoria', *World*, 6 October 1967. Latakgomo 'is a veteran journalist with more than fifty years' experience' who worked for various 'newspapers like the banned *The World* and *Weekend World*, *Post* and *Sunday Post* as Assistant Editor' and 'was founding editor of *The Sowetan*'. In 2009, 'he was inducted into the SAB Sports Journalists Hall of Fame' ('Joe Latakgomo', http://southafrica.co.za/joe-latakgomo.html); Ebrahim Osman, 'The Genesis of Non-Racial Tennis', *Post*, 20 August 2014, https://www.pressreader.com/south-africa/post-south africa/20140820/281767037388902.

9. Latakgomo, 'Athletics, Cricket, Football All Come Easy to Jasmat'.
10. JDS interview.
11. JDS interview.
12. 'Can Dhiraj Beat Abrahams?', *Post*, 20 November 1966.
13. 'Dhiraj Beats Herman Abrahams', *Post*, 27 November 1966.
14. H. Williams, 'Dhiraj Wins in Tennis Thriller', November 1966 (Parvati Soma clippings).
15. 'Dhiraj Beats Herman Abrahams'.
16. 'Jasmat and Lauretta Are Reef's Last Hopes', January 1967 (Parvati Soma clippings).
17. 'Dhiraj Wins Natal Singles Title', *Post*, 16 July 1967.
18. 'Champs Brenda and Jasmat Grab Crowns', January 1968 (Parvati Soma clippings); M. Naidoo, 'Dhiraj – The Magnificent: Clinches Singles Title in Brave Fightback after Attack of Cramps', *Leader*, 12 January 1968.
19. Harold Pongolo, 'Liz Odds-On Favourite to Take 'Vaal Open Title', *Post*, 17 November 1968; Harold Pongolo, 'Here We Go Again...', *Post*, 9 November 1969. Harold Mthutuzeli (HP) Pongolo was 'a pioneer of black sports journalism who wrote for *Drum* magazine, the *Rand Daily Mail* and the *Sunday Times*', as well as for the *Post* (Marthali Brand and Aaron Nicodemus, 'Where Have You Gone', *Mail & Guardian*, 23 December 1999, https://mg.co.za/article/1999-12-23-where-have-you-gone/).
20. Farook Khan, 'Now Abrahams Going to Wimbledon with Dhiraj', *Post*, 28 January 1968. Farook Khan 'enjoyed an illustrious career in journalism and ... worked for the Post Newspapers, *Drum Magazine*, the *Daily News*, *Sunday Tribune*, *Star*, *Pretoria News* and *Cape Argus* ... in Johannesburg, Durban, Pretoria and Cape Town'. He 'blazed a trail as a reporter for over 55 years, and was regarded as one of the most colourful, engaging and wittiest personalities the world of journalism has ever produced in South Africa' (Ismail Suder, 'Journalist Farook Khan is Gone, But I Will Never Forget How He Shaped My Life', *Al-Qalam*, 11 October 2019, http://alqalam.co.za/journalist-farook-khan-is-gone-but-i-will-never-forget-how-he-shaped-my-life/).
21. United Nations Centre Against Apartheid, *Racial Discrimination in South African Sport*, p. 5.
22. Khan, 'Now Abrahams Going to Wimbledon with Dhiraj'.
23. JDS interview.
24. JDS interview.
25. JDS interview.
26. 'Western Province Tennis Championships: Dhiraj Wins Singles, Brenda's revenge', *Cape Herald*, 4 January 1969.

27. Harold Pongolo, 'Dynamic Dhiraj – S.A. Court King Again', *Post*, 12 January 1969; 'Dhiraj Does it Again in Joburg', *Cape Herald*, 11 January 1969.
28. 'Who Will be Sportsman of Year?', *Post*, 10 November 1968.
29. JDS interview.
30. 'So Easy for Jasmat', *Post*, 4 January 1970.
31. 'S.A. Indian Star Challenges Tennis Union', 1969 (Parvati Soma clippings).
32. 'David Samaai Bows Out – At Last', *Leader*, 18 December 1970; 'Third Tourney Best to Date', *Cape Herald*, 19 December 1970.
33. 'David Samaai Bows Out'.
34. 'Youthful Ace Tops Old King', *Post*, 20 December 1970.
35. 'SA Tennis Legend David Samaai Passes Away', 14 June 2019, https://www.news24.com/sport/tennis/atptour/sa-tennis-legend-david-samaai-passes-away-20190614.
36. 'The People's Champion – M. le Cordeur', Stellenbosch University Department of Curriculum Studies, *Education Faculty Newsletter* 1(1) October 2020, http://www.sun.ac.za/english/faculty/education/Curriculum%20Studies%20documents/Newsletter%20October%202020.pdf.
37. 'David Samaai', https://www.atptour.com/en/players/david-samaai/st24/overview.
38. Michael le Cordeur, *The People's Champion: The Story of David Samaai, First Black South African to Play at Wimbledon* (Gansbaai: Naledi, 2021).
39. 'The People's Champion'.
40. 'Dhiraj Brothers Dominate W.P. Open: Jasmet [sic] Takes Singles Title in Strictly Family Final', *Cape Herald*, 2 January 1971.
41. 'Dhiraj Brothers Dominate W.P. Open'.
42. 'Dhiraj Brothers Dominate W.P. Open'.
43. 'Jasmet [sic] Dhiraj the Invincible', *Cape Herald*, 9 January 1971.
44. 'Third Tourney Best to Date'.
45. United Nations Centre Against Apartheid, *Racial Discrimination in South African Sport*, p. 5; 'Those Whites-Only Signs'; R. Williams, 'Race Bar Goes – It's a Promise', *Sunday Times*, 18 April 1971; Sam Ramsamy, 'Foreword' in Osman, *I Think I Have a Story to be Told*, p. ii.
46. 'Dhiraj Bid to Join Players', *Star*, 17 May 1971.
47. David Done, 'Dhiraj Applies', *Rand Daily Mail*, 22 April 1971.
48. 'Approval Given for Dhiraj', *Pretoria News*, 17 May 1971; 'Dhiraj Bid to Join Players'.
49. Williams, 'Race Bar Goes'.
50. 'Dhiraj Bid to Join Players'.
51. 'Tennis Association Spurns Affiliation Scheme'.
52. 'Good Luck Jasmat'.

53. 'Bobat Put Up Brave Display'.
54. Despite considerable effort, including searching of newspaper archives in the UK, results could not be found for all the tournaments in which the Dhiraj Squad members took part. My thanks to my goddaughter Che Ramsden for her valiant endeavours.
55. 'Patricio Cornejo', https://en.wikipedia.org/wiki/Patricio_Cornejo.
56. *Birmingham Daily Post*, 20 May 1971.
57. 'Give Us a Chance Implores Dhiraj', *Leader*, 16 July 1971.
58. 'Give Us a Chance Implores Dhiraj'.
59. D. Pather, 'Dhiraj Shock: Tennis Star May Settle in U.K.', *Leader*, 15 October 1971.
60. Pather, 'Dhiraj Shock'.
61. N. Baird, 'Viren Soma: Tennis Coach', *Islington Faces Blog*, 2013, https://islingtonpeople.wordpress.com/tag/dhiraj-brothers/.
62. 'Former Tennis Legend Receives Recognition', https://www.tennissa.co.za/w/blog/former-tennis-legend-receives-recognition.

Notes to Chapter 14: Hiralal (Dhiraj) Soma

1. HDS interview.
2. D. Moodley, 'Hira Dhiraj Comes Home to Football', *Post*, 23 April 1972.
3. HDS interview.
4. 'Dhiraj Brothers Dominate W.P. Open'.
5. *Times*, 29 April 1971.
6. *Birmingham Daily Post*, 19 May 1971.
7. HDS interview.
8. T. Cox, 'W'ton Tennis Tournament Scare: Matthews Falters Then Wins', *Express and Star*, 8 June 1971.
9. HDS interview.
10. HDS interview.
11. 'Brilliant Charmaine'.
12. HDS interview; The reporting on the match in Moodley, 'Hira Dhiraj comes home to football' is inaccurate; Lenasia Soccer Association, 'The Bluebells United Story', http://lenasiasoccerassociation.weebly.com/bluebells-united-story.html.
13. HDS interview.
14. 'Dedicated Arnie, Plucky Yvette Win SA Titles'.
15. 'Bobat Puts Up Fight but Poole Takes Title', *Post*, 15 July 1973.
16. 'Poole Will Have to Work Hard', *Cape Herald*, 5 January 1974.
17. 'Poole Will Have to Work Hard'.

18. Peter Vale, 'Craig Williamson: The Spy Who Came in for Apartheid', *The Conversation*, 12 April 2017, https://theconversation.com/craig-williamson-the-spy-who-came-in-for-apartheid-76030.
19. In 1982, Williamson commissioned the execution in Mozambique of Ruth First, an outstanding intellectual, author and anti-apartheid militant, who was the partner of Joe Slovo, secretary-general of the South African Communist Party. Subsequently, he posted a letter bomb that murdered ANC anti-apartheid activist Jeanette Curtis Schoon and her six-year-old daughter Katryn in Lubango in Angola, where they lived in exile ('Craig Williamson', https://en.wikipedia.org/wiki/Craig_Williamson).
20. Baird, 'Viren Soma'.
21. HDS interview.
22. HDS interview.
23. Baird, 'Viren Soma'.
24. HDS interview.

Notes to Chapter 15: Alwyn Solomon

1. Lorna Solomon (Rooy, LS) interview. Much of the biographical information on Alwyn Solomon, information on his 1969 tour of Europe and aspects of the 1971 tour is from the interview with Solomon's wife.
2. 'Scholarship for Alwyn Solomons [sic]?', *Cape Herald*, 16 January 1971.
3. B. Cupido, 'Progressive se Resep vir Sukses in Tennis', *Burger*, 28 Januarie 1972.
4. Cupido, 'Progressive se Resep vir Sukses in Tennis'.
5. Pongolo, 'Dynamic Dhiraj'.
6. '1969 Wimbledon (Grand Slam)', http://www.tennisabstract.com/cgi-bin/tourney.cgi?t=1969Wimbledon.
7. 'Sportsman/Sportswoman of the Year Award: Committee Get Down to Business', *Cape Herald*, 30 January 1971.
8. 'Basil d'Oliveira', https://en.wikipedia.org/wiki/Basil_D%27Oliveira.
9. 'Basil d'Oliveira', https://en.wikipedia.org/wiki/Basil_D%27Oliveira.
10. 'Scholarship for Alwyn Solomons [sic]?'
11. 'Grim Yvette Storms to Victory', *Cape Herald*, 28 December 1968.
12. 'Grim Yvette Storms to Victory'.
13. *Rand Daily Mail*, 28 April 1971.
14. LS interview.
15. 'Alwyn Solomon's Back Home Again'.
16. 'Brilliant Charmaine'.
17. 'Dedicated Arnie, Plucky Yvette Win SA Titles'; 'Salute Arnie and Yvette – They're the Greatest'.

18. 'Solomon is Tennis Champ'.
19. 'The Tops in Tennis', *Cape Herald*, 12 January 1974.
20. 'Where Does Lamb Go from Here?', *Cape Herald*, 11 January 1975; 'Fighting Lamb Makes History', *Graphic*, 10 January 1975; 'Cape Tennis Top', *Leader*, 16 January 1976.
21. 'Fighting Lamb Makes History'.
22. 'Cape Tennis Top'; 'Petersen is the Name in SA Tennis', *Cape Herald*, 10 January 1976.
23. 'Boland Tennis Championship Results', *Cape Herald*, 21 December 1976; 'Yvette Petersen Chalks up Yet Another Title', *Cape Herald*, 3 January 1976.
24. 'Cavan Takes the Title in His Stride', *Cape Herald*, 11 January 1977; *Cape Herald*, 14 January 1978.
25. 'Bergman Takes Two Titles', *Cape Herald*, 12 January 1980.
26. 'Results: WP Tennis', *Cape Herald*, 2 January 1982; 'WP Crown for Alwyn', *Cape Herald*, 2 January 1982.
27. 'Anthony is New Champion', *Graphic*, 15 January 1982; Barry Hopwood, 'Anthony Not in Top Gear', *Cape Herald*, 8 January 1983.
28. 'Cavan, Carolissen Make Clean Sweep', *Cape Herald*, 11 January 1986; 'Young Hussein Blasts his Way to Become New SA Singles Champ'; 'Natal Triumph', *Post*, 7–10 January 1987.
29. M. de Bruyn, 'Tennis is in Adam's Genes', *Cape Times*, 20 September 2018.
30. De Bruyn, 'Tennis is in Adam's Genes'.

Notes to Chapter 16: Oscar Woodman

1. 'SA Tennis Legend David Samaai Passes Away'.
2. OW interview.
3. 'Tennis Juniors Smash all the Opposition', newspaper clipping, April 1971; 'Bobat Put up Brave Display'.
4. *Rand Daily Mail*, 28 April 1971.
5. 'Dhiraj Outlasts Top Aussie'.
6. *Times*, 2 June 1971.
7. OW interview.
8. OW interview.
9. 'Brilliant Charmaine'.
10. 'Dedicated Arnie, Plucky Yvette Win SA Titles'.
11. 'Dedicated Arnie, Plucky Yvette Win SA Titles'; 'Salute Arnie and Yvette – They're the Greatest'.
12. 'The Tops in Tennis'.
13. 'Solomon is Tennis Champ'.
14. 'Cavan Takes the Title in His Stride'.

Notes to Chapter 17: Hoosen Bobat

1. T. Reddy, 'Love Match for Tennis Ace: Former Junior Star Turns to Coaching after Successful Business Career', *Independent on Saturday*, 26 November 2006.
2. Reddy, 'Love Match for Tennis Ace'.
3. *Leader*, 22 November 1968.
4. 'Hoosen's Big Chance', *Post*, 11 April 1971.
5. 'Ex-Ace Ossie is no Pushover', *Cape Herald*, 27 December 1969.
6. 'So Easy for Jasmat'.
7. Osman, 'It's Been a Great Year for Juniors'.
8. 'Bobat Flies to Cape to Meet Solomons [sic]', *Graphic*, 11 December 1970.
9. 'Bobat for Lansdowne Tourney', *Leader*, 11 December 1970.
10. 'David Samaai Bows Out'.
11. 'Third Tourney Best to Date'.
12. 'Dhiraj Brothers Dominate W.P. Open'.
13. 'Jasmet [sic] Dhiraj the Invincible'.
14. 'Wimbledon Here We Come!'.
15. Farook Khan, 'Natal Star Shines', *Post*, 23 July 1971; 'Bobat Put up Brave Display'.
16. 'Dhiraj Outlasts Top Aussie'.
17. *Times*, 1 June 1971, 2 June 1971.
18. *Times*, 2 June 1971.
19. JDS interview.
20. 'Hard Luck Chaps'.
21. HB interview.
22. 'Tennis Tourers Growing up Fast'.
23. HB interview.
24. HB interview.
25. Reddy, 'Love Match for Tennis Ace'.
26. Reddy, 'Love Match for Tennis Ace'.
27. John Roberts, 'Tennis: Firebrands, Flour Bombs and Frew', *Independent*, 21 September 1999, https://www.independent.co.uk/sport/tennis-firebrands-flour-bombs-and-frew-1121083.html.
28. HB interview.
29. 'Bobat on Tennis Tour'.
30. Fred Tupper, 'U.S. Clinches Davis Cup Series with South Africa, 3-0', *New York Times*, 17 April 1977, https://www.nytimes.com/1977/04/17/archives/us-clinches-davis-cup-series-with-south-africa-30-us-seals-zone.html.
31. HB interview.
32. HB interview.

33. 'Peter Hain, 'From London to Grahamstown and Contemporary South Africa', 4 September 2015, https://www.ru.ac.za/communicationsand advancement/latestnews/2015/peterhainfromlondontograhamstownandcontemporarysouthafrica.html.
34. Hain, 'From London to Grahamstown and Contemporary South Africa'.
35. HB interview.
36. 'Dhiraj's Squad Fails to Qualify for Wimbledon Test'.
37. HB interview.
38. HB interview.
39. 'Bobat's Year', *Leader*, 31 December 1971.
40. 'Bobat's Year'.
41. Ahmed Bobat, 'Journal of Letters', 1971.
42. HB interview.
43. 'Experiment a Smashing Success'.
44. 'Hustler Hoosen Hammers Asmal', *Leader*, 14 July 1972.
45. 'Dhiraj is Following his Brother'.
46. 'The Tops in Tennis'.
47. HB interview.
48. HB interview.

Notes to Chapter 18: Cavan Bergman
1. 'Bosmont', https://en.wikipedia.org/wiki/Bosmont.
2. 'St Barnabas May Have to Close', 1 October 2000, https://www.news24.com/News24/St-Barnabas-may-have-to-close-20001001.
3. Helena Wasserman, '10 Things We Didn't Know about Trudi Makhaya, Cyril Ramaphosa's New Economic Advisor', *Business Insider South Africa*, 16 April 2018, https://www.businessinsider.co.za/5-things-we-didnt-know-about-the-president-new-advisor-2018-4.
4. Trudi Makhaya, 'Pulling Down Black Excellence', 2014, https://trudimakhaya.co.za/pulling-down-black-excellence/.
5. 'Top Gauteng School May Close', 8 January 2001, https://www.news24.com/News24/Top-Gauteng-school-may-close-20010108.
6. 'Champs Brenda and Jasmat Grab Crowns'.
7. Pongolo, 'Dynamic Dhiraj'.
8. 'Peer Shines', *Leader*, 15 January 1971.
9. 'Tennis Juniors Smash all the Opposition', newspaper clipping, April 1971; 'Juniors Good Start in Britain'.
10. Dowling, 'Dhiraj Meets Bertram in the Next Round'; Dowling, 'First Test for Dhiraj'.

11. 'Dhiraj Outlasts Top Aussie'.
12. *Times*, 1 June 1971.
13. 'Bobat Turned Down'.
14. 'Dhiraj's Squad Fails to Qualify for Wimbledon Test'; 'Hard Luck Chaps'.
15. 'Bob Hewitt', https://en.wikipedia.org/wiki/Bob_Hewitt.
16. CB interview.
17. Gary Curreri, 'Top Tennis Trainer Starts Junior Program', *Florida Sun-Sentinel*, 2 December 2001, https://www.sun-sentinel.com/news/fl-xpm-2001-12-02-0111290686-story.html; 'Charlton Eagle', https://en.wikipedia.org/wiki/Charlton_Eagle.
18. 'Mark Plaatjes', https://en.wikipedia.org/wiki/Mark_Plaatjes.
19. 'Dhiraj is Following his Brother'.
20. 'Hira's Victory', 1973 (Parvati Soma clippings).
21. 'The Tops in Tennis'.
22. 'Where Does Lamb Go from Here?'; 'Fighting Lamb Makes History'.
23. 'Cape Tennis Top'.
24. 'Cavan Takes the Title in His Stride'.
25. *Cape Herald*, 14 January 1978.
26. 'What Now for the Tops in Tennis', *Cape Herald*, 15 January 1979.
27. 'Three in a Row', *Cape Herald*, 13 January 1979; 'Bergman Deserved his Title', *Cape Herald*, 6 January 1979.
28. Barry Hopwood, 'Cavan Turns the Heat on Russell', *Cape Herald*, 29 December 1979; 'Tennis Results', *Cape Herald*, 29 December 1979; 'Cavan Bergman – The Tennis King', *Cape Herald*, 3 January 1981.
29. 'Anthony is New Champion'; K.G. Moodley, 'Hussein Justifies the Nickname and Top Seeding: The King Reigns Supreme', *Post*, 22–25 April 1987; 'WP Crown for Alwyn'; Barry Hopwood, 'Bergman, Anthony Make Amends in Doubles', *Cape Herald*, 1 January 1983.
30. *Cape Herald*, 12 January 1980.
31. 'Bergman Takes Two Titles'.
32. 'Cavan Bergman'.
33. 'Anthony is New Champion'; Barry Hopwood, 'Hats Off to Tennis's Walking Wounded', *Cape Herald*, 12 January 1984.
34. 'Raymond Had Them All Fooled', *Cape Herald*, 15 January 1983.
35. 'Bergman Wins TASA Crown after Five Years', *Graphic*, 13 January 1984.
36. Hopwood, 'Hats Off to Tennis's Walking Wounded'.
37. Hopwood, 'Hats Off to Tennis's Walking Wounded'.
38. 'Young Hussein Blasts his Way to Become New SA Singles Champ'.
39. '"King" Hussein Lets his Racket Do the Talking', *Post*, 13–16 January 1988.
40. This excludes the 1988–1989 tournament, for which results cannot be found in any of the newspapers that reported on non-racial sport.

41. SACOS, 'Tennis Association of South Africa', mimeo, 1988, p. 39, http://www.historicalpapers.wits.ac.za/inventories/inv_pdfo/AG3403/AG3403-A1-4-3-004-jpeg.pdf.
42. SACOS, 'Sportsperson of the Year Award, West End, Port Elizabeth, 24 November 1984', p. 31 (Historical Papers Research Archive, University of the Witwatersrand, Johannesburg).
43. SACOS, 'Sportsperson of the Year Award . . . 1984'.
44. After 1977 the ILTF dropped the L (Lawn) from its name and became the ITF. '2021 TSA Licensed Coaches List', https://www.tennissa.co.za/w/coaches/coaches-listed-alphabetically.
45. '2006 Australian Open – Men's Singles', https://en.wikipedia.org/wiki/2006_Australian_Open_%E2%80%93_Men%27s_Singles.
46. 'Jessica Steck', https://en.wikipedia.org/wiki/Jessica_Steck.
47. 'Amélie Mauresmo', https://en.wikipedia.org/wiki/Am%C3%A9lie_Mauresmo.
48. 'Become a Coach', https://www.tennissa.co.za/w/coaches/become-a-coach.
49. CB interview.
50. Sara Ahmed, *On Being Included: Racism and Diversity in Institutional Life* (Durham: Duke University Press, 2012), pp. 36, 38.
51. 'Squad for World Baseball Qualifiers: Local Baseball Player to Represent South Africa in Australia', *Roodepoort Record*, 4 February 2016, https://roodepoortrecord.co.za/2016/02/04/squad-for-world-baseball-qualifiers/.

Bibliography

Primary Sources

Newspapers
Burger, Cape Argus, Cape Herald, Cape Times, Daily News, Express and Star, Graphic, Independent, Independent on Saturday, Leader, New York Times, Post, Pretoria News, Rand Daily Mail, Roodepoort Record, Scotsman, Star, Sunday Express, Sunday Times, Washington Post

Private collections
Ahmed Bobat, Letters, 1971
Parvati Soma, Newspaper clippings

Official publications
South Africa. *House of Assembly Debates* 11 April 1967, cols 3960-1; 22 April 1971, cols 5050-1; 25 May 1973, cols 7559, 7563, 7783-4

Manuscript Sources
Non-racial Sport History Project Gauteng. 'Let the History be Told', 11 March 2021, https://www.facebook.com/1660909827469680/photos/a.1660915960802400/3071675693059746/?type=1&theater.
United Nations Notes and Documents. Folder: Topical – Cultural Activities and Cultural Boycott, 1983-1992, box 30, Pan Africanist Congress of Azania United Nations Records, National Heritage and Cultural Studies Centre, University of Fort Hare, Alice.
University of the Witwatersrand Historical Papers Research Archive, http://www.historicalpapers.wits.ac.za/inventories/inv_pdfo/AD1137/AD1137-Ea6-1-001-jpeg.pdf.
University of the Witwatersrand Historical Papers Research Archive. AG3403: Non-Racial Sports History Project, Transvaal, 1930s-, http://www.historicalpapers.wits.ac.za/?inventory/U/collections&c=AG3403/R/.

Interviews

Cavan Bergman (CB) 9 March, 11 May and 12 May 2021
Hira (Dhiraj) Soma (HDS) 5 March, 10 May and 24 May 2021
Hoosen Bobat (HB) 1 April, 24 May and 31 May 2021
Jasmat (Dhiraj) Soma (JDS) 8 January and 26 April 2021
Lorna Solomon (née Rooy, LS) 11 May and 13 May 2021
Oscar Woodman (OW) 22 March and 18 May 2021

Videos

Cohen, Barry. 'Let Me Play: The Sewshanker "Papwa" Sewgolum Story', https://www.youtube.com/watch?v=cpBrfb2h90g.
'Discussion: Remembering the Life of SA's Golfer Sewsunker "Papwa" Sewgolum', https://www.youtube.com/watch?v=eZnw6SiemYs.
'Papwa: Golf's Untold Story', https://www.youtube.com/watch?v=IZcxlrShtJg.

Secondary sources

Abrams, Philip. *Historical Sociology*. New York: Cornell University Press, 1982.
Ahmed, Sara. *On Being Included: Racism and Diversity in Institutional Life*. Durham: Duke University Press, 2012.
Alegi, Peter. 'Beyond Master Narratives: Local Sources and Global Perspectives on Sport, Apartheid, and Liberation'. *International Journal of the History of Sport* 37(7), 2020: 559–76.
———. *Laduma!: Soccer, Politics and Society in South Africa*. Pietermaritzburg: University of KwaZulu-Natal Press, 2004.
———. 'Sport, Race, and Liberation Before Apartheid: A Preliminary Study of Albert Luthuli, 1920s–1950s'. *South African History Online*, http://www.sahistory.org.za/archive/sport-race-and-liberation-apartheid-dr-peter-alegi.
Alegi, Peter and Timbs, Liz. 'The Izichwe Football Club: Youth, Sport and Masculinity in Pietermaritzburg, South Africa'. *Journal of Southern African Studies* 45(5), 2019: 963–80.
Alexander, Neville. 'Affirmative Action and the Perpetuation of Racial Identities in Post-Apartheid South Africa'. *Transformation* 63, 2007: 92–108.
———. *An Ordinary Country: Issues in the Transition from Apartheid to Democracy in South Africa*. Pietermaritzburg: University of Natal Press, 2002.
Arsenault, Raymond. *Arthur Ashe: A Life*. New York: Simon & Schuster, 2018.
Badat, Saleem. *Black Student Politics, Higher Education and Apartheid: From SASO to SANSCO, 1968–1990*. Pretoria: Human Sciences Research Council, 1999.
———. *The Forgotten People: Political Banishment under Apartheid*. Johannesburg: Jacana Media, 2012.

———. 'SASO and Black Consciousness, and the Shift to Congress Politics' in *Students Must Rise: Youth Struggle in South Africa Before and Beyond Soweto '76*, edited by Anne Heffernan and Noor Nieftagodien, 98-108. Johannesburg: Wits University Press, 2016.

Barton, John. 'Golf in the Days of Black & White'. *Golf Digest*, 2 October 2007, https://www.golfdigest.com/story/papwa.

Bell, Terry with Ntsebeza, Dumisa. *Unfinished Business: South Africa, Apartheid and Truth*. Observatory: RedWorks, 2001.

Bersell, Matt. 'Sports, Race, and Politics: The Olympic Boycott of Apartheid Sport'. *Western Illinois Historical Review* 8, 2017: 1-31.

Biko, Steve. *I Write What I Like*, edited by Aelred Stubbs. London: Heinemann, 1987.

Bizos, George. *No One to Blame? In Pursuit of Justice in South Africa*. Cape Town: David Philip, 1998.

Black, David and Nauright, John. *Rugby and the South African Nation*. Manchester: Manchester University Press, 1998.

Booth, Douglas. 'Playing the Game? Desegregating South African Sport'. Durban: Development Studies Unit, Centre for Applied Social Sciences, Natal University (Working Paper 18), 1988.

———. *The Race Game: Sport and Politics in South Africa*. London: Frank Cass, 1998.

———. 'The South African Council on Sport and the Political Antinomies of the Sports Boycott'. *Journal of Southern African Studies* 23(1), 1997: 51-66.

Breckenridge, Keith. 'The Book of Life: The South African Population Register and the Invention of Racial Descent, 1950-1980'. *Kronos* 40(1), 2014: 225-40.

Burawoy, Michael. *The Politics of Production: Factory Regimes under Capitalism and Socialism*. London: Verso, 1985.

Carriage, Leigh. 'John Lennon's Imagine at 50: A Deceptively Simple Ballad, a Lasting Emblem of Hope'. *The Conversation*, 8 September 2021.

Carton, Benedict and Morrell, Robert. 'Zulu Masculinities, Warrior Culture and Stick Fighting: Reassessing Male Violence and Virtue in South Africa'. *Journal of Southern African Studies* 38(1), 2012: 31-53.

Case, Maxine. *Papwa: Golf's Lost Legend*. Cape Town: Kwela, 2015.

Chinappa, K. 'The History of the Asiatic Bazaar in Pretoria (1885-1914)'. Honours thesis, University of Durban-Westville, 1984.

Chisholm, Linda (ed.). *Changing Class: Education and Social Change in Post-Apartheid South Africa*. Pretoria: Human Sciences Research Council Press, 2004.

Cleophas, Francois J. (ed.). *Exploring Decolonising Themes in SA Sport History: Issues and Challenges*. Stellenbosch: Sun Press, 2018.

Cohen, Barry. *Let Me Play*. Cape Town: New Voices Publishing, 2020.
Desai, Ashwin (ed.). *The Race to Transform: Sport in Post-Apartheid South Africa*. Pretoria: HSRC Press, 2010.
———. *Reverse Sweep: A Story of South African Cricket since Apartheid*. Johannesburg: Jacana Media, 2017.
———. *Wentworth: The Beautiful Game and the Making of Place*. Pietermaritzburg: University of KwaZulu-Natal Press, 2019.
Desai, Ashwin and Ramjettan, Dhevarsha. 'Sport for All? Exploring the Boundaries of Sport and Citizenship in "Liberated" South Africa' in *Racial Redress and Citizenship in South Africa*, edited by Adam Habib and Kristina Bentley. Cape Town: HSRC Press, 2008.
Desai, Ashwin and Veriava, Ahmed. 'Creepy Crawlies, Portapools, and the Dam(n) of Swimming Transformation' in *The Race to Transform: Sport in Post-Apartheid South Africa*, edited by Ashwin Desai, 14–55. Pretoria, HSRC Press, 2010.
Dlamini, Jacob. *Native Nostalgia*. Johannesburg: Jacana Media, 2009.
Dorfman, Ariel. *Exorcising Terror: The Incredible Unending Trial of General Augusto Pinochet*. New York: Seven Stories Press, 2002.
Faulkner, William. *Requiem for a Nun*. New York: Random House, 1951.
Frederikse, Julie. *The Unbreakable Thread: Non-Racialism in South Africa*. Johannesburg: Ravan Press, 1990.
Fu, Albert and Murray, Martin. 'Sentimentalizing Racial Reconciliation in the "New South Africa": Cinematic Representation of the 1995 Rugby World Cup'. *Black Camera* 9(1), 2017: 22–46.
Galeano, Eduardo. *The Book of Embrace*. London: W.W. Norton, 1992.
Hain, Peter and Odendaal, André. *Pitch Battles: Sport, Racism and Resistance*. London: Rowman and Littlefield, 2021.
Hall, Eric Allen. *Arthur Ashe: Tennis and Justice in the Civil Rights Era*. Baltimore: Johns Hopkins University Press, 2014.
Hamilton, Darrick. 'Neoliberalism and Race'. *Democracy* 53, 2019, https://democracyjournal.org/magazine/53/neoliberalism-and-race/.
Hirson, Baruch. *Year of Fire, Year of Ash: The Soweto Revolt: Roots of a Revolution?* London: Zed Press, 1979.
Hobsbawm, Eric. 'Old Marxist Still Sorting Global Fact from Fiction'. *Times Higher Education Supplement*, 12 July 2002: 18–19.
Hook, Derek. *Fanon and the Psychoanalysis of Racism*. London: LSE Research Online, 2004, http://eprints.lse.ac.uk/2567/1/Fanonandthepscyho.pdf.
Horrell, Muriel. *Laws Affecting Race Relations in South Africa, 1948–1976*. Johannesburg: South African Institute of Race Relations, 1978.
International Olympic Committee. *Olympic Charter*. Lausanne: IOC, 2020.

———. *Olympic Rules and Regulations*. Lausanne: IOC, 1971.
Jung Park, Yoon. 'White, Honorary White, or Non-White: Apartheid Era Constructions of Chinese'. *Afro-Hispanic Review* 27(1), 2008: 123-38.
Kaye, Harvey J. *Why Do Ruling Classes Fear History and Other Questions*. New York: St Martin's Press, 1996.
Kelley, Robin. 'The Role of the International Sports Boycott in the Liberation of South Africa'. *Ufahamu* 13(2-3), 1984: 26-38.
Kennedy-Dubourdieu, Elaine (ed.). *Race and Inequality: World Perspectives on Affirmative Action*. Farnham: Ashgate, 2006.
Khan, Farieda. 'Anyone for Tennis? Conversations with Black Women Involved in Tennis During the Apartheid Era'. *Agenda* 85, 2010: 76-84.
Klee, Juan. 'Multinational Sport Participation Replaces Apartheid Sport in South Africa, 1967-1978: The Role of BJ Vorster and PGJ Koornhof'. *New Contree* 64, 2012: 155-70.
Knowles, Caroline. *Race and Social Analysis*. London: Sage, 2003.
Kollapen, Jody. 'NEPAD's Human Rights Challenge'. *Connecting* February-April 2003.
Kundera, Milan. *The Book of Laughter and Forgetting*. New York: Alfred A. Knopf, 1980.
Lapchick, Richard E. 'The Olympic Movement and Racism: An Analysis in Historical Perspective'. *Africa Today* 17(6), 1970: 14-16.
———. *The Politics of Race and International Sport: The Case of South Africa*. Westport, CT: Greenwood Press, 1975.
Le Cordeur, Michael. *The People's Champion: The Story of David Samaai, First Black South African to Play at Wimbledon*. Gansbaai: Naledi, 2021.
Le Grange, Lesley. 'Decolonising Sport: Some Thoughts' in *Exploring Decolonising Themes in SA Sport History: Issues and Challenges*, edited by Francois J. Cleophas, 15-21. Stellenbosch: Sun Press, 2018.
Leibbrandt, Murray. 'The Human Tragedy of South Africa's Inequality'. *New Frame*, 17 May 2021, https://www.newframe.com/the-human-tragedy-of-south-africas-inequality/.
Levi, Primo. *If This Is a Man*. New York: Orion Press, 1959.
Li, Charmaine. 'Confronting History: James Baldwin'. *Kinfolk*, https://www.kinfolk.com/confronting-history-james-baldwin/.
Llewellyn, Matthew P. and Lake, Robert J. 'The Old Days of Amateurism are Over: The Samaranch Revolution and the Return of Olympic Tennis'. *Sport in History* 37(4), 2017: 423-47.
Marais, Hein. *South Africa Pushed to the Limit: The Political Economy of Change*. Cape Town: UCT Press, 2011.
Mark, Ellen. 'Review of Arthur Ashe and Frank DeFord, *Arthur Ashe: Portrait in Motion*'. *Africa Today* 25(1), 1978: 69-71.

McKinley, Dale T. 'Transformation from Above: The Upside-Down State of Contemporary South African Soccer' in *The Race to Transform: Sport in Post-Apartheid South Africa*, edited by Ashwin Desai. Pretoria, HSRC Press, 2010.
Melucci, Alberto. *Nomads of the Present: Social Movements and Individual Needs in Contemporary Society*. Philadelphia: Temple University Press, 1989.
Merrett, Christopher. *Sport, Space and Segregation: Politics and Society in Pietermaritzburg*. Pietermaritzburg: University of KwaZulu-Natal Press, 2009.
Morgan, Eric J. 'Black and White at Center Court: Arthur Ashe and the Confrontation of Apartheid in South Africa'. *Diplomatic History* 36(5), 2012: 815-41.
Morsy, Soheir. 'Beyond the Honorary "White" Classification of Egyptians: Societal Identity in Historical Context' in *Race*, edited by Steven Gregory and Roger Sanjek, 175-98. New Brunswick, NJ: Rutgers, 1996.
Murray, Bruce and Merrett, Christopher. *Caught Behind: Race and Politics in Springbok Cricket*. Pietermaritzburg: University of KwaZulu-Natal Press, 2004.
Mwirigi. Christopher. 'Transformation and Affirmative Action in South African Sport'. LLM thesis, University of Pretoria, 2010.
'A New Economy Means Undoing the Old One'. *New Frame*, 17 May 2021, https://www.newframe.com/a-new-economy-means-undoing-the-old-one/.
Nicholson, Christopher. *Papwa Sewgolum: From Pariah to Legend*. Johannesburg: Wits University Press, 2005.
Nixon, Rob. 'Apartheid on the Run: The South African Sports Boycott'. *Transition* 58, 1992: 68-88.
Nongogo, Philani. 'The Struggles to Deracialise South African Sport: A Historical Overview'. D.Phil. thesis, University of Pretoria, 2015.
Odendaal, André. 'Reflections on Writing a Post-Colonial History of a Colonial Game' in *Exploring Decolonising Themes in SA Sport History: Issues and Challenges*, edited by Francois J. Cleophas, 1-8. Stellenbosch: Sun Press, 2018.
———. 'Sport and Liberation: The Unfinished Business of the Past' in *Sport and Liberation in South Africa: Reflections and Suggestions*, edited by Cornelius Thomas, 11-28. Alice: University of Fort Hare Press, 2006.
Opperman, Rudolf and Laubscher, Lappe. *Africa's First Olympians: The Story of the Olympic Movement in South Africa 1907-1987*. Johannesburg: South African National Olympic Committee, 1987.
Osman, Ebrahim. *I Think I Have a Story to be Told: The Life of My Days*. Durban, 2014.
Piven, Francis F. and Cloward, Richard A. *Poor People's Movements: Why They Succeed, How They Fail*. New York: Vintage Books, 1979.
Player, Gary. *Grand Slam Golf*. London: Cassell, 1966.

Posel, Deborah. 'What's in a Name? Racial Categorisations under Apartheid and their Afterlife'. *Transformation* 47, 2001: 50-74.
Ramsamy, Sam. 'Foreword' in Osman, Ebrahim, *I Think I Have a Story to be Told: The Life of My Days*. Durban, 2014.
Rawls, John. 'The Best of all Games'. *Boston Review*, 1 March 2008, http://bostonreview.net/rawls-the-best-of-all-games.
Sachs, Albie. 'Foreword' in *Race and Inequality: World Perspectives on Affirmative Action*, edited by Elaine Kennedy-Dubourdieu, ix-xii. Farnham: Ashgate, 2006.
Skinner, Rob. 'The Moral Foundations of British Anti-Apartheid Activism, 1946-1960'. *Journal of Southern African Studies* 35(2), 2009: 399-416.
Southall, Roger. *South Africa's Transkei: The Political Economy of an 'Independent' Bantustan*. New York: Monthly Review Press, 1983.
Steptoe, Tyina. '"What's Going On" at 50: Marvin Gaye's Motown Classic is as Relevant Today as it was in 1971'. *The Conversation*, 18 May 2021.
Swart, Johan. 'The Story of a Remarkable Hindu Temple in Pretoria's Inner City'. *The Conversation*, 22 March 2020.
Thompson, Richard. *Retreat from Apartheid: New Zealand's Sporting Contacts with South Africa*. London: Oxford University Press, 1975.
United Nations Centre Against Apartheid. *Racial Discrimination in South African Sport: Notes and Documents*. New York: United Nations, 1980.
———. 'Response of Artists and Entertainers to Apartheid: A Brief Review', August 1988.
Vahed, Goolam. 'Control of African Leisure Time in Durban in the 1930s'. *Journal of Natal and Zulu History* 18, 1998: 67-123.
Vale, Peter. 'Craig Williamson: The Spy Who Came in for Apartheid'. *The Conversation*, 12 April 2017, https://theconversation.com/craig-williamson-the-spy-who-came-in-for-apartheid-76030.
Valodia, Imraan. 'The Link Between Inequality and Power'. *New Frame*, 18 May 2021, https://www.newframe.com/the-link-between-inequality-and-power/.
Venter, Gustav. 'Discord in the Dressing Room: The Ideological Complexities within Non-Racial Football during the Late 1970s' in *Exploring Decolonising Themes in SA Sport History: Issues and Challenges*, edited by Francois J. Cleophas, 55-65. Stellenbosch: Sun Press, 2018.
———. 'Experimental Tactics on an Uneven Playing Field: Multinational Football and the Apartheid Project during the 1970s'. *International Journal of the History of Sport* 36(1), 2019: 83-103.
———. 'White's Gambit in the Middle Game: Chess, Apartheid, and South Africa's Sporting Isolation in the 1970s'. *International Journal of the History of Sport* 37(7), 2020: 1-15.

Willan, Brian. '"One of the Most Gentlemanly Players that Ever Donned a Jersey": The English Rugby Career of Richard Msimang (1907-1912)'. *Quarterly Bulletin of the National Library of South Africa* 66(3), 2012: 5-16.

Wolpe, Harold. *Race, Class and the Apartheid State*. London: UNESCO/James Currey, 1988.

Index

Aborigines Advancement League 66
affiliation
  international 59, 60, 61, 66, 198–9
  to local tennis unions 75, 79
  to whites-only federation 47, 51, 53, 58–9, 65, 69, 70, 100, 121, 143, 169, 198, 223
African Tennis Association 30
Alegi, Peter 27, 31, 32, 52, 54, 58, 75, 77, 79, 127, 247n.10
Amritraj, Anand 106, *107*, 142
Amritraj, Vijay 106, *107*, 142
Anthony, Raymond 118
anti-apartheid boycotts 56, 61–2, 66, 67–8, 106, 200
anti-apartheid sports organisations conference 11, *see also* SACOS
apartheid
  collaboration 14, 33, 46, 50, 52, 127, 128, 199, 200, *see also* racism, collusion with
  legislation 39, 42, 45, 236n.20
  policy on sport 39–40, 43, 44, 45, 46, 47, 53
archive 25, 31–2, 122
Ashe, Arthur 44, 65, 66–7, 68, 101, 102, *152*, 169, 172, 201
Asmal, Bill 187
Asmal, Cassim *188*
Asmal, Ismail *188*
assimilation and sport 27, 30

Babolat 212
Bacher, Ali 21, 60–1, 127
Bantu Men's Social Centre (BMSC) 29, 30
Bantu Recreational Grounds Association (BRGA) 29, 30
Bergman, Cavan 81, *91*, *134*, *135*, *174*, *176*, *210*, *211*, *214*, *216*, *218*
  coaching involvement 223–4, 227–8, 229
  early life and education 209–11
  employment 217, 223
  experience of racism 226, 227, 228
  family 229
  health 221
  1971 UK tour 109, 116, 212, 215
  1971 UK tour tournament results (summary) 212–13
  sponsorship offer 223
  sportsperson of the year 120, 224
  tennis achievements 118, 120, 124, 211–12, 215–17, 218–22, 224, *225*, 226
  tennis style 86, 88, 215, 217, 218, 219–20, 224
  training 109, 217, 218
Beukes, Danny 180
Bhanabhai, Basil 140
Bhanabhai, Vernon 140, 155, *155*, 160
Bhanabhai family 81, *81*, 82
Bismillah, Nasim 154

269

Black Conciousness movement 11, 52, 74, 76, 94
  and non-racialism 76
black sportspersons
  denial of opportunities to 1, 100, 164
  insufficient recognition of 20, 127, 128
  participation, late nineteenth century 26, 26-7
  tours overseas 51, 79, 133-4, 140-1, 144, 154, 169, 202
  see also individual tours; individual names
Bobat, Ahmed 2, 86, 118, 187, 191
Bobat, Hoosen 91, 133, 134, 135, 155, 184, 187, 188, 191, 192, 193, 195, 196, 214, 216
  coaching 207
  correspondence with family 1971 202-6
  and David Samaai 86, 189
  early life and education 187
  employment 207-8
  European tour 105, 200, 205-6
  funding 74, 205-6
  injury 120, 194, 206
  interests 207, 208
  marriage and family 193, 208, 229
  1971 UK tour highlights 108, 109, 155, 201, 202
  1971 UK tour reflections 111, 112
  1971 UK tour tournament results (summary) 193-4, 203
  scholarship offer 105, 120, 152, 202, 206
  sporting ability 187-8
  tennis achievements 120, 188, 189-91, 193-4, 196, 197-8
  tennis style 86, 201
  university studies 192, 204, 206, 207

  and Wimbledon 1, 99, 99-100, 196-9, 201
Booth, Douglas 39-40, 47, 48, 72, 125
boycott see anti-apartheid boycotts
Bramdaw, Paulin Rai 102
Brown, Pauline 153
Brundage, Avery 48
Brutus, Dennis 29, 62, 62-4, 67, 75, 201, 202, 215
Buxton, Angela 113

Carlos, John 56, 57
Carolissen, Basil 209
Carolissen, Charmaine 118, 209
Carolissen, Darroll 77, 82, 91, 110, 111, 134, 217
Carolissen, Patrick 209
Chalmers, Alf ('Baas') 64, 65, 69, 70, 100, 101, 121, 127, 143, 197, 198-9
class 17, 30, 55, 77, 124
clubs 24, 27, 28, 29, 30, 53, 59, 113, 126, 229
  African 26-7, 29, 75
  coloured 27-8
  post-1994 126
  see also under individual names
coaching and development
  and class differences 55
  lack of 53, 95, 123, 124
  offers of along racial lines 51, 60, 223
Coleman, Anne 135
Collins, John 67
collusion see racism, collusion with
colonialism 35
  effects of 93-4
competition, absence of 94, 95, 111
Coolhurst Tennis and Squash Club 83, 87, 100, 198

Co-ordinating Committee for
    International Recognition in
    Sport (CCIRS) 29, 61
Corrigall, Mary 63
court conditions on tour 83-4, 195,
    201
Cramer, Pat *161*
cricket 60, 61, 62-3, 171
Curren, Kevin 124, 228

Davis Cup
  American zone 150, 200
  coaching 228
  eligibility 51
  exclusion from 64, 69, 73, 200
  participation 44, 69
  selection 53, 70, 147
  team winners 107, 200
De Broglio, Chris 64, 201
decolonisation 34, 35
Desai, Aswin 60
Dhiraj, Hiralal 81, 87, 91, *104, 105,
    133, 134, 135,* 155, *161, 162, 163,
    164,* 216
  as a coach in UK 120, 159, 160,
    161
  employment 154
  family life 158-9, 160, 161, 163-4
  funding support in UK 159-60
  1971 UK tour highlights 108
  1971 UK tour tournament results
    (summary) 156-7
  and soccer 109, 154, 158
  studies 159-60, 161
  tennis achievements 154, 155,
    156-7, 158-9, 160, 161-2, 164
  tennis style 85
  tour 1969 154-5
  tournament on the Netherlands
    Belgium border 106
  tournaments in Germany 105

Dhiraj, Jasmat *80, 81, 87, 91, 93, 133,
    134, 135, 136, 138, 140, 146, 147,
    148, 152, 153,* 171, 173
  Andrew Mlangeni Green Jacket
    award 153
  and Hoosen Bobat 100, 202
  character 115, 151
  coaching in UK 120, 153
  and David Samaai 86
  and Davis Cup 1972 69
  early life and education 136-7, 154
  employment 153
  exile 115-16, 119, 151-3
  family 152, 153
  funding for 110, 141, 152
  inhibitions 92
  and ILTF 198
  name 138-9, 141
  1971 UK tour departure 78-9, 149
  1971 UK tour tournament results
    (summary) 150-1
  1971 UK tour reflections 110-11,
    112
  and SA Open 53
  and SALTU 70, 101, 143
  and SANLTU 65
  and SANROC 116, 153
  and SATPA 147-9
  sportsman of the year (Smirnoff
    Vodka) 143
  tennis style 72, 84-5, 92, 94, 137,
    139, 143, 145-6, 149
  tennis tournament achievements
    137, 139-40, 141, 142, 143-4,
    145-6, 149, 190, 191
  see also Dhiraj Squad
Dhiraj Squad 1, 74, 77, *82, 104, 112,
    114, 115,* 121, *133,* 133-4, *135*
  coaching of 81, 85, 86, *112,* 113,
    114, 118
  composition and lack of diversity
    74-7
  see also individual player names

D'Oliviera, Basil 170-1
Drake, Bill 105
Drysdale, Cliff 79, 146-7, 148
Dunlop Sports 99, 141, 142, 168, 204, 212
Durban Bantu Lawn Tennis Association 30
Durban City Council 54-5
Dutch Lawn Tennis Association 105

Eagle, Charlton 216
equality 18
equity 18-19
Evans, Lee 56
exclusion 75
   from the narrative of tennis 24-5
   in SA sport 14, 31, 36, 153, 171
   tennis 23-4, 25, 57, 69, 75, 92, 197, 200, 201, see also Olympic Games

facilities
   inadequate 55, 60, 188, 195, 197
   improved 48, 51, 223
   post-1994 126
   and social justice 19, 127
   spending on 54
The Fakir (Ranji Nowbath) 54-5
Fanon, Franz 92-3
Federation Cup 54, 58, 64, 65
female participation in tennis 25-7, 28, 76-7, 127, see also Federation Cup
Florian, Jared 105, *105*
Fortuin, Eddie 117
Fortuin, Janice 217
Franklin, Ben 64
Freedom Charter 21

gender 25
Georgeson, C. 112

golf, segregated 40-1
Goolagong, Evonne 66, 91

Hain, Peter 44, 201
history(-ies)
   critical approaches 33, 34
   data sources 3, 30, 31
   periodisation 32, 33
   of sport 31-2, 34
   tennis 25, 26-7, 122
   see also archive
honorary white see *under* race
Hlongwane, Reg 64
Hopwood, Barry 118, 119
Howa, Hassan 11
Huddleston, Trevor 67-8

identity 30, 31
inequality(-ies) 16, 18, 19, 36
   in sport 122-3
   in tennis 124
injustice
   entrenched 14-16
   and power 17, 18, 25
   and redress 3, 4, 18, 19, 23, 35, 128-9
   see also social justice
institutionalisation of leisure 30
International Lawn Tennis Federation (ILTF) 50, 52, 57-8, 64, 65, 70, 100, *101*, 121, 164, 169, 198, 199, 201
International Olympic Committee (IOC) 44, 47, 48, 49, 56, 63, 70, 73
International Table Tennis Federation 61, 227
International University Exchange Fund (IUEF) 160
Invictus 32
isolation of South Africa in sport 44, 59, 68

Jansen, Avril 28
Jeenah, Ahmed and June 74
Johnson, Conrad 180, 191
journalism and journalists 13, 92,
  127, 143, see also media

Kali, Don 52
Katu, Pascalina 119
Kelley, Robin 44
Khan, Farieda 25-6, 27, 28, 123
Khan, Farook 72, 140, 203, 251n.20
Killanin, Lord 48
Koornhof, Piet 44-5
KZN Tennis Association website 24
  account of black players 24-5
  portrayal of history of tennis 25

Lamb, Peter 53
Latakgomo, Joe 250n.8
Lawrence, Trevor 180
Le Grange, Lesley 34-5, 36
Lloyd, John 109
local government spending on sport
  53, 54, 55
Luthuli, Chief Albert 29

Mahomedy, Mohamed *191*
Makhaya, Trudi 210
Manga, Vinoo *104*
Marabastad 137
Marais, Hein 3
master narrative *see* history(-ies)
Mayat, Nasim *188*
McCarthy 119
media 13, 23, 35, 37, 143, 171, *see also*
  journalism and journalists; 1971
  tennis tour
merit 18, 27, 59, 65, 75
Merrett, Christopher 54-5
Messmer, Steve 105

Middleton, Norman 65
Moola, A.Y. *176*
Moosa, Zulecka 208
Mottram, Tony 113, 149
mourning 35, 36
multinational sport 45, 46, 47-8, 52,
  53, 65, 127
  goals 48
multiracial sport 40, 43, 60, 148

Naidoo, M.K. 65, 192, 205
Naidoo, Robbie 124
Naidoo, Selvan 40, 41
Natal Tennis Association 24
1971 tennis tour 114-16
  accommodation and food 81-2,
    103, 104
  apparel 109-10
  coaching 113
  cost 73-4, 77
  entertainment 108, 109
  fear of repression 115
  management 110
  media 72-3, 94-5,
  practice facilities and players 83,
    111-12
  purpose 81, 114
  race 109-10
  secrecy 71-2
  socio-political background to 9-12
  sponsorship 74, 110
  timeline xvi-xvii
  transport during 82, 103
non-racial sport 11, 20, 33, 47, 53,
  57, 61-2, 110, 119, 128, 129
  tennis 50, 58-9, 84, 115, 117, 118,
    120, 124, 149, 224, 228
Non-Racial Sport History Project
  Gauteng 2
Norman, Peter 57

Odendaal, André 23, 25, 31, 33
Olympic Games
  South African suspension/
    expulsion from 32, 43, 44, 48,
    56, 57, 63, 64
Olympic Project for Human Rights
  56
Osman, Ebrahim 24, 50, 53, 58, 72,
  73, 73, 74, 100, 123, 124, *191*,
  192, 198, 199, 200, 203
Osterberg, Bill 159, 160

passports, denial of 71, 79
Patel, D.D. 85, 137
Pather, M.N. 58, 59, 60, 65, 72, 81,
  91, 96, 151, 172, *176*, *191*, 192,
  199, 200, 203
Pickard Commission 126-7
Player, Gary 40, 41, 223
political negotiation, 1990s 125
Pretoria Tamil League 137
privilege 18, 19, 42
Progressive Tennis Club 28, 126, 166,
  167, 209, 210, 212
  champions 209

race 4, 17, 39, 92
  and racial categories 4-5, 39, 66,
    92, 100
  see also whiteness
racism, collusion with 14, 51-2, 53,
  58, 70, 100, 110, 112, 121
racism in sport
  by administrators and
    sportspersons 21, 42, 58, 100,
    101, 121, 127-8, 151, 226
  co-optation 14, 48, 52
  effects of 93-4, 122
  international bodies 60, 61
  in media 92
  tennis 100, 123, 226, 228

  see also golf, segregated
Ramsamy, Sam 224
Rawls, John 111
Reay, Basil 58, 59, 100, *101*, 121, 128,
  140, 198-9, 201
Reddy, E.S. 59
Reeves, Ambrose 67
remembering the past 21-2, 128, 129
restitution for non-racial players 21,
  127, 228
rogue international tours (cricket)
  60-1
Roopnarain, Parbhoo *192*
Rooy, Lorna 177
Rosewall, Ken 86

Samaai, David 86, 133, 138, 144-5,
  145, 146, 179, 188, 189, 215-16,
  224
Schwarz, Alan 148
segregation in sport 30, 38, 40, 41-2,
  43, 44, 45, 54, 60, 95
Sewgolam, Sewsunker (Papwa) 40-1
sexism in sport 25
Smith, Tommie 56, *57*
soccer 30, 43, 51, 52, 123, 126
social justice 18-19, *see also*
  transformation
Solomon, Alwyn 91, *134*, *135*, *167*,
  170, *171*, 173, *174*, 214
  character 86, 174, 217
  as coach 177
  death 119
  early life and education 166, 177
  employment 177
  family life 177-8
  1971 UK tour 173
  1971 UK tour tournament results
    (summary) 172-3
  sporting ability 167, 174, 178
  studies 96, 173, 177

Sunshine Tour, 1969 134, 167, 168, 180, 191
tennis achievements 120, 169, 170, 171, 172, 173, 174-7, 178
tennis style 86, 174, 178
tour of Europe, 1969 167-70
Western Province sportsman of the year 170
Soma, Hiralal Dhiraj *see* Dhiraj, Hiralal
Soma, Hitesh 163, *163*
Soma, Jasmat Dhiraj *see* Diraj, Jasmat
Soma, Viren 163, *163*
South African Council on Sport (SACOS) 11-12, 52-3, 59
debate 25, 52
negotiation 72, 125, 126
players 53, 69, 224
recruitment 25
split 126
South African Indian Lawn Tennis Association 50
South African Lawn Tennis Union (SALTU) 24, 50-2, 53, 143, 224
and Cavan Bergman 223
and Federation Cup 64
and ILTF 50, 57, 58, 65, 100-1, 121, 198, 199
and Jasmat Dhiraj 101, 112, 143
and SANLTU 51-2, 53, 58, 169
SnALTU 58, 59, 69, 70
Wimbledon 196, 198
South African National Lawn Tennis Union (SANLTU) 50, 51, 52, 53, 65, 69
South African Non-Racial Olympic Committee (SANROC) 61, 64, 69, 72, 116, 152, 153, 160, 201, 215, 224
South African Rugby Board 79
South African Sports Association (SASA) 61, 62, 63, 72

South African Students Organisation 76
South African Sugar Association 74
South African Table Tennis Board (SATTB) 61, 71
South African Table Tennis Union 61
South African Tennis Board 50
South African Tennis Coaching Association 228
South African Tennis Players Association (SATPA) 148-9
Southern Africa Lawn Tennis Union (SnALTU) ix, 50, 51, 58, 59, 75, 116, *134*, 143, 172, *176*, *191*, 192, 223
in European tournaments 12, 71-3, 76-7, 81, 96, 111, 134, 211
expulsion/suspension from 69, 191
and formation of TASA 52
name on brochure 59, 70
rejection of subordinate status 58-9, 121
sponsorship/finances 74, 110, 138, 205
women players 76-7
sponsorship 13, 50, 51, 53, 119, 141
Barclays Bank 119
BP 74, 119
Coca Cola 119
Colgate-Palmolive 74
Fred Perry (company) 109, 142
Old Mutual 119
Peugot-Citroen 74
Phillips SA 119
Pick n Pay 119
Rothmans 74, 119
Rubins Sports 172
South African Breweries 74, 119
Stellenbosch Wineries 74
Telefunken 119
Toyota, 119

United Tobacco 119
see also Dunlop Sports
sport
   as social control 28–30
   and society 37–8, 53
   under colonialism 35
   and politics 37–8, 43–4, 46, 66, 68
   see also under apartheid; SANROC
Springbok colours 79
Springbok honours 42, 47
St Barnabas College 209–11
Starkey, Deanna 137
Steve Tshwete Sports Award 59
Sugar Circuit 24
Sunshine Tour, 1969 69, 114, 134, 167, 168, 180, 191

table tennis 61, 71
Tennis Association of South Africa (TASA) 25, 52, 118, 226
   championships 175, 176, 220
   coaching 224
   sportspersons of the year 120, 224
   tennis bodies under apartheid 50–3,
   see also under individual names
Thomas, Joy 173
Thomas, Lynette 209
tournament (Germany) 105–6
   match results 106
tournament (Netherlands)
   informal 103
   match results 104
   scholarship opportunity 105
tournament (border of Netherlands and Belguim)
   match results 106
tournament (1971 tennis tour, UK)
   locations 89, 102
   match results 90, 91–2, 94, 95–8, 102
   results (summary) 150–1, 156–7
   tournaments subsequent to 1971, in SA
   absence of 126
   match results 116–17, 118
transformation
   concept 19–20,
   lack of in tennis 124–5, 127, 228
Truth and Reconciliation Commission (TRC) 13, 36, 122

United Nations Centre Against Apartheid 59

Vahed, Goolam 28, 30
Van der Horst, Frank 52
Vorster, B.J. 11, 43–4, 60

Waring, Frank 60
white administrators 121, 127
white players 24–5, 121, 149
white superiority 65, 79, 94, 226
whiteness 229
whites in sport 42, 47, 55, 70
   spending on 54
Williams, Charmaine 76, 78, 78, *91*, 92, 104, 111, 117, 118, *133*, *134*, *181*, 185, 219
Williams, Owen 222–3
Wimbledon 89, 95, 98–9
   attendance 102, 142, 169
   first SA black player 144, 196
   qualifying 98–9, 142, 143
Wimbledon junior championships 99–101, 168, 196–7
Wisden 61
women in sport 27, 28
   see also female participation in tennis
Woodgate, Billy, 109

Woodman, Oscar 81, *91*, *133*, *135*,
  171, *179*, 180, *183*, *184*, *185*, *196*,
  216
  early life and education 179–80,
    185–6
  emigration to Canada 120, 185
  family 179, *185*, 186
  1971 UK tour highlights 181, 184
  1971 UK tour tournament results
    (summary) 182–3
  personality 86
  soccer 109, 180
  studies 186
  Sunrise Squad 134, 180
  tennis achievements 181, 184–5
  tennis style 86
  tours 109, 180, 184
Woodman, Ossie 179, *179*
Woodman, Valerie *185*, 186

Printed and bound by CPI Group (UK) Ltd, Croydon, CR0 4YY
22/04/2026

14866397-0005